SMART
MOBS

ALSO BY HOWARD RHEINGOLD

The Virtual Community
Tools for Thought
They Have a Word for It
Virtual Reality
Exploring the World of Lucid Dreaming (coauthor)
Higher Creativity (coauthor)
Excursions to the Far Side of the Mind
The Cognitive Connection (coauthor)

SMART MOBS

The Next Social Revolution

HOWARD RHEINGOLD

PERSEUS
PUBLISHING

A Member of the Perseus Books Group

Cataloging-in-Publication Data is available from the Library of Congress
ISBN 0-7382-0608-3

Perseus Publishing is a member of the Perseus Books Group.
Find us on the World Wide Web at http://www.perseuspublishing.com

Perseus Publishing books are available at special discounts for bulk purchases in the U.S. by corporations, institutions, and other organizations. For more information, please contact the Special Markets Department at the Perseus Books Group, 11 Cambridge Center, Cambridge, MA 02142, or call (800) 255-1514 or (617) 252-5298, or e-mail j.mccrary@perseusbooks.com.

Text design by Brent Wilcox
Set in 10.5-point New Caledonia by the Perseus Books Group

First printing, September 2002

4 5 6 7 8 9 10 — 04 03

To Hannah Geraldine Rheingold, my mother and teacher,
who gave me permission to color outside the lines:
Thank you, Mom.

CONTENTS

ACKNOWLEDGMENTS

TO THE FOLLOWING PEOPLE: THANK YOU! I COULD NEVER HAVE DONE
this without you.

Marc A. Smith convinced me that I could weave a book from our many-stranded conversations about cooperation, communication, and computation and then stuck with me to inspire, provoke, support, and educate over the two years it took to do it.

Kevin Kelly, who has patiently pushed, persuaded, edited, and criticized my work for more than a decade, suggested that I turn one of the chapter titles into the name of this book.

My agents, John Brockman and Katinka Matson, who never settle for less, rejected my first two attempts at a book proposal and then found me an editor who understood what I was trying to do.

Nick Philipson at Perseus Books has been this book's champion from the beginning. This was our first book together; I hope it won't be our last.

Moya Mason, researcher extraordinaire, has been intelligent, incisive, meticulous, creative, perfectionistic, and confident. This is our second book together; I hope it won't be our last.

Michele Armstrong transcribed many hours of interviews, not all of which were conducted under ideal conditions.

Jennifer Swearingen is an author's dream—the best copy editor I have encountered.

Bryan Alexander, Timothy Burke, Charles Cameron, Peter Feltham, Gary Jones, Jim Lai, and Michael Wilson were the smartest, best-read, most candid online brain trust I could have hoped for.

Joanna Lemola and Alex Nieminen in Helsinki; Mimi Ito, Joi Ito, and Justin Hall in Tokyo; Judith Donath in Cambridge; and Michael Thomsen in Stockholm were invaluable guides to emerging cultures in their parts of the world. Tim Pozar and Robert Heverly tutored me in the complexities of wireless technology and regulation. Lawrence Lessig alerted me to the attempt to enclose the Internet's innovation commons. David Reed showed me the key connections between social networks, communication networks, and the cornucopia of the commons they make possible.

The people of the Brainstorms community, in both physical and virtual worlds, helped me retain a small residue of sanity and humor during the months I lived in my office.

Rebecca Marks shepherded the book's final production with skill and patience. Lissa Warren, publicist, has been a joy to work with.

Judy and Mamie Rheingold: Without you, what's the point?

How to Recognize the Future When It Lands on You

THE FIRST SIGNS OF THE NEXT SHIFT BEGAN TO REVEAL THEMSELVES TO me on a spring afternoon in the year 2000. That was when I began to notice people on the streets of Tokyo staring at their mobile phones instead of talking to them. The sight of this behavior, now commonplace in much of the world, triggered a sensation I had experienced a few times before—the instant recognition that a technology is going to change my life in ways I can scarcely imagine. Since then the practice of exchanging short text messages via mobile telephones has led to the eruption of subcultures in Europe and Asia. At least one government has fallen, in part because of the way people used text messaging. Adolescent mating rituals, political activism, and corporate management styles have mutated in unexpected ways.

I've learned that "texting," as it has come to be called, is only a small harbinger of more profound changes to come over the next ten years. My media moment at Shibuya Crossing was only my first encounter with a phenomenon I've come to call "smart mobs." When I learned to recognize the signs, I began to see them everywhere—from barcodes to electronic bridge tolls.

The other pieces of the puzzle are all around us now but haven't joined together yet. The radio chips designed to replace barcodes on manufactured objects are part of it. Wireless Internet nodes in cafes, hotels, and neighborhoods are part of it. Millions of people who lend their computers to the search for extraterrestrial intelligence are part of it. The way buyers and sellers rate each other on the Internet auction site eBay is part of it. At least one key global business question is part of it: Why is the Japanese company Do-

CoMo profiting from enhanced wireless Internet services while U.S. and European mobile telephony operators struggle to avoid failure?

When you piece together these different technological, economic, and social components, the result is an infrastructure that makes certain kinds of human actions possible that were never possible before. The "killer apps" of tomorrow's mobile infocom industry won't be hardware devices or software programs but social practices. The most far-reaching changes will come, as they often do, from the kinds of relationships, enterprises, communities, and markets that the infrastructure makes possible.

Smart mobs consist of people who are able to act in concert even if they don't know each other. The people who make up smart mobs cooperate in ways never before possible because they carry devices that possess both communication and computing capabilities. Their mobile devices connect them with other information devices in the environment as well as with other people's telephones. Dirt-cheap microprocessors are beginning to permeate furniture, buildings, and neighborhoods; products, including everything from box tops to shoes, are embedded with invisible intercommunicating smartifacts. When they connect the tangible objects and places of our daily lives with the Internet, handheld communication media mutate into wearable remote-control devices for the physical world.

Within a decade, the major population centers of the planet will be saturated with trillions of microchips, some of them tiny computers, many of them capable of communicating with each other. Some of these devices will be telephones, and they will also be supercomputers with the processing power that only the Department of Defense could muster a couple of decades ago. Some devices will read barcodes and send and receive messages to radio-frequency identity tags. Some will furnish wireless, always-on Internet connections and will contain global positioning devices. As a result, large numbers of people in industrial nations will have a device with them most of the time that will enable them to link objects, places, and people to online content and processes. Point your device at a street sign, announce where you want to go, and follow the animated map beamed to the box in your palm, or point at a book in a store and see what the *Times* and your neighborhood reading group have to say about it. Click on a restaurant and warn your friends that the service has deteriorated.

These devices will help people coordinate actions with others around the world—and, perhaps more importantly, with people nearby. Groups of people using these tools will gain new forms of social power, new ways to organize their interactions and exchanges just in time and just in place. Tomorrow's fortunes will be made by the businesses that find a way to profit from these changes, and yesterday's fortunes are already being lost by businesses that don't understand them. As with the personal computer and the Internet, key breakthroughs won't come from established industry leaders but from the fringes, from skunkworks and startups and even associations of amateurs. *Especially* associations of amateurs.

Although it will take a decade to ramp up, mobile communications and pervasive computing technologies, together with social contracts that were never possible before, are already beginning to change the way people meet, mate, work, fight, buy, sell, govern, and create. Some of these changes are beneficial and empowering, and some amplify the capabilities of people whose intentions are malignant. Large numbers of small groups, using the new media to their individual benefit, will create emergent effects that will nourish some existing institutions and ways of life and dissolve others. Contradictory and simultaneous effects are likely: People might gain new powers at the same time we lose old freedoms. New public goods could become possible, and older public goods might disappear.

When I started looking into mobile telephone use in Tokyo, I discovered that Shibuya Crossing was the most mobile-phone-dense neighborhood in the world: 80 percent of the 1,500 people who traverse that madcap plaza at each light change carry a mobile phone.[1] I took that coincidence as evidence that I was on the right track, although I had only an inkling of how to define what I was tracking. It had not yet become clear to me that I was no longer looking for intriguing evidence about changing techno-social practices, but galloping off on a worldwide hunt for the shape of the future.

I learned that those teenagers and others in Japan who were staring at their mobile phones and twiddling the keyboards with their thumbs were sending words and simple graphics to each other—messages like short emails that were delivered instantly but could be read at any time. When I looked into the technical underpinnings of telephone texting, I found that those early texters were walking around with an always-on connection to the Internet in their hands. The tingling in my forebrain turned into a buzz. When you have a persistent connection to the Internet, you have access to a great deal more than a communication channel.

A puzzling problem troubles those who understand the possibilities inherent in a mobile Internet: The potential power of connecting mobile devices to the Internet has been foreseen and hyped recently, but with the exception of DoCoMo, no company has yet created significant profits from wireless Internet services. The dotcom market collapse of 2001, accompanied by the even larger decline in value of global telecommunication companies, raised the question of whether any existing enterprises will have both the capital and the savvy to plug the Internet world into mobile telephony and make a successful business out of it.

Forecasting the technical potential of wireless Internet is the easy part. I knew that I should expect the unexpected when previously separate technologies meet. In the 1980s, television-like display screens plus miniaturized computers added up to a new technology with properties of its own: personal computers. PCs evolved dramatically over twenty years; today's handheld computer is thousands of times more powerful than the first Apple PC. Then PCs mated with telecommunications networks and multiplied in the 1990s to create the Internet, again spawning possibilities that neither of the parent technologies exhibited in isolation. Again, the new hybrid medium started evolving rapidly; my Internet connection today is thousands of times faster than my modem of the early 1980s. Then the Web in the late 1990s put a visual control panel on the Net and opened it to hundreds of millions of mainstream users. What's next in this self-accelerating spiral of technological, economic, and social change?

Next comes the mobile Net. Between 2000 and 2010, the social networking of mobile communications will join with the information-processing power of networked PCs. Critical mass will emerge some time after 2003, when more mobile devices than PCs will be connected to the Internet.[2] If the transition period we are entering in the first decade of the twenty-first century resembles the advent of PCs and the Internet, the new technology regime will turn out to be an entirely new medium, not simply a means of receiving stock quotes or email on the train or surfing the Web while walking down the street. Mobile Internet, when it really arrives, will not be just a way to do old things while moving. It will be a way to do things that couldn't be done before.

Anybody who remembers what mobile telephones looked like five years ago has a sense of the pace at which handheld technology is evolving. Today's mobile devices are not only smaller and lighter than the earliest cell phones, they have become tiny multimedia Internet terminals. I returned to Tokyo a year and a half after I first noticed people using telephones to send text between tiny black and white screens. On my most recent visit in the fall of 2001, I conducted my own color videoconference conversations via the current version of high-speed, multimedia, "third-generation" mobile phones. Perhaps even more important than the evolution of color and video screens in telephone displays is the presence of "location awareness" in mobile telephones. Increasingly, handheld devices can detect, within a few yards, where they are located on a continent, within a neighborhood, or inside a room.

These separate upgrades in capabilities don't just add to each other; mobile, multimedia, location-sensitive characteristics multiply each other's usefulness. At the same time, their costs drop dramatically. As we will see in later chapters, the driving factors of the mobile, context-sensitive, Internet-connected devices are Moore's Law (computer chips gets cheaper as they grow more powerful), Metcalfe's Law (the useful power of a network multiplies rapidly as the number of nodes in the network increases), and Reed's Law (the power of a network, especially one that enhances social networks, multiplies even more rapidly as the number of different human groups that can use the network increases). Moore's Law drove the PC industry and the cultural changes that resulted, Metcalfe's Law drove the deployment of the Internet, and Reed's Law will drive the growth of the mobile and pervasive Net.

The personal handheld device market is poised to take the kind of jump that the desktop PC made between 1980 and 1990, from a useful toy adopted by a subculture to a disruptive technology that changes every aspect of society. The hardware upgrades that make such a jump possible are already in the product pipeline. The underlying connective infrastructure is moving toward completion.

After a pause to recover from the collapse of the telecommunications economic bubble of the 1990s, the infrastructure for global, wireless, Internet-based communication is entering the final stages of development. The pocket videophone I borrowed in Tokyo was proof that a high-speed wireless network could link wireless devices and deliver multimedia to the palm of my hand. The most important next step for the companies that would deploy this technology and profit from it has nothing to do with chips or network protocols but everything to do with business models, early adopters, communities of developers, and value chains. It's not just about building the tools anymore. Now it's about what people use the tools to do.

How will human behavior shift when the appliances we hold in our hands, carry in our pockets, or wear in our clothing become supercomputers that talk to each other through a wireless mega-Internet? What can we reasonably expect people to do when they get their hands on the new gadgets? Can anyone foresee which companies will drive change and detect which businesses will be transformed or rendered obsolete by it? These questions first occurred to me on that spring day in Tokyo, but I didn't think about it again until another sight on a street halfway around the world from Shibuya Crossing caught my attention.

Sitting at an outdoor café in Helsinki a few months after I noticed the ways that people were using Japanese "i-mode" telephones, I watched five Finns meet and talk on the sidewalk. Three were in their early twenties. Two were old enough to be the younger people's parents. One of the younger persons looked down at his mobile phone while he was talking to one of the older people. The young man smiled and then showed the screen of his telephone to his peers, who looked at each other and smiled. However, the young man holding the device didn't show his mobile phone's screen to the older two. The sidewalk conversation among the five people flowed smoothly, apparently unperturbed by the activities I witnessed. Whatever the younger three were doing, it was clearly part of an accepted social code I knew nothing about. A new mode of social communication, enabled by a new technology, had already diffused into the norms of Finnish society.

At that moment I recalled the odd epiphany I had experienced at Shibuya Crossing the previous spring. Faint lines began to connect the dots. My internal future-detectors switched from a mild tingle to a persistent buzz.

Twice before in the past twenty years I've encountered something that convinced me in an instant that my life and the lives of millions of other people would change dramatically in coming years. On both occasions, I was drawn into a personal and intellectual quest to understand these possible changes. The first experience that propelled me on one of these intellectual expeditions was the sensation of using the graphical user interface that enabled non-programmers to operate computers by pointing and clicking. My 1985 book *Tools for Thought: The History and Future of Mind-Expanding Technology* presented my arguments that the PC could make possible an intellectual and creative expansion as influential as the changes triggered by the printing press.[3]

Within a few years of writing about them, the mind-amplifying gizmos I had futurized about had become part of my own life. My personal computer was a magic typewriter. Then I plugged my PC into my telephone, and I entered into social cyberspace. I spent more and more time online, reading and writing messages to computer bulletin boards, in chat rooms and electronic mailing lists. My 1993 book, *The Virtual Community,* examined the social phenomena I saw emerging from the early days of the Internet era.[4] Because of these previous experiences, I was prepared to pay attention that day in March 2000, when I first watched people in Tokyo thumbing text messages on their mobile phone keypads.

We're only seeing the first-order ripple effects of mobile-phone behavior now—the legions of the oblivious, blabbing into their hands or the air as they walk, drive, or sit in a concert and the electronic tethers that turn everywhere into the workplace and all the time into working time. What if these are just foreshocks of a future upheaval? I've learned enough from past technology shifts to expect the second-order effects of mobile telecommunications to bring a social tsunami. Consider a few of the early warning signs:

- The "People Power II" smart mobs in Manila who overthrew the presidency of President Estrada in 2001 organized demonstrations by forwarding text messages via cell phones.[5]
- A Web site, http://www.upoc.com, enables fans to stalk their favorite celebrities in real time through Internet-organized mobile networks and provides similar channels for journalists to organize citizen-reporters on the fly. The site makes it easy for roving phone tribes to organize communities of interest.
- In Helsinki and Tokyo you can operate vending machines with your telephone and receive directions on your wireless organizer that show you how to get from where you are standing to where you want to go.[6]
- "Lovegety" users in Japan find potential dates when their devices recognize another Lovegety in the vicinity broadcasting the appropriate pattern of attributes. Location-based matchmaking is now available on some mobile phone services.[7]
- When I'm not using my computer, its processor searches for extraterrestrial intelligence. I'm one of millions of people around the world who lend their computers to a cooperative effort—distributing parts of problems through the Internet, running the programs on our PCs while the machines are idle, and assembling the results via the Net. These computation collectives produce enough supercomputing power to crack codes, design medicines, or render digital films.[8]

Location-sensing wireless organizers, wireless networks, and community supercomputing collectives all have one thing in common: *They enable people to act together in new ways and in situations where collective action was not possible before.* An unanticipated convergence of technologies is suggesting new responses to civilization's founding question, How can competing individuals learn to work cooperatively?

As indicated by their name, smart mobs are not always beneficial. Lynch mobs and mobocracies continue to engender atrocities. The same convergence of technologies that opens new vistas of cooperation also makes possible a universal surveillance economy and empowers the bloodthirsty as well as the altruistic. Like every previous leap in technological power, the new convergence of wireless computation and social communication will enable people to improve life and liberty in some ways and to degrade it in others. The same technology has the potential to be used as both a weapon of social control and a means of resistance. Even the beneficial effects will have side effects.

We are moving rapidly into a world in which the spying machinery is built into every object we encounter. Although we leave digital traces of our personal lives with our credit cards and Web browsers today, tomorrow's mobile devices will broadcast clouds of personal data to invisible monitors all around us as we move from place to place. We are living through the last years of the long era before sensors are built into the furniture. The scientific and economic underpinnings of pervasive computing have been building for decades, and the social side-effects are only beginning to erupt. The virtual, social, and physical worlds are colliding, merging, and coordinating.

Don't mistake my estimates of the power of the coming technology with unalloyed enthusiasm for its effects. I am not calling for an uncritical embrace of the new regime, but for an informed consideration of what we're getting ourselves into. We have an opportunity now to consider the social implications of this new technological regime as it first emerges, before every aspect of life is reordered.

Online social networks are human activities that ride on technical communications infrastructures of wires and chips. When social communication via the Internet became widespread, people formed support groups and political coalitions online. The new social forms of the last decade of the twentieth century grew from the Internet's capability for many-to-many social communication. The new social forms of the early twenty-first century will greatly enhance the power of social networks.

Since my visits to Tokyo and Helsinki, I've investigated the convergence of portable, pervasive, location-sensitive, intercommunicating devices with social practices that make the technologies useful to groups as well as individuals. Foremost among these social practices are the "reputation systems" that are beginning to spring up online—computer-mediated trust brokers. The power of smart mobs comes in part from the way age-old social practices surrounding trust and cooperation are being mediated by new communication and computation technologies.

In this coming world, the acts of association and assembly, core rights of free societies, might change radically when each of us will be able to know who in our vicinity is likely to buy what we have to sell, sell what we want to buy, know what we need to know, want the kind of sexual or political encounter we also want. As online events are woven into the fabric of our physical world, governments and corporations will gain even more power over our behavior and beliefs than large institutions wield today. At the same time, citizens will discover new ways to band together to resist powerful institutions. A new kind of digital divide ten years from now will separate those who know how to use new media to band together from those who don't.

Knowing who to trust is going to become even more important. Banding together, from lynch mobs to democracies, taps the power of collective action. At the core of collective action is reputation—the histories each of us pull behind us that others routinely inspect to decide our value for everything from conversation partners to mortgage risks. Reputation systems have been fundamental to social life for a long time. In intimate societies, everyone knows everyone, and everyone's biography is an open, if not undisputed, book. Gossip keeps us up to date on who to trust, who other people trust, who is important, and who decides who is important.

Today's online reputation systems are computer-based technologies that make it possible to manipulate in new and powerful ways an old and essential human trait. Note the rise of Web sites like eBay (auctions), Epinions (consumer advice), Amazon (books, CDs, electronics), Slashdot (publishing and conversation) built around the contributions of millions of customers, enhanced by reputation systems that police the quality of the content and transactions exchanged through the sites.[9] In each of these businesses, the consumers are also the producers of what they consume, the value of the market increases as more people use it, and the aggregate opinions of the users provide the measure of trust necessary for transactions and markets to flourish in cyberspace.

Reputation reports on eBay give prospective auction bidders a sense of the track record of the otherwise anonymous people to whom they may trustingly mail a check. Ratings of experts on Epinions make visible the experience of others in trusting each expert's advice. Moderators on Slashdot award "karma points" that make highly knowledgeable, amusing, or useful posts in an online conversation more visible than those considered less insightful.

Wireless devices will take reputation systems into every cranny of the social world, far from the desktops to which these systems are currently anchored. As the costs of communication, coordination, and social accounting services drop, these devices make possible new ways for people to self-organize mutual aid. It is now technologically possible, for example, to create a service that would enable you to say to your handheld device: "I'm on my way to the office. Who is on my route and is looking for a ride in my direction right now—and who among them is recommended by my most trusted friends?"

Wireless communication technologies and the political regimes that regulate their use are a key component of smart mob infrastructure. One can sit in a restaurant in Stockholm or in the atrium of a business building in San Francisco and connect to unprotected or publicly available wireless networks with a laptop computer. Will ad hoc coalitions of wireless Internet enthusiasts create a grassroots network that can challenge the power of established infrastructure providers?

In Chapter 4, I'll consider how the placeless world of wireless communications is likely to interact with the place-specific networked computer chips that are beginning to infiltrate buildings, furniture, and even clothing. Although pervasive and wearable computers have been predicted and developed for more than a decade, their enabling components are only beginning to become inexpensive enough to trigger a wave of change. After years of kludgey prototypes, wearable computers are on the threshold of becoming fashion items. The first "wearable computing communities" are emerging.

The following chapters chronicle my investigation into technology practices and social theories and my inquiry into what we need to know if we intend to influence the way technological capabilities are exercised. I discuss the likely evolution of mobile devices, the future of pervasive computing, the power of peer-to-peer resource sharing, the study of cooperation, and the science of reputation. I examine the wireless Internet business model, or lack of it, and untangle some of the geek/wonk jargon surrounding regulatory battles over wireless Internet technologies. I explain why today's regulatory battles over the electromagnetic spectrum might be the most important collision of politics and communication technology since the King of England insisted on licensing printing presses.

When I examine the potential of new technologies, I have tried to avoid the dangers of "the rhetoric of the technological sublime," in which the miraculous properties of new tools are extolled to the exclusion of critical examination of their shadow sides.[10] I seek to shine light and also to look into the shadows.

Loss of privacy is perhaps the most obvious shadow side of technological cooperation systems. In order to cooperate with more people, I need to know more about them, and that means that they will know more about me. The tools that enable cooperation also transmit to a large number of others a constellation of intimate data about each of us. In the recent past, it was said that digital information technology, such as the magnetic strips on credit cards, leaves a "trail of electronic breadcrumbs" that can be used to track individuals. In the future, the trail will become a moving cloud as individuals broadcast information about themselves to devices within ten yards, a city block, or the entire world. Although there is room for speculation about how quickly the new tools will be adopted, certainly over the next several decades inexpensive wireless devices will penetrate into every part of the social world, bringing efficiencies to the production of snooping power. The surveillance state that Orwell feared was puny in its power in comparison to the panoptic web we have woven around us. Detailed information about the minute-by-minute behaviors of entire populations will become cost-effective and increasingly accurate. Both powerfully beneficial and powerfully dangerous potentials of this new tracking capability will be literally embedded in the environment.

Cooperative effort sounds nice, and at its best, it is the foundation of the finest creations of human civilizations, but it can also be nasty if the people who cooperate share pernicious goals. Terrorists and organized criminals have been malevolently successful in their use of smart mob tactics. A technological infrastructure that increases surveillance on citizens and empowers terrorists is hardly utopian. Intrusions on individual privacy and liberty by the state and its political enemies are not the only possible negative effects of enhanced technology-assisted cooperation. In addition, profound questions about the quality and meaning of life are raised by the prospect of millions of people possessing communication devices that are "always on" at home and work. How will mobile communications affect family and societal life?

There are opportunities as well as dangers, however, and a major reason I've written this book is my growing belief that what we understand about the future of smart mobs, and how we talk about that future, holds the power to influence that future—at least within a short window of opportunity. The possibilities for the use of smart mob infrastructure do not consist exclusively of dark scenarios. Indeed, cooperation is integral to the highest expressions of human civilization. In counterpoint to the dystopian possibilities I've noted, I introduce sociologists and economists who argue that wireless technologies could make it easier to create public goods, thus affording an unprecedented opportunity for enhancing social capital that can enrich everyone's life.

Just as existing notions of community were challenged by the emergence of social networks in cyberspace, traditional ideas about the nature of place are being challenged as computing and communication devices begin to saturate the environment. As more people on city streets and on public transportation spend more time speaking to other people who are not physically co-present, the nature of public spaces and other aspects of social geography are changing before our eyes and ears; some of these changes will benefit the public good and others will erode it.

Before people who hold stakes in tomorrow's technological civilization can hope to address the social challenges posed by smart mob technologies, we have to know what the issues are, what they imply, and useful ways to think about them. I conclude this book with a strategic briefing for the future, highlighting the strengths, weaknesses, opportunities, and dangers of mobile and pervasive technologies. I believe that our destiny is not (yet) determined by technology, that our freedom and quality of life do not (yet) have to be sacrificed to make us into more efficient components of a global wealth-generating machine.

I also know that beneficial uses of technologies will not automatically emerge just because people hope they will. Those who wish to have some influence on the outcome must first know what the dangers and opportunities are and how to act on them. Such knowledge does not guarantee that the new tools will be used to create a humane, sustainable world. Without such knowledge, however, we will be ill equipped to influence the world our grandchildren will inhabit.

Shibuya Epiphany

The telegraph, like the Internet . . . transformed social and business practices, but it could be used only by skilled operators. Its benefits became available to the public at large only when the telegraph evolved into the telephone—initially known as the "speaking telegraph." The Internet is still in a telegraphic stage of development, in the sense that the complexity and expense of PCs prevent many people from using it. The mobile phone thus promises to do for the Internet what the telephone did for the telegraph: to make it a truly mainstream technology.

Because it used the same wires, the telephone was originally seen as merely a speaking telegraph, but it turned out to be something entirely new. The same mistake is already being repeated with the Internet. Many people expect the mobile Internet to be the same as the wired version, only mobile, but they are wrong . . . . Instead, the mobile Internet, although it is based on the same technology as the fixed-line Internet, will be something different and will be used in new and unexpected ways.

—Tom Standage, "The Internet Untethered"

Thumb Tribes

If you want to experience virtual reality without putting your head in a computer, take the subway to Shibuya station and follow the signs to "Hachiko." Pause near the statue outside the station. This bronze monument to a faithful dog is one of Tokyo's favorite meeting places. In the 1920s, Hachiko accompanied Professor Eisaboru Ueno to this station every morning and waited for Ueno's return. Ueno failed to make his appointment the day he died in 1925, but his pet continued to show up at the station until he died there in 1934. People still hold a festival at the statue every year on the seventh of March.[1] Like other meeting places such as the clock in Grand Central Station in New York City, the statue of Hachiko is an informal coordination point for urban populations—a social focus identified by sociologist Thomas Schelling as an essential element of every city's life.[2]

Hundreds of people mill around Hachiko. Cliques and flocks assemble and diffuse. Couples and octets coalesce, synchronize, and move on. In many ways, Shibuya station resembles every other Schelling point since the Athenian agora. Unlike gathering places of antiquity, however, some of the people milling around Hachiko are invisibly coordinated by flows of electronically mediated messages.

A growing number of people at Shibuya Crossing now divide their attention among three places at the same time. There's the physical world where pedestrians are expected to avoid walking into each other. Surrounding the crowd is an artificial but concrete world, the city as the all-enclosing environment of commercial propaganda described more than thirty years ago as *The Society of the Spectacle*.[3] Less garish but no less influential than the neon and video of the twenty-first-century metropolis are the private channels of the texting tribes, a third sphere in which bursts of terse communications link people in real time and physical space.

If you turn your back to Hachiko and look across the street at the right time, you will see yourself displayed on one of three gargantuan television screens that loom over the intersection. The giant high-definition screens are, in virtual reality parlance, "immersive." That is, when you are at Shibuya Crossing, not only are you perceiving an ever-changing audio-video advertisement, but you are also inside it.

The crosswalk works on the scramble system. Every time the lights turn green, 1,500 people cross from eight directions at once, performing a complex, collective, ad hoc choreography that accomplishes the opposite of flocking; people cooperate with immediate neighbors in order to go in *different* directions. In addition to negotiating split-second coordination with moving strangers, many in this crowd carry on simultaneous conversations with people located elsewhere. When I revisited this place a year and a half after my first encounter with texting, I paused in the center of the intersection during a dozen scramble cycles in order to taste attunement with the hyper-coordinated throngs.

I knew that every technological regime involves people who invent a new tool, people who manufacture and sell it (and their stockholders, and the politicians those stockholders influence), and finally, people who use the technology in ways often unimagined by inventors, vendors, or regulators. Each of these groups owns a different stake and sees the tool from a different perspective. I started my research by interviewing an anthropologist and then met with one of the strategists responsible for "i-mode," Japan's singularly successful wireless Internet service. I also talked with scientists, engineers, marketers, entrepreneurs, journalists, and people on the street.

Two graduate students from Showa Women's University, Tomoko Kawamura and Haruna Kamide, and I were joined on the streets of Tokyo by my friend Justin Hall, a twenty-five-year-old American whose cheery willingness to engage strangers compensated for his rudimentary understanding of the Japanese language. Over a number of days, the four of us directly engaged dozens of *keitai* (mobile telephone) users in an unscientific but illuminating street survey. We started with fourteen-to-twenty-year-olds and then moved on to college-age youth.

A short walk from Harajuku station, La Forêt is a vertical mall catering to young urbanites. The small public space in front of the La Forêt is the informal nexus of the techno-adept, fashion-saturated, identity-constructing, mobile-texting culture. One of the first interviewees we encountered kept her keitai tucked into the rear pocket of her pants. (I noticed a proliferation of tiny pockets in shirts and pants specifically for keitai in Tokyo.) Her hair pointed in forty directions, spliced into carefully composed anarchy by fluorescent-colored baby hair clips. She wore a bow tie. Fashions had flashed through Harajuku like epidemics for decades before texting accelerated the pace of social networking. Our bow-tied informant said that she exchanged around eighty text messages a day, mostly with her three best girlfriends, sometimes with guys. Like many of her friends, she could compose a message with her thumb without looking at it.

We talked with an eighteen-year-old male in baggy purple pants. His hair was casual but immobile in a way that suggested a dab of gel. He wore a camouflage pattern t-shirt and a New York Yankees cap. He messaged guys in his band, "but mostly, my girlfriend." He sent and received a few dozen messages each day. Sometimes, he and his friends sent each other ringtone versions of pop music.

Some girls wore school uniforms but decorated their keitai with iridescent stickers and phrases written in nail polish. Brands were prominent on clothing and accoutrements, but often in an altered form; logos and team insignia were mixed together, adorned with stickers and patches, toys, and charms.

Some call Tokyo texters *oyayubisoku*—"the thumb tribe." Kyodo News service reported a story in the summer of 2001 that revealed an unpleasant side to e-tribalism: Police arrested five teenage members of "Mad Wing Angels," a virtual motorcycle gang that met via texting, included members who didn't own motorcycles, and had never gathered in one place at the same time. The leader had never met the four Tokyo girls she ordered to beat and torture a fifth gang member who asked permission to leave the group in order to study abroad.[4] Clearly, the social ripples of texting were getting into rich ethnographic territory. It was my great good fortune to know an ethnographer who had been exploring it from the beginning— Kawamura's and Kamide's mentor, my old friend Mizuko Ito.

Anthropologist Mizuko Ito has been observing the ways that Tokyo youth use keitai. Stanford graduate Ito, now an associate professor at Keio University, studies "how identity and place are produced through and within digital media infrastructures." I had known her for a decade; Ito's brother, Joichi, was the first person to show me how to create a Web site, circa 1993, and Ito's husband, Scott Fisher, had been a NASA researcher I had interviewed in 1990.[5] I think of the Ito-Fishers as the Tokyo branch of the tribe that lives in the future.

By the time she and I and Kawamura and Kamide conversed in the dining room of Ito's Tokyo residence in 2001, Ito had been interviewing Tokyo teenagers—arguably the most technology-adept cultural experimenters on the planet—for two years. Ito believes that mobile phones triggered an intergenerational power shift in Japan because they freed youth from "the tyranny of the landline shared by inquisitive family members, creating a space for private communication and an agency that alters possibilities for social action."[6] In Japan, adding wired telephone lines to homes is expensive, but it is less expensive for teens to have their own personal mobile numbers.

"The space of the home," Ito noted, "dominated by parents, accommodates their identity as child, but not as friend. It is too small, crowded, and saturated with family interests to be an appropriate place for gathering face to face. The home phone once was a means for parents to monitor and regulate their children's relationships with their peers."[7] Texting made it possible for young people to conduct conversations that can't be overheard. Ito observed teens using this new communication freedom to "construct a localized and portable place of intimacy, an open channel of contact with generally three to five others."[8]

Ito and Kawamura, her research assistant, had interviewed high school and college students, seeking to understand how "keitai refashions the politics of how we view place and time."[9] Explaining that the life of Tokyo high school students is tightly controlled by family and school, Ito elaborated: "Getting a mobile phone grants teenagers a degree of privacy and right of assembly previously unavailable, which they use to construct a networked alternative space that is available from anywhere they are."[10]

Keitai-equipped youth use the parts of the city between their schools and homes as the stage for their alternative social space, staying in touch with friends while traveling from home to school, conducting group communications while shopping, flocking to fast-food restaurants or coffeehouses at fluidly negotiated intervals.

Kawamura and Kamide agreed with Ito that although many Japanese youth have more than one hundred addresses in their keitai's built-in address book, most send the majority of their messages to a small group of three to five peers. The three researchers also noted that many of these messages are of the intimacy-maintaining "thinking of you" variety. The young women they observed casually use text messages to say "good night," "good morning," or even "I'm bored." Similar research, not yet published at the time Ito reached her conclusions, was uncovering similar changes in family power structures in Scandinavia, a distinctly different culture half a world away from Japan.[11]

Kawamura documented communications exchanged by a group of thirty who were organizing a party at a karaoke bar. "As the date grew nearer, the frequency of messages increased. But only four people showed up on time at the agreed place," Kawamura told me. However, dozens of others stayed in touch through voice and text messages while they trickled in. "Kids have become loose about time and place. If you have a phone, you can be late," added Kawamura. Kamide, the other graduate student, agreed that it is no longer taboo to show up late: "Today's taboo," Kamide conjectured, is "to forget your keitai or let your battery die." I later discovered that this "softening of time" was noted for the same age group in Norway.[12] "The opportunity to make decisions on the spot has made young people reluctant to divide their lives into time slots, as older generations are used to doing," agreed another Norwegian researcher.[13]

Has the definition of "presence" become uncoupled from physical places and reassigned to a social network that extends beyond any single location? According to Ito, "As long as people participated in the shared communications of the group, they seemed to be considered by others to be present."[14] In Norway, Rich Ling and Birgette Yttri observed that mobile telephone users in the same age group "were still available to their social network even when participating in another social event."[15]

It is commonly accepted among i-mode watchers that widespread youth adoption accelerated the spread of mobile Internet services throughout Japanese society (by spring 2001, 90 percent of Tokyo-area high school students possessed a mobile telephone—a technology diffusion that exceeded the adoption of the PC in Japan in both rate and scope).[16] Teenagers shared two key characteristics with the wider market of business people and housewives: Most were not already Internet users through desktop PCs, and most viewed keitai as fashion as well as technology. Our informants liked to download new ringtones or query an i-mode site to find out if the boy they just met was astrologically compatible—but none thought of what they were doing as "using the Internet."

Although major global manufacturers like Sony take their cues from the young early adopters in Shibuya and sell their own cultural pastiches back to them, the street kids already take the capabilities of smart mob technologies far beyond the safe boundaries provided by popular brands. Dmitri Ragano reported from Shibuya on this trend six months after my last visit there:

> As the balance of power falls in favor of the Shibuya kids, the technology companies may be increasingly at their mercy. In Japan, young people are beginning to turn away from sites and applications that are officially endorsed by mobile operators and going underground. One dark and strange example of this trend is an independent site called Zavn.net that has gained a sizeable audience and offline momentum with no promotion. The site features a series of original novels about the Japanese phenomenon of *enjo kosai* in which some teenage girls in metro areas like Tokyo have affairs with middle-aged salary men in exchange for money. The stories of Zavn.net are written in punchy, card-size chapters that are intended to be read on a cell phone.[17]

According to Ragano, a café in Shibuya and a film have spun off physical world events based on this underground phenomenon—not entirely what the brand makers planned.

Michael Lewis referred to the "child-centric model of economic development" in *Next: The Future Just Happened,* in describing how the fastest-growing parts of the otherwise ailing Japanese economy derive from teen-centric products and services, from MP3 players and pocket-sized keitai to i-mode mobile Internet services.[18] Although today's 30 million i-mode subscribers come from every age group, Mari Matsunaga, the creative genius who launched this radical service from a staid engineering company, had Tokyo teenagers in mind. I was advised to meet Takeshi Natsuno, the Internet-seasoned marketing executive Matsunaga had hired to help launch the service.

i-mode Uber Alles

In the fall of 2001, NTT DoCoMo's regal modernist reception room on the twenty-seventh floor of Tokyo's Sanno Park Tower felt like the capital of a world, the way dotcom deal making at Buck's restaurant in Woodside, California, felt in 1999 or the way Sony Headquarters felt in 1989. Silent, marble-floored elevators the size of most companies' waiting rooms disgorge cohorts of prospective partners, contractors, and subcontractors into an enormous antechamber with panoramic views of Tokyo. In the center of the room, three banks of receptionists in identical fuchsia outfits take names and gesture toward the ranks of low, square, black leather benches where polyglot hordes wait on all four sides of each bench.

I came to Sanno Park Tower in search of clues about why this company was succeeding while so many others were failing. The telecommunications giants of Europe watched their stock prices crash at the same time they owed $100 billion for the third-generation wireless license fees they paid governments in the 1990s. Portable analog telephones were the first generation of mobile technology. Digital telephones that made use of Internet-like services like short text messages were the second generation. The coming "3G" generation, which required the purchase of government-regulated licenses to use specific chunks of radio spectrum, was thought to be the breakthrough that would usher in the era of the mobile Internet. Although Sweden and Finland granted licenses in "beauty contests" among competitors, other nations conducted auctions. In anticipation of a wireless Internet business explosion, some European companies had staked unprecedented amounts of capital on securing their rights to a piece of the 3G spectrum. Converting those rights into profits, however, was proving to be thorny.

The first 3G trials of wireless networks fast enough for video data to travel in real time to mobile devices was postponed in Europe as telecom infrastructure industries struggled to leap from terrestrial wired networks to wireless media. The hype about the wireless Internet business was beginning to look as empty as the hype about the dotcom industry. There was one notable exception to the failures of wireless Internet schemes. While telecommunications companies faced radical declines in demand after a decade of expansion, one company attracted 28 million users within two years of launching a totally new kind of service. Each of those users pay an average of U.S.$20 monthly for i-mode services—DoCoMo's version of wireless Internet. I sat with the other hopefuls on the big square leather benches in Sanno Park Tower while I waited to meet the director of i-mode strategy. DoCoMo had launched the world's first successful 3G trial three weeks prior to my visit.

Nippon Telephone and Telegraph, DoCoMo's parent company, like AT&T and other telecommunication companies around the world, used to be a monopoly and has always been driven by engineers and bureaucrats. For most of the twentieth century, NTT sold telephone services, licensed headset technologies, and dreamed of delivering services utterly unlike voice telephony. NTT management did realize that the Internet business would be essentially different from the business that had made NTT the largest telco in the world with more than 200,000 employees.[19] When the handset technology and communication network technologies matured to the point where NTT was within sight of launching a wireless Internet service, it was the genius of an NTT executive named Keiichi Enoki to hire someone from outside NTT culture.[20] He turned to a woman, a non-engineer who didn't understand computers and didn't use the Internet.

Mari Matsunaga, at forty-two, had been working for the Japanese company Recruit for twenty years. Her specialty was launching magazines. Enoki proposed that Matsunaga's Internet illiteracy would be an advantage, because the market DoCoMo sought for their new service consisted of people who didn't use the Internet. NTT would provide the engineering expertise. Matsunaga would furnish the marketing genius. Enoki overcame her doubts and convinced Matsunaga to take up the challenge.

Matsunaga needed to hire someone who knew the Internet culture better than she did. She recalled a capable and style-conscious young man who had worked part-time as an assistant editor for one of the Recruit magazines. Takeshi Natsuno later graduated from one of Japan's top universities, and while earning his MBA at the Wharton School in the early

1990s, experienced the Internet culture as it spread among its earliest enthusiasts, American college students. Since his return to Japan, Natsuno had founded a Japanese e-business that was the first to use the Internet as a means of advertising and joined an Internet-focused venture company. "His experience at a venture company," Matsunaga recognized, "had taught him the limitations of businesses that targeted PC users exclusively. The number of users always stalled around the 300,000 mark. But if it was mobile phones instead, there could be millions of potential users."[21]

Natsuno wrote a business plan for Matsunaga that recognized the unique opportunity of marrying mobile telephony with Internet information: "The weakness of mobile phones, and all voice communication tools," Natsuno wrote, "is that they're useless unless you know the right telephone number. The distribution of data via phones, however, would make it possible for users to search for a restaurant or make a dinner reservation. They could also reserve a train or airplane ticket. . . . Ads for companies would no longer be unnecessary information, but essential information that users could be charged for accessing." Natsuno acknowledged Matsunaga's former employer as the inspiration for his i-mode business model: "Consumers are prepared to pay for Recruit magazines, which are essentially a collection of ads. However, in the case of mobile phones, users don't use them for the purpose of acquiring specific information. If we could get the information onto mobile phones, people would start looking at it as a natural extension of using the phone."[22]

Matsunaga insisted that the telephone weigh less than 100 grams and that the basic service should cost less than 300 yen (less than three U.S. dollars) per month. Knowing that "something only comes to life when it's given a name," she came up with the name "i-mode."[23] She remembered that Enoki had said that they weren't designing a service for NTT executives, but for their children. "I got the first positive sign from my family," Enoki recalled. "At that time, the pager was at the peak of its popularity. My daughter used the number pad as a form of data communications. My son could play a new computer game without reading the instructions. Their ability to adapt to new information and use it with ease left a strong impression on me. I was convinced that young people would accept a new data service that would give them the same kind of enjoyment."[24]

The DoCoMo staff in their twenties who had joined the i-mode team convinced the rest of the team of the importance of text communication between mobile telephone users—an abbreviated form of instant email for the small keitai screens. "The young staff members were constantly coming up with new ideas," Matsunaga acknowledged. "One new idea was the addition of symbolic characters. It emerged as an answer to the problem of how to condense meaning and convey feelings in a short email. There had previously been a pager that had sold particularly well. Upon examining the reason for its success, it was discovered that only this particular model offered the symbol of a heart. Just the addition of a heart made a tremendous difference in sales."[25]

Eventually, one of the receptionists directed me to enter another elevator, where I joined those chosen to ascend to chambers on the thirty-third floor. There were crystal decanters and glasses, more views of Tokyo, and a whiteboard at the end of the table. Natsuno entered the room with an energy that didn't flag for the hour and a half we—mostly he—talked. He wore a tailored suit and perfectly dimpled tie. At thirty-six, Natsuno is the youngest of all NTT's top management. His English is perfect, and he makes it clear that he believes what he's selling. He grins often and seems to be authentically happy. Why shouldn't he be? It took AOL more than a decade to acquire 30 million subscribers, but i-mode reached that level in a little more than two years.

As soon as I mentioned in my opening remarks that the NTT video depiction of the future recently shown to me by a PR man was the same one I had seen ten years ago, Natsuno blurted, with surprising glee, "Engineers don't understand the value chain!" He jumped up and drew a diagram on the whiteboard. "I love to use the whiteboard," he exclaimed.[26] Half an hour later, he had taken off his jacket and was still emoting. Nobody who meets him can doubt that Natsuno is an energetic salesman, unafraid of making big claims:

> My role is to coordinate a value chain larger than the world of networks, servers, and handsets NTT is used to. I knew that no single company could provide the entire value chain, so I set out to create alliances and support among third-party developers. I knew how America Online had succeeded. AOL became the number one Internet service where so many others failed because they provided an easy to use interface, useful content developed by others, and ways for users to communicate with each other.[27]

Like AOL, Natsuno offered i-mode users a carefully selected menu of content that would make the new service attractive to mobile telephone customers who weren't Internet-savvy but did want lifestyle-related information: banking services, tickets for events and hotel reservations, weather forecasts and stock market quotes, restaurant guides, transport schedules, games, ringtones, and even fortune-telling services. Natsuno pushed Do-CoMo to provide incentives for developers to create successful sites. This reversed the traditional policy that telephone service operators had used worldwide. Instead of making third-party services advantageous to the operating company at the expense of the entrepreneurs, i-mode made sure that successful i-mode sites would pay off for those who created and maintained them. "This is the Internet way of thinking, not the telecom way of thinking," Natsuno said with a grin.

The ringtone downloads so popular in Harajuku, Natsuno noted, were not just revenue streams; they had initiated millions of users in the process of downloading content. 3G would make it possible to download games, movies, and television news in real time. Millions of people are already on the upgrade path to multimedia capabilities. Who knows what other attractions the tens of thousands of i-mode developers will come up with to make use of that bandwidth?

Three weeks after I visited Natsuno, NTT launched their "i-motion" location-based services that give 3G users and third-party services access to accurate global positioning information.[28] Now, users can employ their telephones to find information relevant to the neighborhood or building they are in at the time. As soon as I heard about i-motion, I recalled a conversation I had with Kenny Hirschhorn, chief strategist for European telecommunication giant Orange. (The sign on Hirschhorn's London office door says "future boy.") Hirschhorn had cautioned me against thinking of the telephone as a device to talk into, urging me instead to think of the mobile telephone as evolving into a "remote control for your life." Hirschhorn's comment made it easier to recognize what Natsuno intends for the future of i-mode.[29]

Before we left the thirty-third floor, Natsuno showed me how to order from the office soft drink machine with my 3G phone. Although I could download cartoons while I sipped my beverage and didn't have to fish in my pocket for change, the menus and buttons seemed too clunky to entice the un-nerdy masses who want a soft drink, not a sequence of screen menus. Nevertheless, Coca-Cola is exactly the kind of "third-party developer" NTT would need to break out of telephony and take the lead in the much-forecasted but yet-to-be-demonstrated "m-commerce" market.

Using your telephone to purchase something from a vending machine or to ask a street sign for directions are examples of how a mobile Internet could be as different from the landlocked Net as telephony was from telegraphy.

The mental models of the smart mob future that I started to form in Tokyo were reinforced in some ways, and had to be revised in other ways, when I spent more time in the other epicenter of mobile and pervasive technology—the Nordic countries.

Virtual Helsinki and the Botfighters of Stockholm

Risto Linturi carried his mobile phone in his hand when he entered the room. Before he sat down, he put the device on the table. At times, Linturi picked up his telephone and gestured with it. Whereas keitai in Shibuya are often tucked away in special pockets or clipped onto belts, they seem to be an extension of the hand in Finland. Indeed, *känny,* the word Finns use to describe their mobile devices, is a diminutive form of "hand."[30] If Tokyo and DoCoMo are the first capitals of the wireless Internet industry, Helsinki and Nokia have been the wellsprings of mobile telephony. Finland leads the world in both Internet connections and mobile phones per capita.[31] Even before the launch of i-mode, Finnish adolescent courtship rituals and the social norms of Finnish business managers had been transformed by the use of short messages known as "SMS."

Helsinki is the color of granite, not neon, and giant televisions don't dominate street crossings, but Finnish citizens have lived the longest with the effects of mobile telephone usage. A few Finnish visionaries, Risto Linturi foremost among them, have been thinking about mobile and pervasive information technologies for some time. Like my Tokyo friends, Linturi is a member of the transnational tribe that lives in the future. As a teenager, he was one of Finland's first PC enthusiasts. Since then, he's been director of technology for Helsinki Telephone and "helped Nokia see the mobile telephone as a general purpose remote control device."[32] Slim, soft-spoken, and deliberate in his choice of words, Linturi is an enthusiast for the technologies he envisions. Like Natsuno and Hirschhorn, he is convinced that mobile telephones are evolving into control devices for the physical world.

Linturi set up a network of sensors in his home outside Helsinki. He monitors the temperature and lighting, locks and unlocks doors, and controls the kitchen appliances and the VCR from wherever he happens to be, using his mobile telephone as a remote control. "People who ring my doorbell when I am away from home can talk to me through my mobile."[33] Linturi's blend of personal enthusiasm and professional optimism reminded me of Mr. Irukuyama, the DoCoMo engineering manager who made his official NTT "vision" presentation with formal aplomb and then proudly showed me how his 3G phone connects to his infant son's webcam.

Linturi, the father of teenage daughters, was one of the first observers of the way young people use text messaging to coordinate their actions: "There are endless calls. 'No, no, it's changed—we're not going to this place, we're going over here. Hurry!' It's like a school of fish."[34] By the time Linturi and I met in May 2001, the term "swarming" was frequently used by the people I met in Helsinki to describe the cybernegotiated public flocking behavior of texting adolescents. In our conversation, Linturi also emphasized that the mobile phones had an effect on older adults: "Managers in Finnish companies always keep their phones on. Customers expect fast reactions. In Finland, if you can't reach a superior, you make many decisions yourself. Managers who want to influence decisions of subordinates must keep their phones open."[35]

Linturi was a principal architect of a project named Helsinki Arena 2000, an experiment connecting mobile telephones to informational "beacons" stationed around the city, providing access to an up-to-the-minute database of the city's geographic information systems.[36] Geographic information systems are the focus of a rich discipline that predates the mobile Internet; using maps as user interfaces to databases makes useful but abstract information easily available and comprehensible.[37] Using location-sensing technologies, mobile devices gave people access to locally relevant portions of a simulation of Helsinki's infrastructure, similar to the "Mirror Worlds" predicted in 1992 by David Gelernter.[38] For the experiment, they modeled twenty-five square kilometers of the city of Helsinki. Cities wired to tell your mobile device where you are and how to get to your destination is Linturi's forecast for a "killer app" of tomorrow's digital cities.

On a previous visit to Helsinki. I had visited a friend whose office was located in a section of town known as Arabianranta ("Arabian Shore"), named after the Arabia brand porcelain factory that had dominated this light industrial area of Helsinki earlier in the century. Like similar urban neighborhoods such as New York's Soho and San Francisco's Multimedia Gulch, Arabianranta's large spaces and cheap rents attracted geeks, designers, artists, students, and entrepreneurs. Restaurants and theaters popped up. Without anyone planning it, a wired ecology of subcultures started aggregating in the same geographic neighborhood. In 1999, IBM, Finland's telecommunications operator Sonera, and the Symbian Alliance—a joint venture including Ericsson, Motorola, Nokia, Matsushita, and Psion—agreed to invest $1 billion to build Helsinki Virtual Village (HVV) in Arabianranta.[39] Since I was already in the neighborhood visiting a friend, I dropped in on Ilkka Innamaa at Digia, a company that was helping design HVV. By 2010, Innamaa claimed, HVV will link 12,000 residents, 700 enterprises with 8,000 employees, via fiber optic cables in their homes and 3G location-sensitive mobile devices.[40] If HVV succeeds, its sponsors plan to roll it out to neighborhoods and suburbs of other cities around the world. All there was to see of it in 2000, however, was a demo video.

"It's too top-down," was Linturi's opinion of HVV. "Open standards should enable people to link devices and services almost automatically." If citizens have the freedom to set up ad hoc wireless networks or to network their houses the way he had, Linturi thinks they will create digital pathways on their own, the way people automatically create pathways between buildings. One school of community design suggests looking for ways to enable people to use resources at hand to create different pathways, instead of trying to predesign their paths through the community.[41] Virtual villages, in this view, create themselves. In Chapter 4 I look more closely at "digital cities" pervaded by sensors, beacons, computers, and communicators. Arena 2000 and HVV might be the earliest representatives of two opposite schools of virtual urban planning: the "grassroots, open system, emergent use" school and the "centrally planned, proprietary system, planned use" school.

Finnish innovators have made significant contributions to Internet technology. Internet Relay Chat, the online social channel connecting countless real-time tribes, was invented in 1988 by Jarkko Oikarinen, a computer science student. The open source software movement's Linus Torvalds started Linux, the community-developed software operating system that is challenging Microsoft, on a server at the University of Helsinki.[42]

Finland's Nokia Oy started as a paper mill on the Nokia River in 1865.[43] By 1999, with $15.7 billion in sales, Nokia had become the world's leading vendor of mobile telephone handsets and infrastructure.[44] Nokia's CEO bet on what was still a distant future technology in 1987, when European technocrats agreed on a mobile telephony technical standard known as Global System for Mobile Communications (GSM). In 1991, Finland's Radiolinja launched the world's first GSM network; within a few years, the penetration of mobile telephones, most of them made by Nokia, had reached 60 percent of the Finnish population.[45]

Built into the GSM standard was the capability of instantly sending short text messages of 160 characters from one telephone to another, using the telephone keyboard to input messages and the small display screen to read them—the Short Message Service (SMS). The first text message was sent in December 1992 in the United Kingdom.[46] By mid-2001, tens of billions of messages were being exchanged worldwide each month.[47] By 2002, 100 billion text messages were being sent on the world's GSM networks each month.[48] Considering that the telephone operators collect a few cents on each message, that's a tidy windfall for what was almost an afterthought in the GSM standard.

The unexpected success of texting was also a sign that people were once again appropriating a communication technology for social purposes, as they had done with voice telephony and with the Minitel in France, where the chat tool was literally stolen from operators by the users, and with email, where it was the driving force behind the growth of the landlocked Internet.[49]

A technical and economic advantage of text messaging is that it is "packet-switched" rather than "circuit-switched." This technical distinction divides the telegraph-telephone era analog network from the Internet and mobile era digital network. Circuit-switched telephone connections require a series of physical switches to link a continuous wired circuit between both parties— think of early twentieth-century films of operators who closed those circuits by plugging jacks into a switchboard. Like data on the Internet, text messages are sent in electronic bursts of data, "packets," that find their own way through the network via "routers" that read the addresses on the packets and forward them. Packets are tiny and are reassembled at the destination, so they can fit in between other messages instead of preempting them the way analog circuits do. This means that far more information can be sent economically from any point on the network to any other because the transport medium efficiently allocates network resources on a bottom-up basis (the packets find their way like autos) rather than an inefficient, centrally planned basis where each conversation requires a devoted circuit (like railroads). This technical advantage makes it less expensive to support massive text-messaging traffic than to support circuit-switched voice traffic. The source of the power of this new medium is the combination of the economic advantages of texting with the way texting supports and is propagated by social networks. The economic leverage that comes from interleaving digital information in this way will come into play again when I look at new wireless Internet technologies that challenge the way the electromagnetic spectrum is regulated.

Texting—referred to by young Finnish enthusiasts with the verb form "tekstata"—surfaced in Finland in 1995 and was discovered by teenagers in 1998.[50] By 2000, Finns were exchanging more than a billion SMS messages annually.[51] Eija-Liisa Kasasniemi, a Finnish folklorist, focused her dissertation research on the text message culture of Finnish teenagers. She and colleague Pirjo Rautianen started collecting data about SMS messaging in the lives of Finnish adolescents. They reported some interesting findings:

> Through SMS teens hate, gossip, mediate, and express longing, even when the writer lacks the courage for a call or in situations where other communication channels are inappropriate. The text message is the backdoor of communication.
>
> The SMS phenomenon has generated its own terminology, customs, and social norms . . . . Perhaps the most surprising feature in the text messaging of Finnish teenagers is the extent to which it incorporates collective behavior . . . . Text messages are circulated among friends, composed together, read together, and fitting expressions or entire messages are borrowed from others.
>
> Teens use the messages to test their limits and step outside the role of a child. Text messaging is a way to share relationships.[52]

In 1997, Pasi Mäenpää and Timo Kopomaa conducted research funded by Nokia and Telecom Finland (which later became Sonera). Their report included observations that resonated with Ito's findings in Japan:

> The mobile phone creates its own user-culture, which in turn produces new urban culture and new ways of life . . .
>
> Spontaneous contacts, which especially the younger interviewees make "ex tempore," tend to be these "where are you" and "whatcha doing" calls. Such chatting hardly resembles real exchange of information or even intercourse, as much as merely sharing one's life with others in real time. It is a question of living in the same rhythm or wave with one's closest friends, the feeling of a continuously shared life.

The repetitive communications by phone are not merely an exchange of information; they also open another world of experience beside, or instead of, the one inhabited at the moment.[53]

I met Finns in their twenties who had grown up with mobile telephony and who now design technologies that could increase social capital rather than dissipate it. They are building a "shared urban living space" that combines a physical location, a virtual community, a mobile social network, and a cooperative organization, "an anti-netcafé, where no screens flicker yet technology is present, where doing together and being together is enabled through a unique social setting."[54] It started when four young men met with an American entrepreneur who wanted to "talk to the young 'Internet dudes' about setting up a netcafé in Helsinki."[55]

When the Finnish Internet dudes started talking about "why netcafés suck so bad," they started dreaming up what they came to call "Aula, an urban living room for the network society." Part entrepreneurial enterprise, part nonprofit attempt to do good, part laboratory for studying mobile culture, Aula was being assembled while I interviewed its creators.

I had spoken with Linturi at the elegant, slightly formal Hotel Kämp. A few blocks away from the Kämp, I met Jyri Engeström, Tuomas Toivonen, and Aleksi Aaltonen at a less elegant, less formal, more hectic and eclectic place. In May 2001, they had secured a small space in the middle of Lasipalatsi and were constructing the physical locus of their community center at one of the city's crucial crossroads—a less spectacular but equally vital counterpart to Shibuya Crossing.

The interior floor space consists of only a few hundred square meters and is L-shaped. Plywood was being cut as we spoke. Naked conduits covered the ceiling. Jyri Engeström, a sociology student in his early twenties, sat amidst construction materials, talking whenever the power saws fell silent. "Netcafés suck because they aren't social places. People don't meet there," he proclaimed.

The young men who turned down the netcafé idea decided to create a public space where "consumption was possible, but not obligatory, and where production and exchange were also present."[56] There would be a coffee machine and a copier/printer, but the participants would operate the machines themselves: a nonprofit Starbucks crossed with a co-op Kinko's. They challenged themselves to design a space where virtual communities and mobile tribes could mingle in the physical world, where technology could help people come together instead of pushing them apart. There would be whiteboards and wireless networks, and the key to get in the door would be an RFID "tag" (an inexpensive microchip with short-range radio broadcast capability) that would allow people to display the social network that connects them to Aula. Various sponsors were rounded up. Until the meeting space was finished and opened in September 2001, the Aula network met online and at cafés. The four people who had met in May 2000 grew to 300 a year later.

Nokia and the recently flourishing Finnish mobile communications industry are experiencing turbulence, but mobile-enabled cultural practices continue to evolve all over Helsinki. Different forms of mobile-enabled culture are emerging in public and in the marketplace—from Arena 2000 to Helsinki Virtual Village to Aula, from adolescent subcultures to transformations in business practice. Finland might be the world's foremost laboratory for mobile society, but it is far from the only one in the Nordic countries. Stockholm, with more mobile phones per person than any city in the world,[57] has its own strong examples of mobile industry, culture, and research. Botfighters, for example.

At a quarter to midnight on one of those late spring evenings when night falls around ten o'clock, I found myself cruising greater Stockholm with four devotees of a game that involves virtual persona, mocking text messages, location-sensing technology, junk food, and continuous banter. They call themselves "the Mob." By their own gleeful confessions, they spend too much of their time chasing game opponents around Stockholm. They first met when three of them ganged up to track down the fourth and destroy his "bot" (a software robot that represents the player). After the virtual battle, the four exchanged good-natured insults via SMS, decided to meet face to face, and instantly became a self-styled gang.

Joel Abrahamsson picked me up in front of my hotel after finishing his day's work as a systems administrator for a Swedish web-hosting firm. He looked up from his mobile phone long enough to greet me. "Oh hell!" was the next thing he said. "My bot got shot." The opponent, Abrahamsson informed me, was less than 400 meters away—perhaps one of the people we could see in the small park in front of my hotel. "Now he is demeaning me by SMS! He better hope he leaves the area before my gang gets here." A small Volvo stopped at the curb, and I jammed in with four young men, all of whom cordially but fleetingly looked up from their phones to greet me.

For all the talk of mobs, gangs, and bot killing, Joel and his friends are mobsters in name only, indistinguishable from other young Swedish males in the info industry.

Earlier, I had visited the Stockholm headquarters of It's Alive, the company that created the world's first location-based mobile game. Sven Halling, the CEO of It's Alive, showed me how Botfighters takes advantage of location-sensing technologies involving mobile phones. Players sign up on a Web site, create a "bot," name it, and arm it with guns, shields, batteries, and detectors. When their mobile telephones are on, the players receive SMS messages about the geographic distance of other players. "When they get close enough to fire," Halling explained, "players get an SMS message from our server, and if their weapons are stronger than their opponent's shield, and their opponent doesn't shoot first, they are credited with a kill." The scores and competitive positions of players are instantly updated on the Web site.

Joel, his sidekick Tjomme, and two fellows named David all work in information technology industries. Fast repartee about the game seemed to be one of the points of playing as a gang. In one respect, it is a variation on the venerable ritual of cruising in automobiles. Botfighters, however, requires laptops and mobile telephones as well as cars. While some players were in their offices or apartments, others, like the Mob, moved around Stockholm on foot, subway, and car. Approximately once an hour, we stopped the car for junk food and leg-stretching. At such times, a laptop would be connected to a mobile phone and players would log on to recharge bots and check game standings.

Mobile phone users are accustomed to paying a few cents for each SMS message they send, and many send hundreds a day. It's Alive charges mobile operators by the number of players who sign up to play the game; players pay It's Alive a monthly fee in addition to the small fee they pay the operator for each message. The game attracts typical gamers like the Mob, males from age twelve to thirty, but it might also serve as a broader platform for social communication if pitched differently. Multiplayer games that can be played while waiting in line, sitting on the bus, and other idle moments could become a driving application for mobile, location-based services. Other location-based mobile telephone games are due to be launched soon in the United States, the United Kingdom, and Scandinavia. France Telecom is running trials of location-based games modeled on treasure hunts rather than shoot-outs.[58]

Stockholm, in May 2001, was buzzing with mobile culture. My hotel hosted weekend private parties, open only to those who could display the right SMS message at the door. One of the party organizers told me that this floating network of hundreds started gathering at a different locale each week after each of four founders sent SMS invitations to everyone in their address books. Svante, a young man of an anarchist persuasion, told me about a cult of fare-jumpers in Stockholm who used SMS broadcast services to warn each other when and where conductors could be found checking fare tickets. Rickard Ericsson opened a laptop on a restaurant table, plugged in his phone, and showed me LunarStorm, a virtual community he launched in January 2000, which grew to 950,000 members by spring 2001—more than 65 percent of the population of Swedish fourteen to twenty-four-year-olds. In the summer of 2001, Ericsson and colleagues added LunarMobil messaging, enabling the tens of thousands of LunarStorm members online at any time to remain in touch with each other when away from their PCs.[59]

Generation Txt

"We Are Generation Txt," proclaims a famous SMS message that has circulated among Filipino youth; another ironic message that recirculated around Manila's social networks said, in Filipino-English texting lingo: "Der is lyf Byond textng. Get 1." (There is life beyond texting. Get one.)[60] In a later chapter, I discuss the events of January 2001, when texting played a role in the "People Power II" revolt against President Estrada of the Philippines. Before 2001, texting had become widespread in the Philippines, with up to 50 million messages exchanged each day.[61] A 2001 *San Francisco Chronicle* story quoted a Philippines telecommunications company source: "Some Filipino teenagers can do it blindfolded. I can't do that—but I can text while driving."[62] Rumors, chain mail, and SMS manifestos regularly ripple through Filipino society. The Philippines might furnish early indicators of the way mobile communications could affect other countries where it is more cost-effective to jump directly to a wireless infrastructure.

An online correspondent reported in spring 2001 on Manila's entrenched "GenTxt":

> Texting is used by this group to send jokes and riddles, to pass out invitations to parties, or merely to say "good morning" to friends with accompanying

graphics of, say, a teddy bear. It is used much like a greeting card sent out to friends morning, noon, and night. Compilations of text messages are even available in bookstores and on the web for those who are not up to creating their own messages.

"Sometimes, I go without lunch just so I could use my allowance to buy a pre-paid call card for my cell phone," says Tammy Reyes, a 17-year old college student. "If I don't receive a text when I wake up or I receive only a few messages during the day, I feel as though nobody loves me enough to remember me during the day."[63]

Although I visited Tokyo, Helsinki, Stockholm, Copenhagen, London, New York, Boston, Seattle, and San Francisco, it became clear by fall 2001 that I would not be able to visit every site of texting outbreaks. I did pay attention when Xinhua News Agency reported that Thailand's largest mobile telephone company's GSM operation was brought down by floods of 2001 Valentine's Day text messages.[64] I took note when "373 million text messages were sent over the Orange network (U.K. and France) in January 2001."[65] I was not surprised to discover that one-fifth of the Italian population owned mobile phones,[66] although I was slightly startled to learn that more than one person in eight has a mobile phone in Botswana.[67]

At around the same time that I was carrying on my own informal investigation, Motorola commissioned U.K.-based writer Dr. Sadie Plant to conduct a study, "On the Mobile: The Effects of Mobile Telephones on Social and Individual life." Plant's research took her to Tokyo, Beijing, Hong Kong, Bangkok, Peshawar, Dubai, London, Birmingham, and Chicago. She reported that in some cases, people use the mobile telephone to maintain family relationships; young people who go off to work in cities can stay in touch with their rural relatives and families scattered around the world. In other cases, young people maintain relationships with friends their parents would disapprove of. Afghans in Pakistan were horrified by the ease with which young Moslem boys and girls, who would never have been allowed to be alone together, can now participate in virtual social relationships via mobile phone. Everywhere she traveled, Plant collected tales of how mobile telephones and texting were changing ways of life in unexpected ways:

On a wooden ship moored in Dubai's busy creek, a Somali trader dozes in the shade of a tarpaulin sheet. He wakes to the opening bars of Jingle Bells. "Hallo? Aiwa . . . la . . . aiwa . . . OK." The deal is done. This trader, Mohammed, exports small electrical goods, including mobile phones, to East Africa. "It's my livelihood," he says of the mobile phone. "No mobile, no business." It multiplies his opportunities to make contacts and do deals as he moves between cities and ports, and the short, instantaneous messages and calls to which the mobile lends itself are perfectly suited to the small and immediate transactions in which he is engaged. He now has access to intelligence about the movements of goods, ships, competitors, and markets. Information that was once way beyond his reach is now at his fingertips.

In remote parts of several developing countries, including Swaziland, Somalia, and the Côte d'Ivoire, the mobile is being introduced in the form of payphone shops in villages which have never had land-lines. In rural Bangladesh, these shops, and the women who run them, have become new focal points in the community.[68]

Why hasn't texting taken off in the United States as a business or as a cultural appropriation? The analysts I consulted laid the blame on competing standards and clueless marketing, including a pricing model that rules out the most likely early adopters. Whereas European operators agreed on the GSM standard, which allows the customer of one company to send SMS messages to any customer of any other company, in the United States text messages can be sent only to certain kinds of telephones, and you can only send messages to people who subscribe to your operator.

I figured David Bennahum would have a theory about the failure of American operators. I knew him as an excellent writer about technologies, but for the past year and a half, he had been a partner with a New York-based venture group that finances wireless infrastructure, technology, and media.[69] I asked him why MCI or AT&T or Sprint hadn't plugged American consumers into mobile Internet culture, and he replied without hesitation, "That would be like expecting General Motors to come up with the Beatles."[70] NTT bypassed its corporate culture by creating DoCoMo and hiring outsider Mari Matsunaga. Scandinavian and Philippine populations surprised unsuspecting telecommunications operators by embracing SMS. The European and Asian adoption of SMS was made possible in large part by pricing policies that made texting less expensive than voice calls. U.S. operators did not bypass their corporate cultures, made text messaging too expensive, failed to bridge barriers that prevented messages from traveling between different operators, and marketed text messaging services to thirtyish executives rather than teenagers.

Despite the corporate culture barrier Bennahum cited, he pointed out that two potentially influential American subcultures have taken to texting. Hip-hop culture, streetwise and fashion-conscious fans of rap music, favor Motorola's two-way pagers, while young stockbrokers, suits, and geeks in the information technology industry favor the BlackBerry wireless pagers from Research In Motion.[71] If the adoption barriers of incompatible technical standards and high prices for texting services disappear, might the cultural practices now incubating in these subcultures reach a tipping point and set off a mainstream fashion epidemic? Will U.S. telecommunications giants learn from DoCoMo and start doing their business in a radically different way? Or will DoCoMo break out from being a successful Japanese brand to becoming a global brand, as Honda and Sony did in previous decades? In December 2000, DoCoMo agreed to pay $9.9 billion for 16 percent of AT&T Wireless,[72] and in 2001 the company set up headquarters in Dusseldorf for the "mobile invasion of Europe."[73]

Mizuko Ito, who has moved between Japan and the United States most of her life, believes unique cultural characteristics of American society contribute to the lack of a mobile texting culture:

> Even urban Americans have immense amounts of private space that can accommodate their full social identities as well as their social networks. Things that many middle class urban Americans have that most middle class urban Japanese don't have include homes large enough to entertain friends and colleagues, private bedrooms for children, kitchens with storage space and appliances, more than one car, extra parking space at home, free parking for cars when out, cheap gas, toll free expressways, PC with Internet access (and space to put a PC in the home), more than one phone line with competitive phone rates (this just recently changed in Japan).
>
> All these items work for the use of private and against the use of street and public spaces. Americans move between private nucleated homes, private transport, and often private offices and cubicles as well, with quick forays in the car to shop occasionally (not daily grocery shopping as in Japan), and use of public space and restaurants has the sense of an optional excursion rather than a necessity. In Japan most people have to meet people outside the home. In Tokyo, I find myself occupying more quasi-public spaces conducive to texting because car usage is prohibitively expensive, my home is small, and it takes a long time on foot and public transportation to get anywhere. The technology of the phone is part of this ecology of other tech-

nologies of place and identity-shaping, and the overall ecology of these technologies is so different in the U.S., working against the adoption of mobile
texting in the Japanese mode.[74]

Other forces, psychological and cultural, undoubtedly are at work in the
United States. The attack on the World Trade Center on September 11,
2001, influenced American attitudes about the devices Americans call "cell
phones." First came dramatic reports that people trapped in burning
buildings and hijacked airplanes had used their personal telephones to call
their families.[75] Then came reports that two-way text pagers, which made
use of a packet-switched data network, remained useful as a lifeline when
most voice calls became impossible in Lower Manhattan.[76] (Packet-switch-
ing had been invented originally as a means of communicating during a nuclear war.[77]) As more Americans start using mobile phones and two-way
messaging for safety in the United States, research from Scandinavia suggests that they will quickly adopt the devices for social communication.[78]

Although it isn't clear yet which company will become the IBM, Microsoft, or AOL of the wireless Internet, or whether American users will
grow a mainstream texting culture, it's clear that mobile telephony, texting,
and mobile Internet services are already affecting social relationships.

Identity Networks, Placeless Spaces, and Other Social Collisions

The mobile Internet may be the first major new communication medium
where the social impacts have been systematically observed from its earliest
stages.[79] I urge caution when generalizing about the broader meaning of
early findings about mobile communications. The methodology of the observations that provide data must be scrutinized. Social, economic, and psychological contexts of the observed cultures must be considered when framing theories about social impacts. Despite these cautions, I am convinced
that some of the first social scientists to look at the mobile communication
subcultures have uncovered useful clues. What follows is a brief review of
the most relevant social scientific observation of mobile telephone use on

- the level of the individual personality, where cognitive and iden-
  tity-related issues emerge;

- the level of the immediate social network and neighborhood, where place and community-related issues emerge;
- the level of the society, where emergent effects of individual usage may influence the zeitgeist, values, and/or power structure of an entire polity, culture, or civilization.

It is worth noting that adolescents, those aged fourteen to twenty, are often the early adopters of mobile communications and are among the first whose identities, families, and communities begin to change. The most obvious explanation for the key role of youth in the diffusion of mobile telephones and texting is that adolescents have adopted a medium that allows them to communicate with peers, outside the surveillance of parents and teachers, at the precise time in their lives when they are separating from their families and asserting their identities as members of a peer group. Another explanation is that young people are comfortable with technologies that didn't exist when their parents were growing up.

Social theorist Erving Goffman wrote about the way people improvise public performances as a way of composing an identity in the presenter's own mind as well as the minds of others.[80] In regard to what Goffman called "the presentation of self," the ways people communicate and the groups they use as audiences for their communicative performances are part of the social machinery they use to construct identities. The groups that individuals belong to define who they think they are. This presentation of self points outward to the group and inward toward the identity of the presenter at the same time, through the same communication acts. Goffman fits well with mobile media because SMS messages, and the choice of who to send it to and how to respond, are used by young people today as the raw material for identity and group-shaping activities.

Researchers studying Norwegian adolescents' use of mobile telephones found that "in Goffmanian terms, the indirect nature of text messages allows one to arrange 'face'."[81] The same researchers noted that chain SMS messages, jokes (often of a sexual nature), and expression of interest in potential boyfriends or girlfriends all have an "expressive" element that constitutes a "confirmation of a relationship. It is a type of social interaction wherein the sender and receiver share a common, though asynchronous experience. When one sends a message it refreshes the contact between the two."[82] Norwegian ethnologist Truls Erik Johnsen claims, "The content is not that important. The message has a meaning in itself; it is a way of showing the recipient you're thinking of him (or her)."[83]

In the next chapter, I'll look more closely at social networks. Note that many youth use social networks as status markers like fashionable clothing or popular music. "Which group do you belong to?" has always been important to adolescents. Researchers Alex S. Taylor and Richard Harper observed 120 participants between ages eleven and eighteen in the United Kingdom and reported that a primary advantage of the phone was the way it enabled young people to demonstrate their membership and status in social networks:

> Both the physical appearance of the phone and the manner in which the phone was used held symbolic value that also supported the demonstration of social networks. . . .
>
> Through the act of using their phones, young people appear to consolidate their peer relationships, differentiate themselves from family or household relations, and contribute to a growing sense of both independence (from family) and collectivity (amongst peers). In short, the collaborative forms of interaction with the device appear to both functionally and symbolically cement the durability of social relationships in local communities.[84]

One of the most obvious early impacts on the level of the immediate social network is the role of texting in youthful mating rituals. Because they can take their time to compose their message, and because they don't have to face rejection in person, young men in Scandinavia and elsewhere have found it easier to ask for dates. A young man sends the object of his attention a blank message, or a bland one such as "that was a nice party." The recipient can choose to ignore the initiation or to respond and thereby signal interest. Younger adolescents have been observed to carry on entire dating relationships exclusively through SMS exchanges.[85]

Text messages and telephones are used as social objects in themselves. Swedish researchers Alexandra Weilenmann and Catrine Larsson noted, as I did, that Scandinavian teenagers often flash the messages on their screens at each other, or even pass the telephone around: "Teenagers thus share the communication they take part in with their co-present friends. Not only the communication but also the phone itself is often shared."[86]

Marko Ahtisaari, one of the young architects of Helsinki's Aula, reiterated the role of the physical device itself in socializing: "The very act of learning to use new mobile social services is social. We learn by being shown, not by reading manuals. The icons and ringing tones used to physically personalize phones are meant to be displayed. The fact that I have Madonna's not-yet-released single as my ringing tone says something about me."[87]

In Italy, the United Kingdom, and Germany, "over half of those surveyed had some form of negative reaction to mobile phone use in public."[88] Sadie Plant quoted Goffman by way of explaining the discomfort associated with overhearing mobile telephone conversations: "A conversation has a life on its own behalf. It is a little social system with its own boundary-maintaining tendencies; it is a little patch of commitment and loyalty with its own heroes and its own villains."[89] Plant notes, "To overhear a conversation is to listen in to one of these worlds. To overhear just one of its sides is to be neither fully admitted nor completely excluded from its world."[90]

Other observers of this phenomenon have referred to Goffman's theories about the different "faces" we present to different audiences:

We believe that talking on a mobile phone in a public place is in part a matter of a conflict of social spaces in which people assume different faces. Mobile phone use often necessitates the interleaving of multiple activities and of multiple public faces. When mobile phone users are on the phone, they are simultaneously in two spaces: the space they physically occupy, and the virtual space of the conversation (the conversational space). When a phone call comes in (or perhaps more pretentiously, when a call is placed out), the user decides, consciously or otherwise, what face takes precedence: the face that is consonant with one's physical environment, or that of the conversational space. The greater the conflict between the behavioral requirements of the two spaces, the more conscious, explicit, and difficult this decision might be.

One's assumption of multiple faces, it would seem, is what is largely at issue for those who find public mobile telephone use disturbing or even offensive. First, choosing to be behaviorally present in a different space from one's physical location may be perceived as inconsiderate by those in the space. Second, a mobile phone user might have to violate (or at least perturb) the social norms of the physical space in order to honor the norms in the conversational space. Finally, perhaps what is most apparent to the public is that the face one presents on the phone is in contrast to the face assumed just before the phone call. This changing act brings to the fore that faces are publicly assumed, which then gives rise to the feeling that the new face and perhaps even the old face are false.[91]

Mizuko Ito pointed out to me that Goffman's theories of the link between identity construction and public performance are useful frames for looking at the people in public places engaged in conversations with people who aren't there: "The way mobile phones locate people in social groups is connected to the way the mobile phone operates in public space. To me these are interconnected points related to how people occupy technologically enhanced social space. The power of the mobile phone to allow people to be connected continuously with their virtual social group is what isolates them from co-present others in the public space, in other words, exclusion as the other side of the coin from affiliation."[92]

In Chapter 8, I'll take up the implications of the "always-on" nature of the mobile Internet, the effects of being continuously available to others, and the way all our formerly idle moments aboard public transit or while walking down the street are now filled with activity. If mobile telephony and texting alone were the only agents of change, the world's cultures would be facing a major shift in norms, relationships, and social power. Today's mobile devices, however, are only part of a larger smart mob infrastructure. "Peer-to-peer" methodologies like the one that made Napster possible are converging on mobile Internet devices, providing opportunities for massive device-to-device collective actions. The emergence of pervasive computation in smart rooms, wearable computers, and digital cities from laboratories into product lines are only beginning to transform today's telephones into the "remote controls for your life" envisioned by Hirschhorn, Linturi, and Natsuno.

The forms of collective behavior enabled or changed by smart mob technology go far beyond the etiquette of where and how to conduct mobile phone calls. The most radical changes are those possible at the level of entire societies. In order to make sense of the technologies I was seeing in media labs and the behaviors I was seeing on the streets, I looked for observers who focused not on small groups, but on the collective actions of entire societies. Fortunately, the years I had spent trying to make sense of virtual communities had led me to thinkers such as Marc A. Smith, now at Microsoft Research. After the streets of Helsinki and Tokyo, and the media labs of Cambridge and California, I headed for Redmond to try to see a bigger picture.

Technologies of Cooperation

Your corn is ripe today; mine will be so tomorrow. 'Tis profitable for us both, that I shou'd labour with you to-day, and that you shou'd aid me tomorrow. I have no kindness for you, and know you have as little for me. I will not, therefore, take any pains on your account; and should I labour with you upon my own account, in expectation of a return, I know I shou'd be disappointed, and that I shou'd in vain depend upon your gratitude. Here then I leave you to labour alone: You treat me in the same manner. The seasons change; and both of us lose our harvests for want of mutual confidence and security.

—David Hume, *A Treatise of Human Nature,* **1739**

The Alchemy of Coopetition

Redmond, Washington, is headquarters of the world's most successful company, mother lode for the world's richest man, and home base of an army of carnivorously competitive software geeks. Despite this intense concentration of mojo, the Microsoft campus is also an unremarkable suburban office park with sidewalks, stands of fir, and lawns separating clusters of three-story buildings. Unlike Sanno Park Tower, the Microsoft campus displays few signifiers of power—aside from the wireless Internet antennae dangling discreetly from light poles. I wasn't sniffing for clues about the industry, although Microsoft might become the dominant player in the wireless Internet industry. I wasn't seeking a peek at future technologies, although the secret gizmos of tomorrow can be found within these buildings. I was searching for hints about the social forces at work in smart mobs.

What scientific knowledge can make sense of swarming teenagers in Finland and texting revolutionaries in Manila? Anthropologist Mizuko Ito and her Scandinavian counterparts helped me to understand group behaviors emerging from use of the mobile telephone. I needed to know more about what these activities could mean for entire societies, so I paid a pilgrimage to my guru in matters cybersociological.

In the ten years I've known him, Marc A. Smith had morphed from UCLA graduate student into Microsoft's research sociologist. In 1992, while I was trying to make sense of virtual communities, I heard about this fellow who had turned Usenet, the Internet's worldwide ecology of virtual communities, into an immense sociology laboratory. Since then, we've stayed in touch regarding social studies of cyberspaces. At Microsoft, Smith has refined the instrument he started building as a grad student—software that maps the social networks woven from a million electronic messages exchanged in 48,000 different conversation groups every day.[1] My question in 1992 was, What do people gain from virtual communities that keeps them sharing information with people they might never meet face to face?

Smith's answer was "social network capital, knowledge capital, and communion"—people can put a little of what they know and how they feel into the online network and draw out larger amounts of knowledge and opportunities for sociability than they put in.[2]

A decade later, I found myself trying to understand what happens when virtual communities migrate from desktop computers to mobile telephones. I wanted to visualize future social forms that could grow out of today's roving bands of mobile texters. How might the intergenerational power shifts illuminated by anthropologists affect power structures and social contracts? Will groups of people find it possible to draw out more than they put into mobile social networks? I was fortunate to be able to turn to someone who had studied both sociology and social cyberspaces. I arrived in Redmond on a rare clear winter day. We left our rain gear inside and engaged in a peripatetic interview. The Cascades sparkled visibly on the horizon. I explained the enabling technologies for smart mobs while we walked.

Smith escorted me into his company cafeteria for coffee—a company cafeteria with its own Starbucks. "The effects of mobile and pervasive technology will reach further into our lives than the Internet has," Smith said in a melodramatic voice, sweeping one arm through the air while reaching into his back pocket with the other hand. Instead of paying cash for our coffees, he placed his wallet on a small pad next to the cash register, triggering a "beep." A chip on a plastic card in his wallet opens doors for Smith and pays for necessities of life within the Microsoft domain. We found a booth. I looked around with the knowledge that we were surrounded by some of the most intelligent and well-caffeinated people in the world.

Smith fell silent, sipped, and rolled his eyes toward the ceiling. "Does the new medium change the way people cooperate?" Smith stated his question again, rolling his gaze back down to eye contact. "That's the big question, and it's not a simple one. Sociologists have developed an entire vocabulary for arguing the technicalities of cooperation. To cast the impacts of mobile and pervasive media in terms sociologists know about, I'd ask how these tools might influence *collective action* and *public goods.*" Marc is good at italicizing the spoken word. Another pause. Another sip.

"Do new modes of communication change the way we see ourselves and how others see us? If you follow the strands of cooperation, public goods, presentation of self, and reputation, you might find that they all tie together." He placed his Tall™ half-caf, hi-fat mocha on the table. "The same conundrum—cooperation exists, but it seems like it shouldn't—has infected discipline after discipline. Biologists, economists, even nuclear warfare strategists became interested in social games."

I asked him why he thought of cooperation when I described mobile and pervasive technologies.

"Whenever a communication medium lowers the costs of solving collective action dilemmas, it becomes possible for more people to pool resources. And 'more people pooling resources in new ways' is the history of civilization in . . . " Pause. ". . . seven words."

We ambled over to the company store, where we found Microsoft employees queued up. Marc queried one of the queued, a guy whose baggy jeans reminded me of Shibuya. "Waiting for new X-Box games," he answered with the happy fervor of a gamer. We skipped the company store and continued our conversation in the Microsoft museum, where we looked at antiques like the fabled Altair, the first personal computer kit. The most amusing exhibit was a photograph of the Microsoft staff in 1978, history's most motley group of billionaire nerds.

I interrupted: "What's a "collective action dilemma?""

"Collective action dilemmas are the perpetual balancing of self-interest and public goods." He held out his hands and made the universal gesture for "balancing."

"And public goods are . . . ?"

"A public good is a resource from which all may benefit, regardless of whether they help create it."

"For example . . . ?"

"For example, public television," Smith answered. "You know those pledge drives?" He dropped to a conspiratorial whisper. "Not everybody who watches public television sends a check." He returned to a normal speaking voice. "A lighthouse that a few build but all use for navigation is a classic example of a public good. So is a park. Breathable air. Sanitation systems."

Smith, at thirty-six, looks a bit like the actor Jeff Goldblum. He's lanky, brilliant, and passionate, and he can't refrain from doing stand-up comedy when he talks. He changes voices to create his own cast of characters. He'll present a case like a lawyer and then switch the imagined courtroom set-ting to an imagined vaudeville stage. Sometimes he appears to be asserting a hypothesis to his thesis committee. Occasionally, he sounds like he is de-fending his budget to Microsoft brass. No wonder he was drawn to the ideas of Erving Goffman—presentation of self, Goffman's material, is Smith's natural métier.[3]

I learned from ten minutes of shtick-laced pedagogy that the people who succumb to the temptation to enjoy a public good without contribut-ing to its provision (or overconsume at the peril of depletion) are called, appropriately, "free riders." I recalled the people in Stockholm who cheat on subway fares by exchanging SMS messages about the location of fare police. Some smart mobs can be organized bands of free riders.

"Does it bother you when someone cuts in front of you at the grocery checkout?" Yes, of course it does. Smith explained that social disapproval of free riders changes the balance of cooperation dilemmas. The notion of reputation, the subject of Chapter 5, "The Evolution of Reputation," de-rives from the utility of knowing whom to trust in a cooperative enterprise and how to warn others about cheaters.

"If everyone, acting in their own interest, free rides, then the public good is never created, or it is overconsumed and goes away. Everyone suf-fers. There's your dilemma. What's good for *you* can be bad for *us*." Smith made the balancing gesture again and then adjusted his gesture to signify "out of balance."

We left the museum and cut across a lawn on our way to his office. "Many public goods, like public health, increase in value the more people share them. But managing collective action is always a struggle. Even where common resources occur naturally, like fishing grounds or pasturelands, free riding seriously threatens their continued sustainability. Most collective goods have a carrying capacity, a rate of consumption beyond which the resource cannot replenish itself. Collectively, groups of people have frequently rushed past this point to total ruin, often aware of exactly what they were doing when they did it. Fishing grounds were overfished, water tables dried up, pasturelands became desert because people faced complex multiplayer games that led each to act rationally for their own gain to the detriment of all."

"This field we're walking on might be a remnant of the first public good that humans found important," Smith declared enigmatically as we walked across a manicured lawn. I could see he was winding up for a story.

"When our ancestors descended from trees, they found themselves on an African grassland called a savanna. One of the things grasslands made possible were big game animals. Hunger drove our forebears to coordinate their actions to bring down animals so large that all the meat couldn't be consumed before it spoiled. In those circumstances, everyone in the group was free to eat—even those who didn't take the risk of hunting. The meat wouldn't be available in the first place unless a few people mustered the gumption to tackle large creatures, but the benefit of the cooperative activity of a few extended to all, even to those who had not participated in the hunt. I think Matt Ridley nailed it when he wrote, 'Big game hunting became the first public good.'"[4]

We entered Smith's office building. "Ridley pointed out in *The Origins of Virtue* that grasslands have been an ongoing theme in human history," Smith remarked in his "you have to read this" voice.[5] Talking with Smith always comes with a price—it can take weeks to finish his reading assignments. After I read the book Smith referred to, I began to see connections between our savanna origins and the desire to own a small lawn, the sport of golf, and the parks we create in the middle of cities. According to Ridley, it's not far-fetched to say that humans are still working out problems our ancestors first encountered on the African grasslands.

Smith held his wallet up to a pad next to the door to unlock the door to his part of the building. "The word *commons* originally denoted pastureland treated as a common resource, where individual herders were free to graze their sheep or cattle. The land can support a limited number of grazing animals. The temptation to graze more than one's share is a rational strategy for an individual herder. But if everyone succumbs to the same temptation, the grass ceases to grow, and the value of the pasture disappears."

I recognized this as the situation Garrett Hardin named in a much-debated article titled "The Tragedy of the Commons," in which Hardin concluded: "Therein is the tragedy. Each man is locked into a system that compels him to increase his herd without limit—in a world that is limited. Ruin is the destination toward which all men rush, each pursuing his own best interest in a society that believes in the freedom of the commons. Freedom in a commons brings ruin to all."[6] Hardin's article provoked a debate that continues to this day: In the face of temptation to behave selfishly, how do people manage to cooperate? Is it necessary to curtail their freedom through some kind of regulatory authority?

The debate surrounding Hardin's tragedy of the commons is a contemporary reprise of an older philosophical conflict. In 1660, Thomas Hobbes argued that humans are so competitive that the only way we can cooperate is for a more powerful competitor to impose a truce. Hobbes called this coercive authority *Leviathan;* subsequently, this logic supported arguments for a strong sovereign.[7] In conflicts over the provision or consumption of common resources, arguments continue to focus on the polarized viewpoints of centralized governmental regulation and decentralized, market-based self-regulation. However, the most salient counterargument to Hobbes is that humans obviously do agree to work together. Decades after Hobbes, John Locke, philosophical mentor to Thomas Jefferson, asserted that humans could govern through social contracts rather than coercive authority.[8]

Since the time of Hobbes and Locke, political philosophers, sociologists, economists, and candidates for public office have argued over the role of central authority in governance, markets, and human affairs. The argument became scientific as well as philosophical when researchers began to systematically observe the way people really do work together. Laboratory investigators began to formulate experiments to probe cooperative behavior. The experiments were based on simple games in which experimental subjects can win or lose money (more about game theory shortly). In the

1950s, economist Mancur L. Olson found that small groups are more likely to exhibit voluntary cooperation in these experimental games than larger groups and that cooperative behaviors increase when the games are repeated over and over with the same groups and when communication is permitted among the participants.[9]

In 1982, Olson wrote, "Unless the number of individuals in a group is quite small, or unless there is coercion or some other special device to make individuals act in their common interest, rational, self-interested individuals will not act to achieve their common or group interests."[10] One unavoidable question remained. Clearly, some groups learn to solve collective action dilemmas to produce public goods or prevent overconsumption. How is this accomplished? Olson provided some hints when he noted that a prominent businessman might finance a lighthouse for the prestige and recognition such an act might win in the eyes of others. Reputation is a recurring leitmotiv in the discourse of cooperation.

In 1990, sociologist Elinor Ostrom argued that external authorities might not be necessary in governing what she called common pool resources (CPRs).[11] Ostrom studied the ways that people shared forestry resources in Japan, pasturelands in Switzerland, and irrigation arrangements in Spain and the Philippines. Ostrom provided examples of communities that have shared public goods for centuries and succeeded in not depleting them. She discovered that in Spanish irrigation-sharing *huertas*, "a portion of the fines is kept by the guards; the Japanese detectives also keep the sake they collect from infractors."[12] To facilitate cooperation, the Spanish synchronize schedules of adjacent water users so they can monitor each other, the Japanese reward those who report infractions, and most successful CPR groups impose social sanctions on cheaters.

In comparing the communities, Ostrom found that groups that are able to organize and govern their behavior successfully are marked by the following design principles:

- Group boundaries are clearly defined.
- Rules governing the use of collective goods are well matched to local needs and conditions.
- Most individuals affected by these rules can participate in modifying the rules.
- The rights of community members to devise their own rules is respected by external authorities.

- A system for monitoring members' behavior exists; the community members themselves undertake this monitoring.
- A graduated system of sanctions is used.
- Community members have access to low-cost conflict resolution mechanisms.
- For CPRs that are parts of larger systems, appropriation, provision, monitoring, enforcement, conflict resolution, and governance activities are organized in multiple layers of nested enterprises.[13]

In the weeks of reading that followed my visit to Redmond, I learned that Hardin has since stated that he should have called it "The Tragedy of the Unmanaged Commons."[14] I also discovered that research continues into the secrets of how successful commons are managed. Ostrom provided an ample and specific agenda for future research: "All efforts to organize collective action, whether by an external ruler, an entrepreneur, or a set of principals who wish to gain collective benefits, must address a common set of problems. These have to do with coping with free-riding, solving commitment problems, arranging for the supply of new institutions, and monitoring individual compliance with sets of rules."[15]

An interdisciplinary community of CPR researchers grew out of Ostrom's work, which built on the findings of Anthony Scott and H. Scott Gordon, who wrote about fisheries in 1954 and 1955.[16] In a paper about the application of CPRs to technology-based, human-created CPRs, such as the Internet, Charlotte Hess pointed out the significance of the emergence of a cross-disciplinary convergence:

> There are centuries of intellectual investigations into the nature of property rights, free riding, overpopulation, efficiency, participation, volunteerism, resource management, organizational behavior, environmental sustainability, social equity, self-governance, transboundary disputes, common fields, enclosure, communal societies, and the common good. What has remarkably changed is the merging of disciplines, the methodologies, the international cooperative approach, and the intentionality of the CPR literature.[17]

CPR research, still in early stages, might be a step toward the "empirically supported theory of self-organizing and self-governing forms of collective action" Ostrom called for in 1990.[18] If people start organizing new forms of collective action through the use of wireless devices, such theories as Ostrom's might help make sense of what we'll see around us.

When I had completed the reading assignments Smith had given me, I called him. The best way to reach Smith is through his mobile telephone. He was waiting to pick up his son from school, trying to log on to an open wireless node from the school parking lot. In addition to being a sociologist, Smith is a hardware and software geek. He pointed out, while walking back and forth in a Redmond parking lot with a handheld computer, that "Ostrom found that some system to monitor and sanction members' actions was a common feature of every successful community. Monitoring and sanctioning is important not simply as a way of punishing rule-breakers but also as a way of assuring people that others are doing their part. Many people are contingent cooperators, willing to cooperate as long as most others do."

Smith reminded me that commitment to cooperate is as important as temptation to free ride; threat of punishment can constrain, but it can't inspire. Something must motivate people to contribute to a public good. While we were talking on the phone, Smith sent me a paragraph from his Ph.D. thesis. He likes to do things like that from his palmtop in parking lots: "A commons can be more than physical resources like fish or pastureland," said his email. I read it while talking to him. Perhaps because I didn't grow up with it, such multitasking tends to require concentration: "A commons," continued Smith's message, "can also be social organizations themselves. Some goods are tangible, like common pastures or irrigation systems; others are intangible goods like goodwill, trust, and identity. Markets, judicial systems, and social capital in communities are all common resources. These resources must be actively reconstructed; where fish will remain in the sea whether they are fished or not, a judicial system or other social contract will not persist without the continued contribution of its participants."[19]

Smith added on the voice track that reputation and peer-to-peer social pressure pay a key role in maintaining CPRs: "Social pressure, from insult to incarceration, to make good on debts or obligations helps communities maintain the essential collective good of trust." Reputation, whether maintained by gossip, ritual behavioral displays, credit bureaus, or online reputation servers, appears to be one of the means by which people negotiate the day-to-day dance of self-interest and public goods.

Identity, reputations, boundaries, inducements for commitment, and punishment for free riders seem to be common critical resources all groups need in order to keep their members cooperatively engaged. These are the social processes most likely to be affected by technology that enables people to monitor reputations, reward cooperation, and punish defection.

The interdisciplinary study of CPRs and the continuing sociological debate about collective action turned out to be only one category of cooperation theory. Parallel inquiry came from different parts of the disciplinary spectrum. A mathematical approach took root in the 1950s and began to bear fruit decades later, when more powerful computers became available. Yet another discourse, which converged with computer modeling, grew up around issues in biological evolution. The surprising results might have remained hidden in think tanks and scientific journals if they had not generated such important implications for human group behavior.

It seemed as if the thread I had started following in Tokyo had turned into a whole ball of yarn by the time I returned from Redmond. My simple inquiry into existing knowledge that might make sense of smart mobs led me to a richer treasury of thinking tools than I had imagined that afternoon Mizuko Ito and I conversed about the thumb tribes of Tokyo.

Mutual Aid, Prisoner's Dilemma, and Other Games People Play

Does cooperation occur exclusively among people, making it the domain of psychologists, sociologists, and anthropologists? Is an emergent property of any population of interacting individuals, landing it in the domain of economists? Or could cooperation be a strategy that genes use to ensure their reproduction, which would make it the domain of biology? The answer to each of these questions appears to be "yes, in part." I caution against concluding that any theory or model will ever predict human social behavior; I recommend these inquiries from different disciplines as a means of understanding aspects of human social processes, not as oracles. Although the genetic influences on social dilemmas might seem distant from the impacts of smart mob technologies, certain motifs crop up at multiple levels when it comes to the tension between self-interest and collective action.

Biological arguments about the role of altruism and the origins of cooperation are rooted in Darwin's discovery of the mechanisms of evolution. If natural selection, a Hobbesian competition to transmit genes to future generations, is the force that sculpts species over millions of years, then genetic disposition toward cooperation should have been bred out of all species long ago. The philosopher who argued for the place of cooperation when evolutionary theory was first debated was a swashbuckling geographer and anarchist, Peter Kropotkin. Kropotkin, a Russian prince, was selected by the czar for elite training at an early age and later led a secret life writing pseudonymous anarchist pamphlets until he was arrested. After escaping czarist prison, Kropotkin ended up in London, where he contested the idea that competition was the sole driving force of evolution.

The naturalist Thomas H. Huxley championed Darwinian theory in Kropotkin's day, especially in his 1888 essay "The Struggle for Existence," which promoted competition as the most important driver of human evolution.[20] Kropotkin asserted that Huxley's interpretation of Darwinian theory was misconstrued and inaccurate. The publication of Huxley's essay was the impetus for Kropotkin to begin writing *Mutual Aid: A Factor of Evolution* as a reply to Huxley, and the subsequent series of articles that eventually made up Kropotkin's most famous book were originally published in the same journal, *The Guardian*.[21]

Cooperation, Kropotkin claimed, has been observed extensively in the animal kingdom. Horses and deer unite to protect each other from their foes, wolves and lions gather to hunt, while bees and ants work together in many different ways. Since Kropotkin's day, corroboration for some of his ideas has surfaced, and interest in Kropotkin's biological work, long eclipsed by his anarchist writing, was revitalized when biologist Stephen J. Gould concluded that Kropotkin had been onto something.[22] Symbiosis and cooperation have indeed been observed at every level from cell to ecosystem.

Kropotkin also contended that humans are predisposed to help one another without authoritarian coercion. A centralized government, he insisted, is not needed to set an example or to make people do the right thing. People were doing so before the rise of the state. In fact, Kropotkin maintained that it is government that represses our natural tendency for cooperation. His belief in the principle of grassroots power was strong enough to land him in the czar's prison.

Kropotkin wrote of the temporary guilds of the Middle Ages—cooperative, "just in time" groups formed by the union of like-minded individuals who shared a common goal and space. These groups could be found aboard ships, at the building sites of large-scale public construction projects such as cathedrals, and anywhere "fishermen, hunters, travelling merchants, builders, or settled craftsmen—came together for a common pursuit."[23] After leaving port, the captain of a ship would gather the crew and passengers on deck, tell them that they were all in this together and that the success of the voyage was dependent upon all of them working as one. Everyone onboard then elected a "governor" and "enforcers," who would gather "taxes" from those who broke the rules. At the end of the voyage the levies would be given to the poor in the port city.

Kropotkin's uncontestable observation that cooperation crops up all over biology eventually fomented a revolution in evolutionary theory in the 1950s and 1960s. Marine biologist George Williams stated the problem posed by the cooperative behavior exhibited by social insects: "A modern biologist seeing an animal doing something to benefit another assumes either that it is being manipulated by the other individual or that it is being subtly selfish."[24] If every organism seeks only to benefit itself against all, why would bees sacrifice themselves for the hive, as they clearly do?

In 1964, social insect specialist William Hamilton came up with an answer now known as "kin selection": Because bees are sisters (in fact, bees share more genes than sisters do), saving the life of several hivemates at the cost of one's own is a net gain in the number of the same genes transmitted to future generations.[25] The most radical interpretation of kin selection was popularized by Richard Dawkins's book *The Selfish Gene* in a startling formulation: "We are survival machines . . . robot vehicles blindly programmed to preserve the selfish molecules known as genes."[26]

The difference between predisposition and predestination is outside the scope of this book, but I recommend contemplating another of Hobbes's statements in regard to the behavior of insects versus that of humans: "The agreement of these creatures is natural; that of men is by covenant only, which is artificial; and therefore it is no wonder if there be somewhat else required."[27] The "somewhat else required" to achieve human cooperative behavior is as important as evolutionary influences and is the focus of its own discipline. And the bulk of the "artificial" part is what we now call "technology."

Those "covenants" mentioned by Hobbes turn out to be tricky because humans play elaborate games of trust and deception. Economists have long sought the mathematical grail that could predict the behavior of markets. In 1944, John von Neumann and Oskar Morgenstern's *Theory of Games and Economic Behavior* provided, if not a grail, a means of looking at the way people compete and collude, cooperate and defect, in competitive situations.[28]

John von Neumann was arguably the most influential but least-famous scientist in history, considering his fundamental contributions to mathematics, quantum physics, game theory, and the development of the atomic bomb, digital computer, and intercontinental ballistic missile.[29] Von Neumann was a prodigy who joked with his father in classical Latin and Greek at the age of six, was a colleague of Einstein at Princeton's Institute for Advanced Study, and was perhaps the most brilliant of the stellar collection of scientists gathered at Los Alamos to undertake the Manhattan Project. Jacob Bronowski, a Manhattan Project colleague, recounted that von Neumann had told him, during a taxicab ride in London, that "real life consists of bluffing, of little tactics of deception, of asking yourself what is the other man going to think I mean to do. And that is what games are about in my theory."[30]

Game theory is based on several assumptions: that the players are in conflict, that they must take action, that the results of the actions will determine which player wins according to definite rules, and that all players (this is the kicker) are expected to always act "rationally" by choosing the strategy that will maximize their gain regardless of the consequence to others. These are the kind of rules that don't fit real life with predictive precision, but that do attract economists, because they map onto the behavior of observable phenomena like markets, arms races, cartels, and traffic.

After World War II, von Neumann joined other mathematicians and economists to brainstorm game theory at a mundane building that still houses the same institution near the Santa Monica beach. The RAND Corporation was the first think tank, where intellectuals with security clearances thought about the unthinkable, as RANDite Herman Kahn referred to the craft of thermonuclear war strategy.[31] Because the arms race seemed to be closely related to the kind of bluff and counter-bluff described by game theory, the new field became popular among the first nuclear war strategists. In 1950, RAND researchers came up with four fundamental elements of Morgenstern- and von Neumann-style games: Chicken, Stag Hunt, Deadlock, and Prisoner's Dilemma. Keep in mind that although they can be described as stories, they are represented by exact mathematical equations.

Chicken is the game portrayed in movies about juvenile delinquents: two opponents rush toward oblivion, and the one who stops or swerves first loses. Deadlock is endless betrayal: Each player refuses to cooperate, ever. The next two are more interesting. Stag Hunt was first described by Jean Jacques Rousseau in 1755: "If it was a matter of hunting deer, everyone well realized that he must remain faithfully at his post; but if a hare happened to pass within reach of one of them, we cannot doubt that he would have gone off in pursuit of it without scruple and, having caught his own prey, he would have cared very little about having caused his companions to lose theirs."[32] Stag Hunt is a classic illustration of a problem of provisioning a public good in the face of individual temptation to defect to self-interest. Should a hunter remain with the group and bet on the smaller chance of bringing down large prey for the entire tribe or break away from the group and pursue the more certain prospect of bringing a rabbit home to his own family?

The fourth game hatched at RAND has grown into an interdisciplinary Schelling point. The game was invented in 1950 by RAND researchers Merrill Flood and Melvin Dresher.[33] A few months after Flood and Dresher invented the game, a RAND consultant named it at a seminar at Stanford University. Tucker described the game situation: "Two men, charged with a joint violation of law, are held separately by the police. Each is told that (1) if one confesses and the other does not, the former will be given a reward . . . and the latter will be fined . . . , (2) if both confess, each will be fined . . . . At the same time, each has a good reason to believe that (3) if neither confesses, both will go clear."[34]

Over the years, the popular version has changed Tucker's rendition of Prisoner's Dilemma. Threatening jail sentences is a better story than offering rewards. Remember that the prisoners are "held separately" and unable to communicate, so they can only guess what the other prisoner is likely to do. The prisoner who testifies against his partner will go free, and the partner will be sentenced to three years. If both prisoners decide to testify against each other, they will both get a two-year sentence. And if neither testifies, they will both receive a one-year sentence. Because this is game theory, each player is interested only in his own welfare. Rationally, each player will conclude that testifying will take a year off his sentence, regardless of what the other player does. Defecting will prevent a player from being a sucker—remaining loyally silent while the other player rats out. However, if they both refuse to testify, they could both get away with only one year. There's the dilemma: Each player, acting in his own interest, brings a result neither player prefers.

The mathematical version represents the results of the two players' strategies, pitted against each other in the form of a table. Each row represents a strategy for one player and each column represents a strategy for the other player. The pairs of numbers in the table cells represent the respective payoffs for the players. The payoffs are structured so that, in the RAND researchers' original terms, the *reward* payoff for mutual cooperation is greater than the *punishment* payoff for mutual defection; both are greater than the *sucker's* payoff for cooperating when the other player defects and less than the *temptation* payoff for defecting when the other player cooperates. All four of the RAND social dilemmas are variations of the same model: Reverse the sucker and temptation payoffs, and Prisoner's Dilemma becomes Chicken. Switch reward and temptation payoffs, and Prisoner's Dilemma becomes Stag Hunt.

	B cooperates	B defects
A cooperates	2,2	0,3
A defects	3,0	1,1

In 1979 political scientist Robert Axelrod grew interested in cooperation—a turning point in the history of smart mob theory:

> This project began with a simple question. When should a person cooperate, and when should a person be selfish, in an ongoing interaction with another person? Should a friend keep providing favors to another friend who never reciprocates? Should a business provide prompt service to another business that is about to be bankrupt? How intensely should the United States try to punish the Soviet Union for a particular hostile act, and what pattern of behavior can the United States use to best elicit cooperative behavior from the Soviet Union? There is a simple way to represent the type of situation that gives rise to these problems. This is to use a particular kind of game called the iterated Prisoner's Dilemma. The game allows the players to achieve mutual gains from cooperation, but it also allows for the possibility that one player will exploit the other, or the possibility that neither will cooperate.[35]

The Prisoner's Dilemma game takes on interesting new properties when it is repeated over and over ("iterated"). Although the players cannot communicate their intentions regarding the current move, the history of previous decisions becomes a factor in assessing the other player's intentions. In Axelrod's words, "What makes it possible for cooperation to emerge is the fact that the players might meet again. This possibility means that the choices made today not only determine the outcome of this move, but can also influence the later choices of the players. The future can cast a shadow back upon the present and thereby affect the current strategic situation."[36] "Reputation" is another way of looking at this "shadow of the future."

Axelrod proposed a "Computer Prisoner's Dilemma Tournament" pitting computer programs against one another. Each program would make a choice to cooperate or defect on each move, thus gaining points according to the game's payoff matrix. Each program could take into account the history of its opponent's prior moves. Axelrod received entries from game theorists in economics, psychology, sociology, political science, and mathematics. He ran fourteen entries against each other and against a random rule, over and over. "To my considerable surprise," Axelrod reported, "the winner was the simplest of all the programs submitted, TIT FOR TAT. TIT FOR TAT is merely the strategy of starting with cooperation and thereafter doing what the other player did on the previous move."[37] If the opponent cooperates on the first move, then TIT FOR TAT cooperates on the next move; if the opponent defects on the first move, then TIT FOR TAT defects on the next move. If the opponent switches from defection to cooperation, TIT FOR TAT switches from defection to cooperation on the following move, punishing the opponent but forgiving it.

Axelrod invited professors of evolutionary biology, physics, and computer science to join the original entrants on a second round. Designers of strategies were allowed to take into account the results of the first tournament. TIT FOR TAT won again. Axelrod found this intriguing:

> Something very interesting was happening here. I suspected that the properties that made TIT FOR TAT so successful in the tournaments would work in a world where any strategy was possible. If so, then cooperation based solely on reciprocity seemed possible. But I wanted to know the exact conditions that would be needed to foster cooperation on these terms. This led me to an evolutionary perspective: a consideration of how cooperation can emerge among egoists without central authority. The evolutionary perspective suggested three distinct questions. First, how can a potentially cooperative strategy get an initial foothold in an environment which is predominantly noncooperative? Second, what type of strategy can thrive in a

variegated environment composed of other individuals using a wide diversity of more or less sophisticated strategies? Third, under what conditions can such a strategy once fully established among a group of people, resist invasion by a less cooperative strategy?[38]

Tinkering with the game simulation revealed an answer, at least on the game-theoretic level, to Axelrod's first question: Within a pool of entirely uncooperative strategies, cooperative strategies evolve from small clusters of individuals who reciprocate cooperation, even if the cooperative strategies have only a small proportion of their interactions with each other. Clusters of cooperators amass points for themselves faster than defectors can. Strategies based on reciprocity can survive against a variety of strategies, and "cooperation, once established on the basis of reciprocity, can protect itself from invasion by less cooperative strategies. Thus, the gear wheels of social evolution have a ratchet."[39]

Axelrod, a political scientist at the University of Michigan, wasn't a biologist, so he called "selfish gene" biologist Richard Dawkins in England, who told him to speak to William Hamilton, discoverer of kin selection in insects, who, unknown to Axelrod until then, was also at the University of Michigan. Hamilton recalled a Harvard graduate student, Robert Trivers, who had presented evidence for reciprocity as the mechanism that enables self-interested individuals to cooperate.[40] The "shadow of the future" enabled individuals to do favors for others, who would do favors for them in the future. Years before Axelrod and TIT FOR TAT, had Trivers uncovered the link between self-interest and cooperation? The publication of Axelrod's *The Evolution of Cooperation* ignited interest in the biological basis of cooperation.[41]

In 1983 biologist Gerald Wilkinson reported that vampire bats in Costa Rica regurgitate blood to share with other bats who had been less successful in their night's hunt and that bats played TIT FOR TAT, feeding those who had shared in the past and refusing those who had not shared.[42] Wilkinson suggested that the bats' frequent social grooming rituals furnished a means by which this social memory functioned.

In related research, Manfred Milinski performed a clever experiment with a species of small fish called sticklebacks.[43] Schools of sticklebacks send out scouting pairs to assess the danger posed by nearby predators. Why would an individual dart out from the safety of the school to probe the reactions of a fish that would like to eat it? Milinski noted that each pair of sticklebacks probing a predator took turns moving toward the larger fish in short darting movements. If the predator showed interest, the scouts scooted back to the school. Milinski proposed that the turn taking was an example of the Prisoner's Dilemma. He tested his hypothesis by putting a mirror near a predator in an aquarium. Lone sticklebacks reacted in a TIT FOR TAT–like manner when observing what their mirror image did; that is, when they darted forward or backward spontaneously, they repeated the action after seeing their image.

Later, when discussing zero-sum games versus non-zero-sum games, I'll point out the ways that cooperative and competitive behaviors are nested within one another. Recall the first public goods, where early hunters may have cooperated in order to bring down game but reverted to more competitive strategies such as dominance hierarchies when it came to allocating that meat (although one of the oft-quoted observations about the emergence of food sharing is that "the Inuit knows that the best place for him to store his surplus is in someone else's stomach"[44]).

Cooperation and conflict are both aspects of the same phenomenon. One of the important ways that humans cooperate is banding together into clans, tribes, and nations in order to compete more effectively against other bands. Cooperators can thrive amid populations of defectors if they learn to recognize each other and interact with one another. Are Ostrom's "clearly defined group boundaries" another way of cooperators learning to recognize each other? Cooperators who clump together can outcompete noncooperative strategies by creating public goods that benefit themselves but not the defectors. One time-tested way of inducing a group to work together is to introduce an external threat. Cooperative enterprise and intergroup conflict have coevolved because the ability to recognize who is inside and who is outside a group's boundaries is integral to both intragroup cooperation and intergroup conflict.

Reciprocity, cooperation, reputation, social grooming, and social dilemmas all appear to be fundamental pieces of the smart mob puzzle. Each of these biological and social phenomena can be affected by, and can affect, communication behaviors and practices. Prisoner's Dilemma and game theory are not "answers" to questions of cooperation; rather, they are tools for understanding human social dynamics. Together with CPR theory, game-theoretic and other computer-modeling approaches open windows onto the kinds of group behavior that might emerge with smart mob technologies.

Inventing the Innovation Commons

The most successful recent example of an artificial public good is the Internet. Microprocessors and communication networks were only the physical part of the Net's success formula; cooperative social contracts were also built into the Net's basic architecture. The Internet is both the result of and the enabling infrastructure for new ways of organizing collective action via communication technology. This new social contract enables the creation and maintenance of public goods, a commons for knowledge resources.

The personal computer and the Internet would not exist as they do today without extraordinary collaborative enterprises in which acts of cooperation were as essential as microprocessors. The technologies that support tomorrow's smart mobs were created over three decades by people who competed with each other to improve the value of their shared tools, media, and communities of practice. And for most of this era, "value" translated into "usefulness," not price per share of stock. A brief detour into the history of personal computing and networking illuminates more than the origins of smart mob technologies; the commons that fostered technical innovations is also the fundamental social technology of smart mobs. It all started with the original hackers in the early 1960s.

Before the word "hacker" was misappropriated to describe people who break into computer systems, the term was coined (in the early 1960s) to describe people who *create* computer systems. The first people to call themselves hackers were loyal to an informal social contract called "the hacker ethic." As Steven Levy described it, this ethic included these principles:

> Access to computers should be unlimited and total.
> Always yield to the Hands-On Imperative.
> All information should be free.
> Mistrust authority—promote decentralization.[45]

Without that ethic, there probably wouldn't have been an Internet to commercialize. Keep in mind that although many of the characters involved in this little-known but important history were motivated by altruistic concerns, their collaboration was aimed at creating a resource that would benefit all—starting with the collaborators who created it. Like other creators of public goods, the hackers created something that they were eager to use for their own purposes.

The Internet was deliberately designed by hackers to be an innovation commons, a laboratory for collaboratively creating better technologies. They knew that some community of hackers in the future would know more about networks than the original creators, so the designers of the Internet took care to avoid technical obstacles to future innovation.[46] The creation of the Internet was a community enterprise, and the media that the original hackers created were meant to support communities of creators.[47] To this end, several of the most essential software programs that make the Internet possible are not owned by any commercial enterprise— a hybrid of intellectual property and public good, invented by hackers.

The foundations of the Internet were created by the community of creators as a gift to the community of users. In the 1960s, the community of users was the same as the community of creators, so self-interest and public goods were identical, but hackers foresaw a day when their tools would be used by a wider population.[48] Understanding the hacker ethic and the way in which the Internet was built to function as a commons are essential to forecasting where tomorrow's technologies of cooperation might come from and what might encourage or limit their use.

Originally, software was included with the hardware that computer manufacturers sold to customers—mainframe computers attended by special operators. Programmers were required to submit their programs to the operators in the form of punched paper cards. When technology and political necessity made it possible for programmers to work directly with computers, an explosion of innovation occurred.

Credit Sputnik for the way computers changed. In 1957, motivated by the groundbreaking entry of Soviet technology in orbit, the U.S. Department of Defense created the Advanced Research Projects Agency. ARPA hired an MIT professor by the name of J.C.R. Licklider to lead an effort to leapfrog over existing computer technology. ARPA contractors created software that would display the results of computations as graphical displays on screens instead of printouts. Most importantly, they created software "operating systems" that enabled the community of programmers/users to interact directly with computers.

An operating system (OS) coordinates the interaction between a computer's hardware and application software. Early interactive operating systems were known as "time-sharing" systems because they took advantage of the speed of electronic computation to divide the computer's "attention" among groups of programmers. The computer's processor would switch between each user for a fraction of a second, giving each user the impression that he or she was the sole user. Because they were connected to the same computer, programmers working on ARPA projects quickly developed a sense of community. They started inventing ways to send each other messages from their individual terminals through the shared computer. Email and virtual communities are both rooted in the ancestral "hacks" the time-sharing programmers created to communicate among themselves.

The bill for these innovations was paid by ARPA grants. The hackers created tools for one another, competing to share the best hacks with the community, giving American taxpayers and the rest of the world an astonishing return on investment. At MIT in the early 1960s, inventing interactive computing was a collective enterprise. Essential programs were stored on punched paper tape and kept in an unlocked drawer; any hacker could use the program, and if he found a better way to do what the program was intended to do, he would revise the program, change the tape, and put it back in the drawer.[49]

In the late 1960s and early 1970s, several developments set off the next frenzy of innovation. Licklider and others started planning an "intergalactic network" to connect the geographically scattered ARPA computing centers.[50] From the beginning, the network's architects knew they were creating a communication medium as well as a means of connecting remote computers.[51] By the mid-1970s, government laboratories and big corporations were joined by a new player in the computer game: teenage hobbyists. In 1974, the Altair, the first personal computer kit, became available, and "homebrewing computing" hobbyists began meeting in Palo Alto. The Homebrew Computer Club received a famous letter in 1976 from twenty-one-year-old Bill Gates, complaining that homebrewers were using the programming tool that his new company, Microsoft, had created for the Altair without paying him for it.[52] Software, Gates declared, was not a public good you kept in a drawer, tinkered with, and shared; it was private property. Bill Gates stuck by his declaration, and by the 1990s he had become the world's richest man by selling the operating system used by 90 percent of the desktop computers in the world.

In 1969, AT&T Bell Labs pulled out of ARPA's Multics operating system project, and several Bell Labs programmers who missed the sense of community started working on their own unofficial OS project. Programmer

Ken Thompson created a game on a small computer that had come into his hands, in the process writing a "kernel" that would end up growing into the OS that collaborator Brian Kernighan named Unix in 1970. The name was a pun on the abandoned Multics project.[53] The Unix creators made their source code publicly available to other programmers and invited collaboration in creating software that could make Unix more useful, a decision that gave birth to a whole new way of developing software. Computer software is distributed for use in the form of "object code," a translation of the original ("source") program into a human-unreadable but machine-executable collection of zeroes and ones. By distributing the source code, the Unix creators made it possible for other programmers to understand how the software works and to make their own modifications—harking back to the days of the paper tape in the unlocked drawer. Ken Thompson started duplicating Unix source code and utilities on magnetic tapes, labeling and documenting them with the words "Love, Ken," and mailing the tapes to friends.[54]

Unix software became the OS of the Net. In turn, the Internet created a rich environment for Unix programmers to establish one of the earliest global virtual communities. Dennis Ritchie, one of the Unix creators, wrote: "What we wanted to preserve was not just a good environment in which to do programming, but a system around which a fellowship could form. We knew from experience that the essence of communal computing, as supplied by remote-access, time-shared machines, is not just to type programs into a terminal instead of a keypunch, but to encourage close communication."[55]

However, in 1976, AT&T halted publication of Unix source code; the original, eventually banned, books became "possibly the most photocopied works in computing history."[56] At around the same time the Unix community was coalescing, MIT's Artificial Intelligence research laboratory changed the kind of computers it used. This was a blow to the MIT hacker culture, because their software tools were rendered useless. At the same time, many of the early AI researchers were leaving for private industry to get involved in the techno-bubble of the time, the commercial AI boom and eventual bust. One holdout at MIT, deprived of his beloved programming environment, resistant to the commercialization of what he considered public property by AT&T and Microsoft, was Richard Stallman.

Stallman vowed to write an OS that would be as portable and open as Unix, but which would be licensed in a way that would maintain its status as public goods. Stallman, founder of the Free Software Foundation, started creating GNU—a recursive acronym that stands for "GNU's Not Unix." Stallman, who owns little property and has no home other than his office, devoted himself thereafter to what he called "free software" (and emphasized that he meant "free as in free speech, not free beer").[57]

Stallman hacked the legalities of the copyright system as well as created the first source code for a free OS. He released the software he created with a license known as the GPL (General Public License). The GNU GPL enables others to copy, distribute, and make changes to software, as long as innovators don't prevent others from doing the same thing. Stallman called the new kind of license "Copyleft."[58] Like the paper tape in a drawer at MIT, GPL software is free for anyone to use, and anyone is free to build on it, but only if they keep the source code of the software open for others to use and improve.

Creating an operating system is not a simple enterprise. By 1991, GNU was a complete OS, with the exception of its most essential part, known as the kernel. Linus Torvalds, a student at the University of Helsinki, started to write his own kernel. Based on GNU, all of Torvalds's code was open according to the GPL, and Torvalds took the fateful step of posting his work to the Net and asking others for help. The kernel, known as Linux, drew hundreds, then thousands of young programmers. By the 1990s, opposition to the monolithic domination of the computer operating system market by Microsoft became a motivating factor for rebellious young programmers who had taken up the torch of the hacker ethic.

"Open source" refers to software, but it also refers to a method for developing software and a philosophy of how to maintain a public good. Eric Raymond wrote about the difference between "cathedral and bazaar" approaches to complex software development:

> The most important feature of Linux, however, was not technical but sociological. Until the Linux development, everyone believed that any software as complex as an operating system had to be developed in a carefully coordinated way by a relatively small, tightly knit group of people. This model was and is typical of both commercial software and the great freeware cathedrals. . . . Linux evolved in a completely different way. From nearly the beginning, it was rather casually hacked on by huge numbers of volunteers coordinating only through the Internet. Quality was maintained not by rigid standards or autocracy but by the naively simple strategy of releasing every

week and getting feedback from hundreds of users within days, creating a sort of rapid Darwinian selection on the mutations introduced by developers.[59]

Software deliberately created as a public good is the reason you can type www.smartmobs.com instead of a string of numbers to see this book's Web site; the Internet's "domain name" system depends on BIND software, probably the most widely used software that nobody owns and everybody uses.[60] When it was time for the ARPAnet to grow into a network of networks, the programming wizards who created the Internet's fundamental protocols understood that decisions they made about this software would affect future generations of innovators. They created the first protocols for sending data around the network in a way that had profound social effects: "The basic argument is that, as a first principle, certain required end-to-end functions can only be performed correctly by the end-systems themselves. . . . The network's job is to transmit datagrams as efficiently and flexibly as possible. Everything else should be done at the fringes."[61] (Think of a "datagram" as a little chunk of content that has an address on it.)

By adhering to one of the principles Ostrom had recognized—in complex social systems, the levels of governance should nest within each other—Internet architects hit upon the "end-to-end" principle that allows individual innovators, not the controllers of the network, to decide what to build on the Internet's capabilities.[62] When Tim Berners-Lee created World Wide Web software at a physics laboratory in Geneva, he didn't have to get permission to change the way the Internet works, because the computers that are connected (the "fringes"), not a central network, is where the Internet changes. Berners-Lee simply wrote a program that worked with the Internet's protocols and evangelized a group of colleagues to start creating Web sites; the Web spread by infection, not fiat.[63]

In 1993, Marc Andreesen and other programmers at the U.S. National Center for Supercomputing Applications (NCSA) released Mosaic, the "browser" software that made the Web accessible through a point-and-click interface. Key Mosaic programmers moved from NCSA, a public institution that puts its software into the public domain, to Netscape, Inc., which "closed" the browser code. Marc Andreesen became a zillionaire when Netscape went public in 1994. As the Internet industry skyrocketed from nowhere to "the greatest legal accumulation of wealth in history,"[64] the Web was also emerging as a noncommercial effort by programmers who had not been born when the ARPAnet was invented. Volunteers started exchanging software to improve the Web server that NCSA programmers had created. Just as the browser is the software used to navigate the Web, the Web server is the software used to publish information on the Web. These volunteer programmers agreed that keeping free, open-source Web server software available was key to maintaining the spirit of innovation.

Brian Behlendorf cofounded the virtual community of volunteers who maintain the open-source software that still powers 60 percent of the Web servers in the world. Because the earliest noncommercial Web server software required many "patches"—additional software added to a program to fix a bug—Behlendorf organized an online coalition of programmers to share patches. Because it was a "patchy" program, they decided to call the software Apache. He's now the CEO of Collabnet, one of the rare surviving dotcoms that uses open-source methods for commercial software development. In 1998, IBM based its e-business product line on Apache and subsequently announced a billion-dollar budget to support open-source software development.

Perhaps the largest incubator of online social networks and the oldest global virtual community, Usenet, is also an example of a gigantic long-functioning anarchy—a public good that exists on minimum enforcement of cooperation. In 1979, Duke University grad students Jim Ellis and Tom Truscott, and Steve Bellovin at University of North Carolina, created the first link between Duke and UNC.[65] Unix-to-Unix copy protocol, a communication tool that came bundled with every copy of Unix, made it possible for computers to exchange files over telephone modem connections. Every day or hour, one computer would automatically dial the modem connected to another computer and exchange messages that had been composed by computer users at either end; each computer would relay messages that had been passed to them until they reached their destination, like a bucket brigade. This kind of public email, known as "postings," or "posts," is readable by anyone who subscribes to the appropriate topical interest group known as a "newsgroup." The self-organizing global conversation network began to spread among university and industry computer centers, relaying messages around the world through ad hoc dial-up arrangements.

To join Usenet, a computer system operator only needed to get a "feed" from another computer system that would transmit and relay messages to and from the system's users. That single agreement to send messages back and forth in an agreed format is the extent of Usenet's enforced cooperation. There is no central control, either technical or social. "Whatever order exists in the Usenet is the product of a delicate balance between individual freedom and collective good," is how Marc Smith put it.[66] This anarchy, now over twenty years old, became spectacularly successful after 1986, when the news feed began to propagate through Internet-linked sites with high-speed connections rather than ad hoc relay networks of dial-up connections. Usenet exchanged 151 million messages, contributed by 8.1 million unique identified users in 2000. Each day, more than 1 million messages are exchanged among more than 110,000 unique participants via 103,000 newsgroups.[67]

Will the Internet remain a decentralized, self-organized commons as the fixed network infrastructure upgrades to wireless connection technologies? Lawrence Lessig, distinguished professor at Harvard and Stanford law schools, is alarmed at technical and legal movements now underway that might change the characteristics that enabled the Internet to thrive. Intrigued by Lessig's book, *The Future of Ideas,* I talked with him directly in his office at Stanford's law school.[68] Lessig was dressed casually in black jeans and a blue cardigan sweater. I noticed five different coffee containers on his desk. I asked him whether it was proper to think of the Internet as the kind of common pool resource that Hardin and Ostrom had written about.

Definitely! The resource that was held in commons was the right to innovate. That resource was held in commons because the architecture of the Internet prevented the owner of the network from vetoing innovations in content or applications that they didn't like. The end-to-end principle meant that the network itself had no power to discriminate. That meant anybody could take advantage of the commons created by connecting all these computers together to develop new ideas and applications that everybody could have access to. And that's what happened. The value of the Internet came from no single institution or company, but from the collective innovations of millions of contributors.

I asked Lessig why he is worried about the future.

The innovation commons is being corrupted by changes that are being made at the architecture level. These changes are accomplished by allowing future versions of Internet software protocols to abandon the end-to-end principle, enabling the network owners to decide which applications will be permitted to run over the network and which applications won't. Coaxial cable owners that offer high-speed Internet access already prevent their users from running servers or hosting Web pages and are preventing content that competes with the cable owner's own content from running on their parts of the Internet. The AT&T–MediaOne merger created a huge cable infrastructure that AT&T controlled. AOL-Time-Warner created a huge cable infrastructure that AOL controlled, and now they're trying to put them both together into a single cable infrastructure for a large part of the Internet. As cable providers consolidate ownership, they are increasingly asserting their right to decide how people can use the network.

Four months after Lessig and I talked, the Federal Communications Commission launched a campaign to expand deployment of high-speed Internet access by reclassifying the cable modem business as an "information service" that would not require open access with the rest of the Internet to connect with their lines.[69] At the same time, the cable television industry pressed the FCC to prevent local governments from requesting that a portion of bandwidth be set aside for public, educational, and governmental uses.[70] In March, 2002, the FCC ruled in favor of the cable industry, dropping the requirement that cable operators allow competitors to use their networks and removing the power of local governments to request public resources in exchange for monopoly access to the local community.[71]

Lessig and I talked about technical and legal changes that might affect the wireless Internet of the future; that discussion continues in Chapter 6, "Wireless Quilts." He did have this to say in regard to the enabling technologies for smart mobs:

New ways to think about connecting information services and people on the network now seem to be possible with wireless technologies, but what has to be preserved is the right to innovate about how these different ways of connecting to the Net can be used. The right to connect all sorts of devices to the network to do things that were never imagined by the people who built the network will assure a broad range of innovation around the mobile Internet. Are we going to move toward a controlled wireless world, where the equivalent of telephone companies or cable companies get to decide what we do on our wireless devices? It will be innovative relative to what wireless devices were five years ago, but still it will be innovative only as far as the controlling companies believe benefits them. Or will we adopt an architecture for wireless where nobody gets to decide for everyone what the technology can and cannot be used for? Once we construct an innovation commons there, I think we could see the next great revolution of innovation in wireless Internet technology.

Who Knows Who Knows Who? Social Networks as Driving Forces

A few years ago, Marc Smith introduced me to his colleague Barry Wellman, a master of a discipline Smith knew would interest me—social network analysis. I learned that people were studying social networks decades before computer networks or mobile telephones were invented and that Wellman claimed that "computer networks are social networks."[72] His research and hypotheses about the connections between online and face-to-face social networks mapped perfectly onto many questions that had cropped up when I was investigating social cyberspaces. When Wellman visited California, he and I walked in an oak forest and chatted about the ways physical places and cyberspaces influence one another. Wellman has a quiet manner and a dry sense of humor, and he doesn't shrink from making bold claims. Wellman's claims came back to me when I looked for the social underpinnings of smart mobs.

Every time someone interacts with another person, there is the potential to exchange information about people they both know. The structure of everyone's links to everyone else is a network that acts as a channel through which news, job tips, possible romantic partners, and contagious diseases travel. Social networks can be measured, and interconnections can be charted, from relationships between interlocking boards of directors of major corporations to terrorist networks. One of Wellman's claims is that "we find community in networks, not groups."[73] He explained that "a group is a special type of network: densely-knit (most people are directly connected), tightly-bounded (most ties stay within the densely-knit cluster), and multistranded (most ties contain many role relationships)," and he challenged conventional thinking about how people cluster socially:

Although people often view the world in terms of groups, they function in networks. In networked societies, boundaries are permeable, interactions are with diverse others, connections switch between multiple networks, and hierarchies can be flatter and recursive. The change from groups to networks can be seen at many levels. Trading and political blocs have lost their monolithic character in the world system. Organizations form complex networks of alliance and exchange rather than cartels, and workers report to multiple peers and superiors. . . . Communities are far-flung, loosely-bounded, sparsely-knit, and fragmentary. Most people operate in multiple, thinly-connected, partial communities as they deal with networks of kin, neighbours, friends, workmates and organizational ties. Rather than fitting into the same group as those around them, each person has his/her own "personal community."[74]

Does "personal community" remind anyone of those teenagers in Scandinavia and Pakistan, Tokyo and Manila, maintaining a stream of text messages with small groups of five to eight close friends as they go about their lives? I think Wellman's mapping of traditional social network analysis onto social cyberspaces can be applied to mobile cyberspaces, as well:

Complex social networks have always existed, but recent technological developments in communication have afforded their emergence as a dominant form of social organization. When computer-mediated communication networks link people, institutions and knowledge, they are computer-supported social networks. The technological development of computer networks and the societal flourishing of social networks are now in a positive feedback loop. Just as the flexibility of less-bounded, spatially dispersed social networks creates demand for the world wide web and collaborative communication, the breathless development of computer networks nourishes societal transitions from little boxes to social networks. I define "community" as networks of interpersonal ties that provide sociability, support, information, a sense of belonging, and social identity. I do not limit my thinking about community to neighbourhoods and villages. This is good advice for any epoch and especially pertinent for the twenty-first century.[75]

Wellman foresees that "the person—not the place, household or workgroup—will become even more of an autonomous communication node" and points out that "people usually obtain support, companionship, information and a sense of belonging from those who do not live within the same neighborhood or even within the same metropolitan area. People maintain these community ties through phoning, writing, driving, railroading, transiting and flying. . . . The person has become the portal."[76] The Internet facilitates the creation and management of multiple, personal social networks.

What connects the technical properties of computer networks and the communication properties of social networks? When I started posing this question in my own social network, all the most interesting links led to Reed's Law, a mathematical formulation discovered by David P. Reed. When I educated myself about Reed, I knew I had to meet him. He had been one of the authors of the Internet's end-to-end principle; Reed had been the senior scientist of Lotus Corporation, and in affiliation with MIT's Media Lab, he has become one of the instigators of the "open spectrum" movement, a radical rethinking of the way wireless communications are regulated. When I visited Media Lab in the fall of 2001, Reed and I met at the lab and continued our conversation over lunch, where he recalled how he first discovered his law.

Reed's Law relating social networks and computer networks is the most recent in a series of fundamental discoveries about the driving forces of computers and networks. In the social sciences, prediction is necessarily fuzzy. In the economics of computer-mediated social networks, however, four key mathematical laws of growth have been derived by four astute inquirers: Sarnoff's Law, Moore's Law, Metcalfe's Law, and Reed's Law. Each law is about how value is affected by technological leverage.

Sarnoff's Law emerged from the advent of radio and television networks in the early twentieth century, in which a central source broadcasts from a small number of transmitting stations to a large number of receivers. Broadcast pioneer David Sarnoff pointed out the obvious: The value of broadcast networks is proportionate to the number of viewers.[77]

The often-cited Moore's Law is the reason electronic miniaturization has driven the hyper-evolution of electronics, computers, and networks. In 1965, Gordon Moore, cofounder of Intel and one of the inventors of the microprocessor, noted that the number of elements that could be packed into the same amount of space on a microchip had doubled every year. Moore forecast that the number of elements would double every eighteen months in the future.[78] Anything that doubles and redoubles grows large very quickly, from 2,250 elements in Intel's first microprocessor of 1971 to 42 million elements in the Pentium 4 processor thirty years later.[79] Computers and electronic components have driven industrial growth for decades because they are among the rare technologies that grow more powerful and less expensive simultaneously. Without the efficiencies described by Moore's Law, the PC, the Internet, and mobile telephones would have been impossibly large, unintelligent, and expensive.

What happens when you link devices based on Moore's Law? When ARPA wizards gathered at the Xerox Palo Alto Research Center (PARC) in the early 1970s to create the first personal computers, one of the engineering aces, Bob Metcalfe, led the team that invented the Ethernet, a high-speed network that interconnected PCs in the same building.[80] Metcalfe left PARC, founded 3Com, Inc., cashed out, and came up with Metcalfe's Law, which describes the growth of value in networks. The math is simple and is based on a fundamental mathematical property of networks: The number of potential connections between nodes grows more quickly than the number of nodes. The total value of a network where each node can reach every other node grows with the square of the number of nodes. If you have two nodes, each with a value of one unit, the value of joining them is four units. Four interconnected nodes, each still worth one unit, is worth sixteen units when networked, and one hundred nodes is worth one hundred times one hundred, or ten thousand. When value increases exponentially more quickly than the number of nodes, the mathematical consequence translates into economic leverage: Connecting two networks creates far more value than the sum of their values as independent networks.[81]

David Reed has a graying beard and a wicked twinkle in his eye. He's not the type of fellow to pound the table to make a point. He's more the kind of fellow who genially proves he is right with equations on a whiteboard. As we sipped lobster bisque in Kendall Square, I asked him what led him to Reed's Law.

"I had the first 'eureka' when I thought about why eBay was so successful."[82]

eBay, which has turned out to be the only hugely profitable e-commerce business, doesn't sell any merchandise; it provides a market for customers to buy and sell from each other.

eBay won because it facilitated the formation of social groups around specific interests. Social groups form around people who want to buy or sell teapots or antique radios. At that time, I had been reading Fukuyama about social capital.[83] Fukuyama argues in his book *Trust* that there is a strong correlation between the prosperity of national economies and social capital, which he defines as the ease with which people in a particular culture can form new associations. I realized that the millions of humans who used the millions of computers added another important property—the ability of the people in the network to form groups. I remembered that when it became possible to send and reply to entire groups in email, it became possible to create ad hoc discussions. Since then, all sorts of chat rooms, message boards, listservs, buddy lists, auction markets, have added new ways for people to form groups online. Human communication adds a dimension to the computer network. I started thinking in terms of group-forming networks (GFNs). I saw that the value of a GFN grows even faster—much, much faster—than the networks where Metcalfe's Law holds true. Reed's Law shows that the value of the network grows proportionately not to the square of the users, but exponentially.[84]

That means you raise two to the power of the number of nodes instead of squaring the number of nodes. The value of two nodes is four under Metcalfe's Law and Reed's Law, but the value of ten nodes is one hundred (ten to the second power) under Metcalfe's Law and 1,024 (two to the tenth power) under Reed's Law—and the differential rates of growth climb the hockey stick curve from there. This explains how social networks, enabled by email and other social communications, drove the growth of the network beyond communities of engineers to include every kind of interest group. Reed's Law is the link between computer networks and social networks.

Reed, using his law to analyze the value of different kinds of networks, believes he has discovered an important cultural and economic shift. When a network is aimed at broadcasting something of value to individuals, like a television network, the value of services is linear. When the network enables transactions between the individual nodes, the value is squared. When the same network includes ways for the individuals to form groups, the value is exponential:

> What's important is that the dominant value in a typical network tends to shift from one category to another as the scale of the network increases. Whether the growth is by incremental customer additions or by transparent interconnection, scale growth tends to support new categories of "killer apps," and thus new competitive games.
>
> We can see this scale-driven value shift in the history of the Internet. The earliest usage of the Internet was dominated by its role as a terminal network, allowing many terminals to selectively access a small number of costly time-sharing hosts. As the Internet grew, much more of the usage and value

of the Internet became focused on pairwise exchanges of email messages, files, etc., following Metcalfe's Law. And as the Internet started to take off in the early '90s, traffic started to be dominated by newsgroups, user-created mailing lists, special interest web sites, etc., following the exponential GFN law. Though the previously dominant functions did not lose value or decline as the scale of the Internet grew, the value and usage of services that scaled by newly dominant scaling laws grew faster. Thus many kinds of transactions and collaboration that had been conducted outside the Internet became absorbed into the growth of the Internet's functions, and these become the new competitive playing field.

What's important in a network changes as the network scale shifts. In a network dominated by linear connectivity value growth, "content is king." That is, in such networks, there is a small number of sources (publishers or makers) of content that every user selects from. The sources compete for users based on the value of their content (published stories, published images, standardized consumer goods). Where Metcalfe's Law dominates, transactions become central. The stuff that is traded in transactions (be it email or voice mail, money, securities, contracted services, or whatnot) is king. And where the GFN law dominates, the central role is filled by jointly constructed value (such as specialized newsgroups, joint responses to RFPs, gossip, etc.).[85]

Reed believes that there is a direct connection between the kind of social capital that Fukuyama discusses and the way people use the Internet as a group-forming network. This connection is the reason why esoteric technical and legal arguments about the end-to-end principle and wireless regulation might have a large effect on everybody in the world. If the innovation commons is open to many in the future, as it has been in the past, a "cornucopia of the commons" could make it possible for many to benefit. Or those who have concentrated capital in existing infrastructures and corporations might manage to enclose the commons and reserve that power of innovation by technically excluding future innovators. The first battle has already been fought over Napster. The established interests won, triggering an effort by innovators to invent knowledge commons that can't be enclosed.

The "cornucopia of the commons" is a consequence of Reed's Law taking advantage of Moore's Law. My journey into the universe of peer-to-peer ad-hocracies that combine the powers of computation with the growth capabilities of online social networks started innocently enough, when I stumbled onto a plot to find life in outer space.

Computation Nations
and Swarm Supercomputers

Peer-to-peer networks are composed of personal computers tied together with consumer Internet connections, each node a quantum zone of
uncertainty, prone to going offline whenever its owner closes his laptop
and chucks it into a shoulder-bag. . . . Peer-to-peer networks aren't owned
by any central authority, nor can they be controlled, killed, or broken by a
central authority. Companies and concerns may program and release software for peer-to-peer networking, but the networks that emerge are
owned by everyone and no one.

They're faery infrastructure, networks whose maps form weird n-dimen-
sional topologies of surpassing beauty and chaos; mad technological hairballs
run by ad-hocracies whose members each act in their own best interests.

In a nutshell, peer-to-peer technology is goddamn wicked. It's esoteric.
It's unstoppable. It's way, way cool.

—Cory Doctorow, "The Gnomes of San Jose"

ETs, Worms, and 'Zillas

I stumbled into my first peer-to-peer ad-hocracy when I visited a friend's office in San Francisco one night in 1999. It was a quarter past midnight during the peak of the dotcom era, which meant that the crew was going full
blast at the witching hour. Nevertheless, I couldn't help noticing that the
screens on the few unoccupied desks in the block-square geek farm
seemed to be talking to each other. Animated graphical displays danced in
bright colors on dozens of monitors.

When he noticed what I was noticing, my friend explained that the computers were banding together. When nobody was using them, the PCs were swarming with other computers around the world in an amateur cooperative venture known as SETI@home—a collective supercomputer spread all over the Net.

"What are they computing?" I asked.

"They're searching for extraterrestrial communications," he replied.

He wasn't kidding.

Community computation, also known as "distributed processing" or "peer-to-peer (p2p)" computing, had already been underway for years before Napster evoked the wrath of the recording industry with this new way of using networked computers. Whereas Napster enabled people to trade music by sharing their computer memory—their disk space—distributed processing communities share central processing unit (CPU) computation cycles, the fundamental unit of computing power. Sharing disk space does no more than enable people to pool and exchange data, whether it is in the form of music or signals from radio telescopes. CPU cycles, unlike disk space, have the power to compute—which translates into the power to analyze, simulate, calculate, search, sift, recognize, render, predict, communicate, and control. By the spring of 2000, millions of people participating in SETI@home were contributing their PCs' processors to crunch radio astronomy data.[1] They did it voluntarily, because finding life in outer space would be "way, way cool." And perhaps because cooperating on that scale is a thrill. The thrill made even more sense when I learned that all the computers in this office were part of a team, competing and cooperating with other geek farms around the world to contribute computations to the group effort.

Keep one thing in mind as we travel through the p2p universe: A great deal of peer-to-peer technology was created for fun—the same reason the PC and the Web first emerged from communities of amateur enthusiasts. When the suits, the bucks, and the corporations move in, the noncommercial and cooperative origins of technologies tend to be forgotten. Yet, venture capitalists would never have paid attention to the Web in the first place if a million people had not created Web pages because it was a cool thing to do (i.e., the creators would gain prestige among their peers) and because a little bit of cooperation can create resources useful to everyone. It's the same old hacker intoxication of getting a buzz from giving tools away and then coming back to find that someone else has made the tool even more useful.

The power of peer-to-peer methodology is a human social power, not a mechanical one, rooted in the kind of passion that enthusiasts like Cory Doctorow demonstrate when he says: "In a nutshell, peer-to-peer technology is goddamn wicked. It's esoteric. It's unstoppable. It's way, way cool." Although Doctorow hadn't been born when system administrators started receiving tapes in the mail, labeled "Love, Ken," he was expressing the same spirit that drove Unix and the creation of the Internet and the Web. People don't just participate in p2p—they *believe* in it. Hardware and software make it possible, but peer-to-peer technology is potent because it grows from the collective actions of large numbers of people. Like Cory, some people grow passionate about this kind of technology-assisted cooperation. The people who created the Web, and before that, the Internet and the PC, knew that passion. It's what author Robert Wright calls "non-zero-sumness"—the unique human power and pleasure that comes from doing something that enriches everyone, a game where nobody has to lose for everyone to win.[2]

Today, millions of people and their PCs are not just looking for messages from outer space and trading music but tackling cancer research, finding prime numbers, rendering films, forecasting weather, designing synthetic drugs by running simulations on billions of possible molecules—taking on computing problems so massive that scientists have not heretofore considered them.

Distributed processing takes advantage of a huge and long-overlooked source of power.[3] It is a kind of technical windfall. In a sense it's found energy, analogous to the energy savings that come from building more efficient appliances and better insulated buildings. Computation power can be multiplied, without building any new computers, simply by harvesting a resource that until now had been squandered—the differential between human and electronic processing speeds.

If you type two characters per second on your keyboard, you're using a miniscule fraction of your machine's power. During that second, most desktop computers can simultaneously perform hundreds of millions of additional operations. Time-sharing computers of the 1960s exploited this ability. Now, millions of PCs around the world, each one of them thousands of times more powerful than the time-sharing mainframes of the '60s, connect via the Internet. As the individual computers participating in online swarms become more numerous and powerful and the speed of information transfer among them increases, an expansion of raw computing power looms, an expansion of such magnitude that it will certainly make possible qualitative changes in the way people use computers.

Peer-to-peer sociotechnical cooperatives amplify the power of the other parts of the smart mobs puzzle. Peer-to-peer collectives, pervasive computing, social networks, and mobile communications multiply each other's effects: Not only are millions of people now linking their social networks through mobile communication devices, but the computing chips inside those mobile devices are growing capable of communicating with radio-linked chips embedded in the environment. Expect startling social effects when the 1,500 people who walk across Shibuya Crossing at every light change can become a temporary cloud of distributed computing power.

In the summer of 2000, I visited David P. Anderson, technical instigator of the Search for Extraterrestrial Intelligence (SETI) project. I knew I had arrived at the right place when I spotted the WELCOME ALL SPECIES doormat. The University of California Space Sciences Laboratory in the Berkeley Hills is still the mother ship of community computation, nerve center of the largest cooperative computing effort in the world.

Search for Extraterrestrial Intelligence (SETI) is a privately funded scientific examination of extraterrestrial radio signals in search of messages from alien civilizations. More than 2 million people worldwide donate untapped CPU time on their PCs to analyze signals collected by a radio telescope in Puerto Rico. The telescope pulls down about 50 billion bytes of data per day, far more than SETI's servers can analyze. That's where community computing comes in. SETI@home participants install client software (a program they download from the Net and run on their home computer; the client communicates automatically with the central "server" computer in Berkeley). The client software downloads a small segment of radio telescope signals and processes it, looking for interesting patterns consistent with intelligent life. When the task is complete, the program uploads the results to SETI@home headquarters and collects a new chunk of digitized space signal to search. When the computer's user logs into the machine, the SETI@home client goes dormant, awakening again when the human user pauses for more than a few minutes.

It was a sunny day, so Anderson and I sat on a terrace outside the Space Sciences Laboratory. The California hills had turned summer tawny. We could smell the eucalyptus forest on the hills below us. Behind Anderson, I could see a panoramic view of San Francisco Bay. If I worked in this building, I would take as many meetings as possible on the terrace. Anderson, tall, dark-haired, with the lank and sinew of a long-distance runner, takes his time thinking about a response and then tends to speak in perfectly formed paragraphs.

I asked him how SETI@home started. "In 1995," Anderson recalled, "I was contacted by a former Berkeley grad student named David Gedye. Inspired by documentaries about the Apollo moon landing, an event that made people all over the world feel that human beings were taking a collective step forward, Gedye wondered what contemporary project today might have a similar impact and hit upon the idea of harnessing the public's fascination with both the Internet and the SETI program."

In mid-1999, SETI@home clients were made available online for free downloading. "It's been a wild ride since then," says Anderson. "We were hoping for at least 100,000 people worldwide to get enough computer power to make the thing worthwhile. After a week, we had 200,000 participants, after four or five months it broke through a million, and now it's past 2 million."[4]

Although SETI@home put distributed computing on the map, it wasn't the first such attempt to link computers into a cooperating network. In the early 1980s, I searched for the future in the library of the Xerox Palo Alto Research Center. Some of the most interesting reading was in the distinctive blue-and-white bound documents of PARC research reports. I wasn't technically knowledgeable enough to understand most of them, but one of them, written in largely nontechnical English, had an intriguing title, "Notes on the 'Worm' Programs—Some Early Experience with a Distributed Computation," by John F. Shoch and Jon A. Hupp.[5] The report was about experiments with a computer program that traveled from machine to machine on a local network, looking for idle CPUs, sneaking in computations when the processor was not in use, and then retreating to the mother ship with the results when humans started using the machines.

I was intrigued by the authors' acknowledgment that they were inspired by a 1975 science fiction novel: "In his book *The Shockwave Rider,* John Brunner developed the notion of an omnipotent 'tapeworm' program running loose through a network of computers—an idea which may seem rather disturbing, but which is also quite beyond our current capabilities. Yet the basic model is a very provocative one: a program or computation that can move from machine to machine, commandeering resources as needed, and replicating itself when necessary."[6]

It took decades for the telecommunication pipelines that linked computers to become fast enough, and for the computer processors to become powerful enough, to enable truly useful distributed computation power. In 1985, Miron Livny proposed that idle workstations could be used for distributed work.[7] A few years later, Richard Crandall, now Distinguished Scientist at Apple, started testing gargantuan prime numbers with networked NeXT computers.

"One day at NeXT engineering headquarters," Crandall recalled when I talked with him in 2000, "I looked at these idle computers, and it occurred to me that machines have no business sleeping. I installed software that allowed the computers to perform computations when machines were idle and to combine their efforts across the network. I called it Godzilla. But we got a legal warning from the company that owned the rights to the name Godzilla. So we renamed it 'Zilla."[8]

Crandall wanted to work on a specific task: searching for very large prime numbers. Crandall and two colleagues completed the deepest computation ever performed in order to answer a yes-or-no question: Is the 24th Fermat number (which has more than 5 million digits) prime?[9] "It took 100 quadrillion machine operations," Crandall proudly estimates. "That's approximately the same amount of computation Pixar required to render their computer-animated feature film *A Bug's Life*. With that level of computational effort you can create a full-length movie or get a yes or no answer about an interesting number." Number theory, he asserted, has a history of surfacing ideas that are interesting only to contemporary mathematicians but then turn out to be essential to some practical problem a few centuries later. I later discovered that Crandall's interest in prime numbers had led to his patent for an algorithm that Apple uses for encryption.[10]

One classic example of a computationally intense problem is computer weather simulation. In addition to being technically difficult, weather simulation has become an important tool in the highly charged political debate surrounding global warming and other human-initiated kinds of climate change. Myles R. Allen of the Rutherford Appleton Laboratory in Chilton, England, proposed applying distributed computation to climate simulation.[11] Allen appealed to a sense of civic spirit among those who read his Web site: "This experiment would introduce an entirely new form of climate prediction: a fuzzy prediction, reflecting the range of risks and probabilities, rather than a single 'best guess' forecast. And we don't have the computing resources to do this any other way. So, if you're lucky enough to have a powerful PC on your desk or at home, we're asking you to do your bit so the right decisions get taken on climate change." Allen received 15,000 replies within two weeks.

On their Web site, Allen and colleagues explain their objectives and methodology:

> Predictions of climate change are made using complex computer models of the ocean and atmosphere of the Earth. Uncertainties arise in these predictions because of the interactions between physical processes occurring on many different scales (from the molecular to the planetary). The only systematic way to estimate future climate change is to run hundreds of thousands of state-of-the-art climate models with slightly different physics in order to represent uncertainties. This technique, known as ensemble forecasting, requires an enormous amount of computing power, far beyond the currently available resources of cutting-edge supercomputers. The only practical solution is to appeal to *distributed computing* which combines the power of thousands of ordinary PCs, each PC tackling one small but key part of the global problem![12]

Another category of difficult problem has direct appeal to people who don't care about giant prime numbers or life in outer space but would highly appreciate a new medicine. Creating new synthetic medicines for a spectrum of diseases, including AIDS and cancer, requires three-dimensional modeling of the ways complex molecules fit or fold together. With very large numbers of possible molecules to simulate, multiplied by very large numbers of ways they can assume shapes, sifting the possible molecules for promising pharmaceuticals has been prohibitively slow. A variety of voluntary and for-profit distributed computation enterprises are addressing the computational needs of "rational drug design."

SETI@home instigator David Anderson became Chief Technology Officer of a for-profit enterprise, United Devices, which offers incentives such as frequent flier miles and sweepstakes prizes to individuals who become members and supply CPU cycles to corporations and research facilities.[13] Chip maker Intel sponsors a "philanthropic peer-to-peer" program. United Devices, together with the National Foundation for Cancer Research and the University of Oxford, enables participants to contribute their CPU cycles to drug optimization computations involved in evaluating potential leukemia medicines from Oxford's database of 250 million candidate molecules.[14] Whereas Intel's first supercomputer, built in the 1990s for Sandia National Laboratory at a cost of $40–$50 million, is capable of one teraflop (one trillion floating point operations), the United Devices *virtual* supercomputer is aiming for fifty teraflops "at almost no cost."[15] In 2002, with the help of 1.35 million PC users who had joined the United Devices effort, an Oxford University team searched through 3.5 million potential anthrax-treating compounds and came up with 300,000 possible new drugs. "We managed to search the complete dataset in just four weeks instead of years," one of the researchers noted. "Having that big set to start with means we've come up with drug compounds that the pharmaceutical companies would never have thought of."[16]

As of 2002, a rainbow of distributed computation efforts were underway. An incomplete list includes the following:

- Entropia (http://www.entropia.com), a commercial enterprise like United Devices, provides computing cycles for life sciences research and more mundane applications such as financial and accounting calculations.
- Folderol (http://www.folderol.com) uses human genome data and volunteers to put medically crucial protein-folding computations in the public domain.
- Distributed.net (http://www.distributed.net), according to instigator David McNett, started out as "a loose coalition of geeks that came together in 1997 to crack one of RSA corporation's encryption techniques." This virtual supercomputer has succeeded in solving cryptographic challenges—an important part of determining whether e-commerce schemes are sound—and has become a linchpin in the provision of personal privacy and national security.
- Folding@home (http://www.folding@home.org) is a Stanford University project aimed at understanding the structure of protein in order to develop better treatments for diseases. In March 2002, the popular search engine Google bundled a Folding@home client with the custom search tool it distributes to millions of users.[17]
- SaferMarkets (http://www.safermarkets.org) seeks to understand the causes of stock market volatility ("You and Your PC Can Help Stabilize the Global Economy").
- Evolution@home (http://www.evolutionary-research.org) searches for genetic causes for extinction of species.

Distributed computation is only one example of how peer-to-peer arrangements can assemble scattered resources to create collective goods. Disk space is another resource that can be shared over the Net. File sharing, however, is not about the quantity of computer disk space that p2p memory can aggregate but about the social arrangements that enable the members of a p2p community to copublish and share information. Napster is probably the most well known example of a p2p arrangement for sharing the contents of individual participants' disks—challenging traditional notions of intellectual property and the existing commercial music industry in one stroke.

Peer-to-Peer Power

The story of the "killer app"—the software application that turns an underused technology into an industry—is a central and recurring myth of Silicon Valley culture. The PC was a toy for geeks and gamers until the electronic spreadsheet transformed it into a business tool.[18] Email and the Web were the killer apps of the Internet. And Napster was the killer app that awoke the world to the disruptive potential of p2p power. When millions of college students started trading music files in the new MP3 digital recording format, they strained the carrying capacity of large-scale university Internet connections, alerted the vested interests in the existing intellectual property industry that a frontal assault had been launched on their livelihood, and demonstrated that teenagers can ignite world-changing p2p ad-hocracies.

While finishing his freshman year at Northeastern University, Shawn Fanning spent a lot of time hanging out with other geeks on Internet chat channels. He noticed that his friends were going to some trouble to exchange music files encoded in the new MP3 digital format. Fanning decided to create software that would allow people to search the Internet for the MP3 files they had trouble finding and to exchange them. He incorporated some clever ideas that were circulating in the p2p world, such as building an enormous distributed database by enabling every user to make some disk space available to the file-sharing community. Because they liked music and didn't like to pay for it and had PCs and high-speed Internet connections, college students drove the Napster epidemic.

Fanning founded Napster, Inc. in May 1999, dropped out of school, and moved to northern California during the height of the dotcom bubble. Pictures of his stubbly head became an icon in the entrepreneurial pantheon. Napster quickly became the world's largest community for sharing music files because it allowed easy searching, had a user-friendly interface, let the users communicate with each other through instant messaging and chat rooms, and enabled them to share each other's bookmarks. The social network multiplied the impact of the network of computer storage. At its height, 70 million users were trading 2.7 billion files per month.[19]

The social system for sharing resources was as revolutionary as the application of p2p technology to distributed file sharing. In an article titled "The Cornucopia of the Commons," Dan Bricklin, the inventor of VisiCalc, the killer app of PCs in the early 1980s, pointed out: "The genius of Napster is that increasing the value of the database by adding more information is a natural by-product of each person using the tool for his or her own benefit. No altruistic sharing motives need be present, especially since sharing is the default. . . . In other words, nobody has to think of being nice to the next guy or put in even a tiny bit of extra effort."[20]

Naturally, the Recording Industry Association of America (RIAA) wasn't happy about millions of downloads of songs that had formerly fed revenues into their companies. Some recording artists, most notably the band Metallica, also became outraged at this sudden threat to their livelihood. The legal battle began.

In July 2001, Judge Patel of the Ninth Circuit Court ordered Napster to remain offline until it had shown that it could effectively block the trading of any copyrighted work. Metallica and rapper Dr. Dre settled their legal disputes with Napster, ending all legal actions between the parties. It was agreed that the artists would have final say over which of their songs could be shared on the platform, with the provision that they would make certain "material available from time to time." In September 2001, a proposed settlement was announced between Napster and the National Music Publishers' Association (NMPA), in which Napster agreed to turn into a fee-based service with the music being licensed by the publishers to the users. However, by that time, downloads of music from alternative file-sharing services outnumbered Napster at its peak, and the fee-based service never took hold.[21] Napster filed for bankruptcy in June 2002.

Although judicial counterattacks killed Napster, other ad hoc networks that enrich their participants—arguably at the expense of intellectual property that belongs to others—thrived. Like other driving technologies of the age of smart mobs, p2p technology is undergoing rapid evolution.

The post-Napster generations of file-sharing schemes directly addressed Napster's perceived weaknesses.

The main problem with Napster, from a p2p purist's perspective, is that it was not designed to be truly a decentralized network. Although Napster users stored all the music files they exchanged on their own disks, the users had to go through a central server in order to find the music they wanted and to connect with the users who had it. Having control of that central server was what made Napster a business worth investing in. Like the telephone company, Napster aimed to profit by introducing its users to each other. Having control of the central server is what made Napster, Inc.'s owners vulnerable from a legal standpoint.[22]

Gnutella was specifically designed by Tom Pepper and Justin Frankel of Nullsoft to be a totally decentralized system, with no central server.[23] According to the company origin myth, "The name Nullsoft was chosen by Justin Frankel in 1995 to label software that he would develop for fun in his free time."[24] In 1997, Frankel began working on a software client that would enable people to play MP3 music. Later that year, Frankel connected with Tom Pepper, who hosted a Web site for Winamp, the MP3 player Frankel had developed. The Winamp software, released as shareware (free to download, with payment on the honor system), was wildly successful. Just as the Mosaic browser made the World Wide Web instantly popular, Winamp multiplied Napster's success. America Online acquired Nullsoft in 1999.

While technically an AOL employee, Frankel set out to create an unbustable, untraceable, perhaps even indestructible file-sharing program. Frankel and his partner Pepper had definite social goals for Gnutella when they created it in March 2000.[25] The owner of Nullsoft, AOL, was reportedly unhappy about this innovation, but by the time AOL tried to shut it down, the enabling software protocols were out of the bag.[26] It's no wonder AOL tried to shut down GnutellaNet before it could propagate. It enables the sharing of not only music files but video, text, pornography—anything that can be transformed into digital format. Unlike Napster, there is no deep-pockets single owner to hold responsible. Gnutella claimed to avoid the legal vulnerability of Napster by making the owners and controllers everyone who uses the Gnutella client software. The GnutellaNet Web site proclaims that the Gnutella service was designed to be "anonymous," "designed to survive a nuclear war," and "withstand a band of hungry lawyers."[27] It is possible that GnutellaNet's creators underestimated the opposition. Hollywood joined the recording industry in an all-out assault on file sharing when broadband connections made it possible to exchange pirated videos as well as music.

Because Gnutella users connect to other users and not to a central server, the users' personal computers act both as clients and as servers. The Gnutella "servent" software is composed of a mini–search engine combined with a file system. In describing how the network of Gnutella users serves as a search engine and file-sharing facility for its users, the founders compare it to the game of "telephone":

> When you say to GnutellaNet, "Hey, find strawberry-rhubarb pie recipes," you are actually saying, "Hey, my close friends, could you tell me if you've seen any recipes for strawberry-rhubarb pie? And while you're at it, ask your close friends too. And ask them to ask their friends." It's obvious that after just a few rounds of this, you've got a lot of friends working on finding that recipe! And, it's pretty much impossible for any one person to know who asked the question in the first place.
>
> So suppose some guy, 6 degrees from you (your friend's friend's friend's friend's friend's friend), has the world's best recipe for strawberry-rhubarb pie. He tells the guy who asked him. That guy tells the guy who asked him . . . And ultimately the answer gets back to you. But only one person in the whole world knows that you're the original person who asked. And guess what? In GnutellaNet, we even fix that. The guy you asked originally doesn't even know that you're the person who's really asking the question.[28]

The central dogma of p2p-as-cult is "every client a server." In the opinion of some observers, this is not so much an innovation as a return to one of the Web's founding principles. In "Gnutella and the Transient Web," Kelly Truelove describes Gnutella's effect on the Web:

> The Gnutella protocol restores the Web's original symmetry, enabling even transient computers to effectively participate as servers. It's far from a complete solution, and alternative systems may eclipse it. Nonetheless, this simple and idiosyncratic protocol is currently in the vanguard of the emergence of the transient Web. The transient Web has the potential to be every bit as disruptive as the conventional "permanent" Web, and possibly more so.[29]

The value of Gnutella depends on the voluntary cooperation of its users, who need to give information to the system as well as to use the information they find through the system. This is increasingly difficult with such a large and anonymous user population. Gnutella's weakness is, you guessed it—free riding. In "Free Riding on Gnutella," Eytan Adar and Bernardo A. Huberman report that Gnutella has a significant amount of free riding in its system: Nearly 70 percent of Gnutella users share no files, and nearly 50 percent of the system's resources are contributed by the top 1 percent of users. The architecture of the system allows for anonymity and decentralized control, but it does not structurally encourage cooperation, rendering it vulnerable to the "tragedy of the commons."[30] The question that remains: Does p2p technology enable people to build public goods that can withstand large amounts of free riding, or will free riding end up destroying the p2p cornucopia?

Jim McCoy, founder and CEO of Mojo Nation, set out to create a file-sharing system that added three important new features: First, cooperation is structurally encouraged by requiring users to contribute at least as much as they take away; second, not only are queries anonymous, but nobody knows where specific files are stored; third, the "swarm distribution" model breaks up files into large numbers of small segments, distributed throughout the network. Swarm distribution makes it easier to find the most popular material and ensures its availability, even though the servers are only transiently available.[31]

Mojo Nation shares the advantages of other open source software such as Linux; because the source code is available to any programmer who wants to tinker with it, an ever-growing community of developers improves the software. The downloadable client is used to publish and retrieve information from Mojo Nation—the collection of users who run the software at any moment. Mojo Nation brings together trust management, security through encryption, and a distributed accounting system.

Mojo Nation incorporates an economy of incentives, using micropayments called "Mojo" to reward users for distributing and uploading files to the network. Every user is expected to contribute something, whether it is system resources or digital cash, for the transactions they make within the community. Users earn Mojo by acting as a server, allowing their bandwidth or disk space to be used, or providing other services. A market mechanism enables buyers and sellers to determine prices, and prices can be advertised. As a result, users create a reputation system of sorts since the quality of service and the reliability of service providers is constantly under review and tracked by agents, which check for good connectivity and proximity to resource providers.

All files that are distributed on Mojo Nation are broken into hundreds or thousands of pieces, and no files are stored in their entirety in a single location. When a user requests a file, it is automatically downloaded in parallel streams from the nearest peers that have chunks of it available. If a peer is offline, it is likely that another peer will have the needed chunk. Documents that are requested more frequently are distributed more widely, minimizing bottlenecks that would slow down the system when a majority of users try to download the most popular files simultaneously. Encryption is used to cover the tracks of people making requests and to make it impossible for participants to know exactly what content they are storing on their PCs as part of their contribution to the system. Mojo Nation ceased operations as a commercial enterprise in February 2002, replaced by the noncommercial Mnet project.[32]

The first peer-to-peer networks linked social networks into cooperative ventures that shared computing cycles, files, and bandwidth. The next generations of p2p sociotechnology include p2p systems that share decisions and judgments.

Sheep That Shit Grass

Cory Doctorow, thirty-year-old online auction addict, Internet jack-of-all-symbol-manipulating trades, and award-winning science fiction writer, is also the most enthusiastic p2p proponent I've met. When I learned that he was working on a p2p scheme that would enable people to share their decisions about what they find interesting, I called him. He was living in Toronto at the time. A year later, I found his name while looking through a list of publicly accessible wireless Internet links in San Francisco (see Chapter 6, "Wireless Quilts"). The combination of p2p and wireless technology and his passionate defense of online collective action drew me to Doctorow's Potrero District apartment. I suspected he had some ideas about where p2p might be heading, and I wasn't disappointed.

The hallway leading to Doctorow's apartment is decorated with his landlord's collection of faux-Tiffany lamps, Star Trek commemorative plates, and what Doctorow calls "framed assemblage sculptures made from symmetrically arranged junk jewelry." Doctorow's own apartment is filled with paper ephemera from Disney parks. Indeed, it turns out that his interest in Disney memorabilia was one of the motivations for creating OpenCOLA.

Here is Doctorow's "elevator pitch" for OpenCOLA:

The idea is that you have a folder on your desktop, you put some things in it you like, and it will fill up with things that you'll *probably* like. It figures out what you'll probably like by finding peers in the network who have taste similar to you and telling you what they think is good. The software fetches documents from peers and from various Internet servers, puts them under the noses of people that it thinks will like them, then watches what the peers do when they get them: Do they attend to them, or do they throw them away? These implicit, observed decisions are aggregated and the result is a "relevance-switched" network where documents automatically migrate to the attention of people who'll probably like them, based on human decisions.[33]

Doctorow, in addition to being cofounder and chief evangelist for Open-COLA, is a winner of the John W. Campbell award for new science fiction writers. He has a beard, chain-smokes, and seems to pull epigrams from the air. My favorite Doctorow epigram is his description of Napster as a solution to the tragedy of the commons dilemma. Doctorow refers to Napster users, who provide the same resource that they consume, as "sheep who shit grass."

I sat on Doctorow's couch while he smoked filter cigarettes and spun rants in response to my inquiries. Above his head, perched on a shelf high on one wall, is the small box that quietly provides wireless Internet access to any nearby geek who knows the node is there. His notions about finding something interesting in the seething chaos of the Net are sufficiently novel that it took a while to wrap my mind about the idea. "Relevance switching" is a way of creating your own self-updating map of the network by querying the social networks of people who share your interests.

Doctorow and two friends in Toronto ran a technical services company during the dotcom era. Like many contract service companies, they yearned to create something to call their own. Doctorow and his partners, John Henson and Grad Conn, wanted to create a tool that they personally lusted after—some kind of software agent that "would keep us abreast of things we were interested in, and would inform us about things we *should* be interested in."

They looked at how search engines help people find things by indexing every document on the Internet and at how some collaborative filtering tools (like the one Amazon uses) are able to recommend books or music people might like by looking at the tastes of people who make similar choices. Would it be possible to build a collaborative filter that would include every document, music, graphic, video, and software program on the entire Internet, and at the same time take into account the tastes of every person on the Net, somehow keeping track of how all other people's tastes compare with one's own? Why not think big?

Computers make complicated tasks easier to handle. However, some kinds of tasks always remain too complicated for state-of-the-art computing technology. Doctorow and his partners soon realized that they could create software to do what they proposed, but it would be impractical to apply it to the entire Net. "We were going to have to buy servers bigger than the entire Internet," is how Doctorow put it. That's where Doctorow's passion for collecting pop culture artifacts came in.

Ever since I was really young, I've collected vintage Disney theme park crap. In Toronto you'd find one piece per year at a yard sale or a thrift store. Then I found Auctionweb, which is what eBay was called at the beginning, and I found dozens of items, then thousands. I started to build long, in-depth query strings, and eventually I ended up with a 20 kilobyte long URL that I would paste into my browser at 5:00 A.M. Eastern time, the only time of night or day when their servers were idle enough to run my query. Half an hour later the host computer at Auctionweb shrank 5,000 listings to 50 that would truly interest me. Eventually I couldn't even do that anymore, because there was no time when their servers were idle enough to run my monster query.

I was ready to give up when I hit upon a better strategy. I started keeping a record of every person who had ever bid against me in the past and then found out what they were bidding on now. Then I would look at who was bidding against the people who were bidding against me and examine what *they* were bidding on now. Not only did that strategy turn out to be a great means of finding vintage Disney theme park stuff, as you can see by looking around my apartment, but it was also an amazing means of discovering stuff that I didn't know I was looking for! I would bid on the little silver badge from the conductor's hat on the Disney railroad, which went up to $300, and there was no way I was going to buy it for that much, but it hooked me into the bidding patterns of people who bid on vintage railroad stuff, which I found quite charming and beautiful.

Like SETI@home, OpenCOLA requires a population of volunteers. While you put documents in a folder on your computer, waiting for similar documents to appear, others must do the same. Your client probes through your map of the network (and through the maps of those you know about) for other people's folders (a process referred to in the search business as "spidering"), looks at the record of what these other people (peers) have accepted (by saving the files somewhere) and rejected (by discarding the files). OpenCOLA refers to these records as people's "caches"—a file in their OpenCOLA folder where the record of their save-or-discard decisions is stored.

> Having discovered a group of peers on the network, the next thing my agent does is to spider [automatically search] whatever they have in their folders, pull in their caches, and team up with them to discover the places where they found those things. If you and I both like *Wired News,* our peers team up to spider *Wired News* periodically, discover new documents and bring them to the attention of one or the other of us, and based on what one or the other of us do, bring it to the other person's attention or just round-file it. The last thing the OpenCOLA agent does with documents is to bring them back to my attention and observe what I do with them. When I file them, it knows that I like them; when I throw them away, it knows that I didn't. And it either upgrades or downgrades other peers' ability to recommend documents to me based on what I've done.

Doctorow notes that the cooperative nature of the system he describes doesn't rely on any pledges of altruism or enforced sharing. Simply looking for material and then deciding whether to keep it or not creates information that is useful to others. Each participant in the network cooperates by keeping a file of their decisions available to others, which is part of a self-interested behavior of keeping a folder open to be filled with interesting documents; keeping that folder open both invites contributions and provides information to others who seek it.

> The thing that defines peer-to-peer, I think, is the degree to which the power of the technology depends on Metcalfe's Law. In the end, a word processing program is only a word processing program whether you're the only user or the millionth user; its utility doesn't change. Napster is not Napster if you're the only user. Napster is nothing more than a folder full of MP3s if you're the only user. Napster doesn't tell you to share your files, but the system is arranged so that the files you have plundered are available for others to plunder during the time you have the software running so that you can plunder more files. The problem is congestion; the more users you have, the

harder your network is to connect to. What a peer-to-peer network can do is provide a commons where the sheep shit grass, where every user provisions the resource he consumes.

Grids and Ad-hocracies

Ad-hocracies among cooperating individuals spread out across the world are not the only ways to take advantage of p2p power. Consider the idle disk space and CPU cycles on all the thousands of computers owned by a big company in a single building or worldwide. If computers were heaters, almost every computer-using enterprise is running them at full capacity and keeping the windows open, leaking energy into the air. United Devices and other commercial providers help these companies apply their own in-house computing technology to appropriate tasks, re-capturing that otherwise-wasted computational potential. While voluntary virtual communities create supercomputers to cure cancer or look for messages from outer space, insurance companies crunch actuarial statistics or petroleum companies run geological simulations. Even more significantly, major corporate and government-sponsored research programs are looking at distributed processing as a new paradigm for the provision of computing power in the future. The notion of "grid computing" has attracted powerful sponsors. Several governments and corporations have started programs to create "farms" of networked computers that could provide computing resources on demand—more like the way electricity is delivered than the way computers have traditionally been marketed.

Some criticize the movement toward grid computing as an attempt to return to the days of the mainframes, when the computer priesthood, not the users, controlled access to computer power. It wouldn't be the first time that a voluntary grassroots movement turned into an operating division of IBM. When IBM, the bastion of the mainframe, was confronted by the invention of the PC by Xerox PARC and Apple, they decided to embrace it and mainstreamed what had been a technological counterculture by introducing their own version. When the open source movement challenged Microsoft and other purveyors of proprietary software through the cooperative efforts of distributed teams of programmers working on software that was open to all to use or modify, IBM mainstreamed the movement by spending a billion dollars to create their own open source tools, products, services, and processes.[34] Microsoft has built features of grid computing into its .Net initiative, and in February 2002, IBM announced its support for open-source grid-computing platforms and proclaimed that it would "grid-enable" its existing products.[35]

For years, clustering microprocessors in the same physical environment (rather than distributing them across the Net) has been the foundation of "massive parallel" approaches to creating large quantities of computing power. Other than the computers that the National Security Agency doesn't talk about, the most powerful computers continue to be those used by major U.S. nuclear weapons research laboratories; the fastest current supercomputer is the 8,000-processor cluster at Lawrence Livermore National Laboratory, known as ASCI White.[36] In 1995, the I-WAY experiment used high-speed networks to connect seventeen sites across North America to explore grid computing.[37]

Perhaps the most significant news in the grid computing effort is that astrophysicist Larry Smarr has enlisted the governor of California to finance what Smarr calls "the emerging planetary supercomputer."[38] Smarr has a track record when it comes to creating as well as forecasting the next paradigm in computation. He founded the National Center for Supercomputer Applications (NCSA) in 1985. Part of the project involved finding ways to link the nation's five supercomputing centers through high-speed Internet connections. In 1993, another part of the NCSA research resulted in the creation of Mosaic, the browser software that detonated the explosive growth of the Web.[39] His latest sponsor, funded by $300 million in state and private financing, is the Center for Information Technology Research in the Interest of Society (CITRIS). "He imagines bridges that are covered with a fabric of computerized sensors that will automatically tell engineers where earthquake damage has occurred, or a world in which intelligent buildings whisper directions to visitors on the way to their destinations."[40] CITRIS will focus on new kinds of sensors, distributed computing software, and advanced wireless Internet.

Like the digital computer itself, grid computing is seen as a tool for fundamental research, like the microscope, telescope, or particle accelerator. Britain is building a national grid, linking research centers from Edinburgh to Belfast. Companies reported to be experimenting with internal grids include Pfizer, Ericsson, Hitachi, BMW, Glaxo, Smith-Kline, and Unilever.[41]

With ad-hocracies, national defense research, and major corporations all experimenting with different approaches, it isn't hard to forecast grid computing as the emerging paradigm in computation. What is less clear is whether some single winner or cartel of big players will dominate the scene to the point where ad-hocracies are squeezed out or marginalized or whether industrial-scale and strictly amateur p2p efforts will coexist. The legal counterattack against p2p technologies has barely begun, and its first effort, the success of the recording industry in shutting down Napster, was a stunning first strike. In 2001, a college computer technician in Georgia who contributed his school's idle processing power to distributed.net was charged by the FBI with computer theft and trespass.[42] In 2002, the technician was fined $2,100 and sentenced to a year's probation.[43] Because cable television infrastructure providers are regulated differently than telephone companies, legal observers such as Lawrence Lessig fear that broadband Internet service providers will move to block p2p activities over their parts of the Internet.[44]

Peer-to-peer technologies and social contracts are reconverging with both the clouds of mobile devices that are spreading through the world and the mesh of sensors and computing devices that are increasingly embedded in the environment. In the early 1990s, the visions of "virtual reality" modeled a world where humans would explore artificial universes that would exist inside computers. Less widely reported were even wilder speculations of a world of the early twenty-first century where the computers would be built into reality, instead of the other way around.

The Era of Sentient Things

Consider writing, perhaps the first information technology: The ability to capture a symbolic representation of spoken language for long-term storage freed information from the limits of individual memory. Today this technology is ubiquitous in industrialized countries. Not only do books, magazines and newspapers convey written information, but so do street signs, billboards, shop signs and even graffiti. Candy wrappers are covered in writing. The constant background presence of these products of "literacy technology" does not require active attention, but the information to be conveyed is ready for use at a glance. It is difficult to imagine modern life otherwise.

Silicon-based information technology, in contrast, is far from having become part of the environment. More than 50 million personal computers have been sold, and nonetheless the computer remains largely in a world of its own. It is approachable only through complex jargon that has nothing to do with the tasks for which people actually use computers. The state of the art is perhaps analogous to the period when scribes had to know as much about making ink or baking clay as they did about writing.

—**Mark Weiser, "The Computer for the 21st Century," 1991**

When Computers Disappear

Scott Fisher has been putting computers on his head for as long as I've known him. In 1983 at the Atari Research laboratory, I watched Fisher's group dramatize ways people might use computers in the future. Fisher pretended to put something on his head.[1] Then he swiveled his head as if he were looking around. In 1990, when Fisher got his chance to build "head-mounted displays" for NASA, he invited me to stick my own face inside a computerized helmet in order to peer around "virtual reality." Cyberspace had arrived! It turned out to look like a cartoon, but that's another story.

In 2001 I found myself walking around a campus outside Tokyo, my head enclosed by a helmet once again. The world I peered at this time looked almost exactly like the same one in which my body resides, not a cartoon galaxy far away. The physical world I experienced through Dr. Fisher's latest helmet, however, had a few features reality never included before. Instead of substituting a virtual model in place of the physical world, the twenty-first-century version added information to the physical world.

I walked up to a real tree at Fisher's test site. If I had kept walking, I'd have bumped into a branch. An icon hovered in the air at eye level next to the tree trunk, like a tiny fluorescent UFO. I pointed my mobile telephone at the icon. A picture of Scott Fisher and the words, "Hello, Howard!" appeared. The text message floated in space as if it were projected on a transparent screen. Fisher left this message for me at this tree yesterday, sending it from his home computer in Tokyo. He explained that I could have read an explanation of some aspect of the tree, examined the tree's hidden roots, even looked at a recent satellite image of the field I was stumbling around.

In 1991, the artificial world I explored was a three-dimensional computer graphic simulation I could navigate (carefully, because I was blind to the external world) and manipulate by way of a computerized glove. In contrast, Fisher's 2001 foray into "wearable environmental media" was an example of "augmented reality"—one of many current efforts to mingle virtual and physical worlds. Other investigators I visited at IBM's Almaden laboratory in California, MIT Media Lab in Cambridge, Sony's Tokyo Computer Science Laboratory, and Ericsson's wireless lab outside Stockholm used mobile phones, digital jewelry, physical icons, and other technologies for combining bits and atoms, digital personae and physical places.

Different lines of research and development that have progressed slowly for decades are accelerating now because sufficient computation and communication capabilities recently became affordable. These projects originated in different fields but are converging on the same boundary between artificial and natural worlds. The vectors of this research include the following:

- Information in places: media linked to location

- Smart rooms: environments that sense inhabitants and respond to them
- Digital cities: adding information capabilities to urban places
- Sentient objects: adding information and communication to physical objects
- Tangible bits: manipulating the virtual world by manipulating physical objects
- Wearable computers: sensing, computing, and communicating gear worn as clothing

Information and communication technologies are starting to invade the physical world, a trend that hasn't yet begun to climb the hockey stick growth curve. Shards of sentient silicon will be inside boxtops and dashboards, pens, street corners, bus stops, money, most things that are manufactured or built, within the next ten years. These technologies are "sentient" not because embedded chips can reason but because they can sense, receive, store, and transmit information. Some of these cheap chips sense where they are. The cost of a global positioning system chip capable of tracking its location via satellite to an accuracy of ten to fifteen meters is around $15 and dropping.[2]

Odd new things become possible. Shirt labels gain the power to disclose what airplanes, trucks, and ships carried it, what substances compose it, and the URL of a webcam in the factory where the shirt was manufactured. Things tell you where they are. Places can be haunted by intergenerational messages. Virtual graffiti on books and bars becomes available to those who have the password.

Radio, infrared, and other invisible signaling technologies already enable chips to transfer information to other people and to devices elsewhere in the room or on the other side of the world. Cheap sensors are learning how to self-organize on bodies, in buildings, across cities, and worldwide via wireless networks. The first conference on "Sensor Networks for Healthcare, the Environment, and Homeland Defense" was held in 2002.[3] There are already more than 200 billion chips in the world. The next 200 billion chips will be able to talk to each other and to us. As the president of Bell Labs said in a 2000 speech, "When your children become roughly your age . . . a mega-network of networks will enfold the entire earth like a communication skin. As communication becomes faster, smaller, cheaper and smarter in the next millennium, this skin, fed by a constant stream of information will . . . include millions of electronic measuring devices all monitoring cities, roadways, and the environment."[4] In February 2002, the Chief Technology Officer of Intel announced that in the near future, Intel will include radio transponder circuitry in *every chip* Intel manufactures.[5]

Watch smart mobs emerge when millions of people use location-aware mobile communication devices in computation-pervaded environments. Things we hold in our hands are already speaking to things in the world. Using our telephones as remote controls is only the beginning. At the same time that the environment is growing more sentient, the device in your hand is evolving from portable to wearable. A new media sphere is emerging from this process, one that could become at least as influential, lucrative, and ubiquitous as previous media spheres opened by print, telegraphy, telephony, radio, television, and the wired Internet. Media spheres grow from technologies that provide channels for symbolic communication, commercial exchange, and group formation. Media spheres include industries and financial institutions, scientists and engineers, content providers and consumers, regulatory infrastructures, power structures, civic impacts, social networks, and new ways of thinking.

Pervasive media bring the power of surveillance together with the powers of communication and computation. Other people will be snooping on those who use mobile and pervasive media. In some cases, the snooping will be consensual and mutually beneficial. In other cases, it will be everything feared by Orwell and more—tele-torture, to pick one horrible possibility (combining the satellite-tracked ankle cuffs used on some offenders today with the remotely controllable electrical shocking device used in some dog collars). There are important questions about pervasive surveillance:

- Who snoops whom? Who has a right to know that information?
- Who controls the technology and its uses—the user, the government, the manufacturer, the telephone company?
- What kind of people will we become when we use the technology?

The kind of world we will inhabit for decades to come could depend on the technical architecture adopted for the emerging mobile and pervasive infrastructure over the next few years. For example, if the power to encode information as a shield against surveillance is vested in billions of individuals and literally built into the chips, the situation that arises is radically different from a world in which a few have the power to snoop on many. That power is what is at stake in political conflicts over encryption laws.

Although the issue is most often cast as "privacy," arguments over surveillance technology are about power and control. Will you be able to use the capabilities of smart mob technologies to know everything you need to know about the world you walk through and to connect with those groups who could benefit you? Will you be allowed to cooperate with anyone your wearable computer helps you choose? Or will others know everything they need to know about you through the sensors you encounter and information you broadcast? Different answers to those questions lead to different kinds of futures. The answers will be determined in part by the way the technology is designed and regulated in its earliest stages.

A few years after I encountered VR at NASA, and a few miles north, I met a fellow who thought about the opposite of virtual reality. He wanted to make computers, not the real world, disappear. His name was Mark Weiser, and although he built on the work of predecessors, he is acknowledged for asking the first critical questions about the technology he was helping bring into existence: "If the computational system is invisible as well as extensive, it becomes hard to know what is controlling what, what is connected to what, where information is flowing, how it is being used, what is broken (versus what is working correctly, but not helpfully), and what are the consequences of any given action (including simply walking into a room)."[6]

"Here, carry this pad," Weiser said when I visited him in 1994, handing me an artifact I didn't understand at the time. It fit nicely in the palm of my hand and had a small screen. As we walked from room to room in the Xerox Palo Alto Research Center, fabled birthplace of the personal computer, a large screen in the rooms we entered showed our location and the location of other researchers around the lab.

Weiser smiled frequently. He wore red suspenders. I quickly learned that any computer we approached in any part of the laboratory displayed his personal computer files when he walked up to it and put his PARCpad down. "Ubiquitous computing," or "ubicomp," Weiser called it, "is invisible, everywhere computing that does not live on a personal device of any sort but is in the woodwork everywhere."[7] The notion of a future where every desk, wall, home, vehicle, and building possesses computational powers was radical for 1988, when the research effort started. Weiser insisted that the implications of such a future were serious enough to consider long in advance.

Weiser, former chief technologist at PARC, died in 1999, on the cusp of the era he had foreseen. In 1991, Weiser declared: "The most profound technologies are those that disappear. They weave themselves into the fabric of everyday life until they are indistinguishable from it."[8] Knowing that it would take decades for technology and economics to catch up with his extrapolations, Weiser asked in a provocative *Scientific American* article how our lives might change if every object and environment contained microchips that could communicate with each other and with mobile devices.[9]

When Weiser and I performed the primary social ritual of the modern worker—the consumption of caffeinated beverages—he pointed out PARC's online coffeepot. The communal coffeepot has played a historic role in the development of pervasive computing: A PARCpad affixed to the coffeepot signaled other people nearby via the local network whenever a fresh pot was ready. The introduction of this simple sensor catalyzed coffeepot conversations among the researchers. There are now uncounted thousands of webcams in the world. The first one was aimed at a coffeepot. Researchers at the University of Cambridge wanted to see if a fresh pot was ready without walking down the hall, so they aimed a digital camera at the coffeepot and rigged it to send periodic snapshots. Because they sent the pictures via the Web, the Cambridge researchers also made the coffeepot visible to anyone else in the world who cared to look.[10] Millions of people did. Since then, webcams have proliferated. The first network-connected examples of ambient intelligence were associated with a social networking ritual. Online coffeepots were early smart mob technologies.

Weiser forecast that computers of the twenty-first century would become invisible in much the same way electric motors did in the early 1900s: "At the turn of the century, a typical workshop or factory contained a single engine that drove dozens or hundreds of different machines through a system of shafts and pulleys. Cheap, small, efficient electric motors made it possible first to give each machine or tool its own source of motive force, then to put many motors into a single machine."[11] For the better part of a century, people have lived among invisible electric motors and thought nothing of it. The time has come to consider, as Weiser urged us to do, the consequences of computers disappearing into the background the way motors did.

It wasn't until I started looking into smart mobs that I saw the connection between ubicomp and two of the characters I had encountered ten years ago, when I wrote about the emerging field of virtual reality. The central idea of VR—that computer graphics and sensor-laden clothing would enable people to immerse themselves in lifelike artificial worlds— fascinated even those who didn't care about computers. It was a metaphor for the way computers and entertainment media were surrounding people with artificial worlds. The past ten years of VR have not been as exciting as the original idea was or as I had thought they would be. Whether or not researchers ever succeed in creating truly lifelike worlds, many of the technologies, capabilities, and issues that grew out of VR research contributed to the development of smart mob components such as pervasive computing and wearable computers. Sometimes, a technological development appears to dead-end, when it is really in the process of sidestepping.

When I first looked into the origins of virtual reality, I came across a curious book that was part science, part art, part futurist manifesto. In 1991 I took a train and then a bus to the University of Connecticut at Storrs to see what the book's author, Myron Krueger, had built with analog electronic circuits and video cameras in a room behind the university's natural history museum.[12] He had been working on something he called "artificial reality"—the title of his 1983 book—since the late 1960s.[13] The enabling technologies to manifest his ideas properly wouldn't come along for decades. As an artist and an engineer, he was able to look beyond the horizon of what new media would do *for* people to glimpse what it might do *to* people. In 1977, he wrote something about "responsive environments" that speaks directly to those who attempt to build "smart rooms" and pervasive computing:

> We are incredibly attuned to the idea that the sole purpose of our technology is to solve problems. It also creates concepts and philosophy. We must more fully explore these aspects of our inventions, because the next generation of technology will speak to us, understand us, and perceive our behavior. It will enter every home and office and intercede between us and much of the information and experience we receive. The design of such intimate technology is an aesthetic issue as much as an engineering one. We must recognize this if we are to understand and choose what we become as a result of what we have made.[14]

I was reminded of another VR researcher when I started rethinking pervasive computing: Warren Robinett, a soft-spoken fellow with a touch of a southern drawl who proposed that head-mounted displays could be used to extend human senses instead of immerse them in an artificial environment.

Robinett had designed the software for NASA's VR prototypes. One evening in 1991, when I was visiting the University of North Carolina VR lab in Chapel Hill, Robinett asked, "What if you could use VR to see things that are normally beyond human perception?" At that time I was editor of the *Whole Earth Review,* so I commissioned Robinett to write an article. While I was researching smart mobs, I was surprised to find Robinett's article cited as one of the first descriptions of what is now known as "augmented reality."[15] Robinett proposed connecting the head-mounted display to a microscope, telescope, or a video camera equipped with gear that could make infrared, ultraviolet, or radio frequencies visible.

Today's research on "smart rooms" and "digital cities" uses computation and communication to extend the idea of "responsive environments," as Krueger forecast. Today's "wearable computing" addresses Robinett's proposal to use computer-aided media to extend human capabilities. These different technical approaches have radically different political consequences.

Alex Pentland, now Academic Head of MIT Media Lab, directed research into both the responsive environment (Krueger) and extended senses (Robinett) approaches when he directed both the "Smart Rooms" and "Smart Clothes" projects, which he described as examples of "The Dance of Bits and Atoms":

> There is a deep divide between the world of bits and the world of atoms. Current machines are blind and deaf; they are unaware of us or our desires unless we explicitly instruct them. Consequently, only experts use most machines, and even they must spend most of their time battling arcane languages and strange, clunky interface devices.
>
> The broad goal of my research is merge these worlds more closely and intimately, primarily by giving machines perceptual abilities that allow them to function naturally with people. Thus machines must be able to recognize people's faces, know when they are happy or are sick, and perceive their common working environment. I call this Perceptual Intelligence, a type of situation awareness, Roughly, it is making machines know who, what, where, when and why, so that the devices that surround us can respond more appropriately and helpfully.
>
> To develop and demonstrate this idea, my research group and I are actively building Smart Rooms (i.e., visual, audio, and haptic interfaces to environments such as rooms, cars, and office desks) and Smart Clothes (i.e., wearable computers that sense and adapt to the user and their environ-

ment). We are using these perceptually-aware devices to explore applications in health care, entertainment, and collaborative work.[16]

"Bits and atoms" is a major theme at MIT's Media Lab. Ivan Sutherland started it in 1965 with his dramatic statement that "the ultimate display would, of course, be a room within which the computer can control the existence of matter. A chair displayed in such a room would be good enough to sit in. Handcuffs displayed in such a room would be confining, and a bullet displayed in such room would be fatal."[17] While others at Media Lab work in the "Things That Think" or "Tangible Bits" programs —ways to create Sutherland's chair, if not the hypothetical bullet—Pentland and his colleagues built the first smart room in 1991.[18]

Cooltown and Other Informated Places

On a warm October day in 2001, I drove to the end of a country road. Atop a hill, past the "caution livestock" sign, behind a security gate, I found a bright green, fragrantly fresh-cut lawn surrounded by unpopulated, summer-brown foothills stretching to the horizon. Except for owning their own hill, IBM's Almaden Research Laboratory was a low-key affair. Jim Spohrer signed me in and escorted me into what one journalist had called "Big Blue's Big Brother Lab."[19] We talked on our way to his office.

Spohrer had taken a sabbatical from Apple Computer's Learning Communities group in 1994 with the intention of finding something new to work on. He was particularly interested in the future of education. Walking on a trail, he asked a fellow hiker the name of a plant. "The hiker said that he didn't know, but his friend probably did. While I waited for the friend to come down the trail, I realized that I had a cell phone and a computer. It occurred to me that if I could add a global positioning system, then the person who knew the plant could geo-code the message. Why not make the entire world into a geo-spatial informational bulletin board? I got back to Apple and started building prototypes."[20]

What emerged was a proposed infrastructure called WorldBoard. In 1996, Spohrer wrote:

What if we could put information in places? More precisely, what if we could associate information with a place and perceived the information as if it were really there? WorldBoard is a vision of doing just that on a planetary scale and as a natural part of everyday life. For example, imagine being able to enter an airport and see a virtual red carpet leading you right to your gate, look at the ground and see property lines or underground buried cables, walk along a nature trail and see virtual signs near plants and rocks.[21]

Spohrer raised the bar for technical difficulty by wanting to see the information in its context, overlaid on the real world. WorldBoard, Spohrer noted, combined, and extended the ideas of Ivan Sutherland, Warren Robinett, and Steven Feiner. Sutherland had invented computer-generated graphics in his MIT Ph.D. thesis in 1963.[22] Computer graphics came a long way in forty years, from Sutherland's first stick figure displays to today's computer-generated feature films. Another prototype that Sutherland developed in the 1960s, the "head-mounted display," took a less dramatic development path.[23] Sutherland realized that synchronized computer displays, presented optically to each eye, yoked to a device for tracking the user's location and position, could create a three-dimensional computer graphic either as an artificial world or as an overlay on the natural world.

One of Sutherland's prototypes used half-silvered mirrors that enabled the computer to superimpose graphical displays on physical environments. While most VR researchers pursued "immersive" VR, Steven Feiner at Columbia University continued the line suggested by Sutherland's semitransparent mirrors. The Columbia group in the early 1990s worked on models of an office of the future in which head-mounted displays superimposed information on physical components. A repair technician, for example, could use such a system to see a wiring diagram projected on the machine, or a plumber could see through a wall to the location of the main pipes.[24]

Spohrer set out to assemble "the technology of augmented reality, the art of special effects, and the culture of the information age" to make a "planetary chalkboard for twenty-first-century learners, allowing them to post and read messages associated with any place on the planet."[25] It is not hard to imagine a server computer storing information associated with every cubic meter of the earth's surface; computer memory is cheap. Geographic positioning systems could make handheld or wearable devices location-aware. Wireless Internet access would mean that a user could access the server computer and add or receive information about specific geographic locations.

WorldBoard servers would define computer codes that could be used to associate information of all kinds with the six faces of a virtual cube, one meter on a side. A user's device would combine the coordinates of the cube's location and one of the cube's faces with a channel number, along with a password, then transmit or receive information about that place through a mobile device. That transmitted information could be spatial co-ordinates for projecting a virtual overlay onto an object in space, or an animation, text, music, spreadsheet, or voice message. The client software that runs on users' devices would include "a mobile capability to author and access the information associated with places on a planetary scale. A location-aware device with navigation, authoring, and global wireless communication capabilities would be needed."[26]

When I started looking for similar research, I found it everywhere. In 2001, researchers at the Social Mobile Computing Group in Kista, Sweden, presented their GeoNotes system, which enables people to annotate physical locations with virtual notes, to add signatures, and to specify access rights.[27] Jun Rekimoto and his colleagues at Sony described in 1998 "a system that allows users to dynamically attach newly created digital information such as voice notes or photographs to the physical environment, through mobile/wearable computers as well as normal computers. . . . Similar to the role that Post-it notes play in community messaging, we expect our proposed method to be a fundamental communication platform when mobile/wearable computers become commonplace."[28] It isn't clear yet which standard will dominate, but it is clear that first-rate scientists and major institutions all over the world are working on ways to link information and places.

After the global geo-coding infrastructure and the client software, the third element of Spohrer's vision was "WorldBoard glasses," which would make it possible to perceive information in place, "co-registered" with the physical environment so that it would look like a perfect overlay. When Spohrer moved to IBM's research laboratory, he brought his vision with him. Several professional-quality posters on the walls of his office illustrated different Almaden research initiatives into "Digital Jewelry," "Location-Based Services," "WorldBoard," and "Wearable Computing." We walked down the hall to the office of Ismail Haritaoglu, who handed me the prototype of what he called the "InfoScope: Link from Real World to Digital Information Space."[29]

Haritaoglu gave me an off-the-shelf hand-held computer with an off-the-shelf digital camera attachment, connected to a stock model digital cellular phone. Haritaoglu pointed out some signs on the wall outside his office. I picked one in Chinese, which I don't read. Following his directions,

I pointed the lens of the device in my hand at the sign on the wall, clicked the shutter, pressed some buttons on the telephone, and in a few seconds, the English words "reservation desk" appeared on the screen of the Info-Scope. "We use computer-vision techniques to extract the text from the sign," Haritaoglu explained. "That requires processor power." The telephone sent the picture to a computer on IBM's network, which crunched the numbers to parse the characters out of the image, crunched the numbers to translate the text, and sent it back to the device in my hand. In the near future, there will be sufficient processor power to enable the device itself to crunch the translation, but that won't matter so much when all the processing power you want is available online, wirelessly.

After we left Haritaoglu's office, Spohrer told me about research into "attentive billboards"—display screens that use optical recognition techniques to learn where people are looking and to detect characteristics of the people who look at the billboard: "There's a display at the checkout counter for people waiting in line," Spohrer explained. "The billboard looks back at them as they gaze at ads and news, extracts information about their sex, age, and race, and adjusts the display accordingly. When grandma walks up, it can show the knitting advertisement, and when you walk up in your leather gear, it can show a motorcycle. Attentive billboards can recognize where you are looking and even extract your facial expression to guess whether you are happy or sad."

When I started investigating the combination of mobile communication and pervasive computing, it didn't take long to discover the R&D hotspots; they are always the places where the authors of the most interesting papers work. I began to believe that a new technological infrastructure really is in the process of emerging when I saw how IBM, Hewlett-Packard (HP), Nokia, Ericsson, Sony, and DoCoMo conduct similar R&D. From Almaden, the trail led to Silicon Valley's Cooltown, Helsinki's Virtual Village, Stockholm's HotTown, and a couple of labs in Tokyo.

CoolTown, HP's pervasive computing effort, is built around the Web as the universal medium for linking physical and virtual worlds. CoolTown is in the same building where Bill Hewlett and David Packard's offices are enshrined as they left them. After a ritual pilgrimage to the eerily time-frozen temples of the founders, I came to a door marked by a highway sign that said "CoolTown City Limits." Gene Becker, a strategist for HP's Internet and Mobile Systems Lab, a maestro of the studiously casual demo, welcomed me into what looked like an ordinary meeting room.

Becker pointed his modified Kyocera Smartphone at the projector, and the room's Web page popped up on the wall screen. "We call it 'e-squirting' when we transmit URLs from our personal devices to another device in the environment," he explained. The projector and printer each had radio-linked Web servers built into them. "Imagine walking into any meeting room in this building, or the world, and displaying your presentation on the screen, or printing documents on the local printer. CoolTown is a test bed for a future in which every person, place, or thing can be connected wirelessly, anywhere in the world, through the Web."

I asked Becker about the neo-retro aluminum radio console on a table in the corner. Becker pointed his phone at it, and music started playing. "You can play your own music from any radio that's equipped to communicate with you. Stick a Web server inside a device, and suddenly the Web and browsers become your universal remote control for that device."

CoolTown researchers use barcode readers, radio-frequency identity tags, wireless Internet links, Web servers on chips, infrared beams, handheld computers, and mobile telephones to create an ecology of "Web-present objects." Although the original ubicomp researchers knew it would take a decade for the price of chips to drop low enough, they didn't know in 1988 that the Web would come along to provide a worldwide infrastructure. By assigning URLs and wireless Web servers to physical objects, HP researchers are looking at what happens to life in a city, a home, and an office when the physical world becomes browsable and clickable.

Think of all the public places where inexpensive chips could squirt up-to-the-second information of particular interest to you—such as the time your flight leaves and animated directions to your destination in an unfamiliar city—directly to your phone. "You could look through a physical bookstore, tune into 'virtual graffiti' associated (through the Web) with every book, and read reviews from your book club or see how people who like the same books you like rate this one," said Becker. Point your handheld computer at a restaurant, and find out what the last dozen customers said about the food. Point your device at a billboard, and see clips of the film or music it advertises, and then buy tickets or download a copy on the spot. Not only will products and locations have Web sites, but many will have message boards and chat rooms.

Recognizing that it's impractical to put signal beacons everywhere in the world, and cognizant of the privacy implications of location-based services, CoolTown researchers came up with virtual beacons called Websigns.[30]

Websigns are a combination of information and geo-coded coordinates, stored in a database available through the Web, like WorldBoard except your mobile device doesn't interact directly with a world map on a server in real time. Instead, you download the entire database of all the local Websigns to your mobile device. You could easily store information about tens of thousands of up-to-date locations for an entire city on a handheld device. Your device knows where it is located at all times. It looks at the database, and without signaling anyone but you, it tells you what virtual beacons are available. Nobody but you knows exactly where you are when you query the database because it's in your hand, not out on the Web. CoolTown's use of "semantic location" for Websigns is an existence proof that privacy protection can be designed into potentially intrusive technology.

Who owns access to your devices, either to push information at you or to pull information from you? Some of the answers will emerge from political processes, but many of them are sensitive to technical design decisions. In that regard, the designs that dominate early in the growth of a technology can have disproportionate power over the way the technology will affect power structures and social lives. What control will you have over whose sensors and beacons can talk or listen to your device? Who will have the right and the power to leave messages in places? HP asserts that using the Web as a standard for connecting mobile and pervasive technologies is essential for maintaining open and affordable access.

Becker was candid: "We don't want any company to gain unfair architectural control over how the physical and virtual worlds are connected. That's one reason why we're moving some of the software we've developed into an open source development community. We want to see a world like the early days of the Web, where anybody with the skill and interest and some ideas can create novel applications for themselves or their friends or make a business out of it." If today's mobile telephone morphs into something more like a remote control for the physical world, social outcomes will depend on whether the remote control device's software infrastructure is an open system, like the Web, or a closed, proprietary system.

My previous exploration of VR research made it easier to identify the most interesting recent explorations of the "magical glasses" Robinett and Spohrer dreamed of using. I discovered that in 1997, a group of computer scientists at Columbia University, led by Steven Feiner, collaborating with Anthony Webster of Columbia's Graduate School of Architecture, Planning, and Preservation, made a navigable virtual model of the Columbia campus, "a prototype system that combines the overlaid 3-D graphics of augmented reality with the untethered freedom of mobile computing."[31] Wearing the proper apparatus enabled users to access information about specific places as they strolled around the campus. The real-time position-sensing capabilities necessitated headgear and a backpack full of equipment. I learned that at Keio University outside Tokyo, Professor Scott Fisher of DoCoMo's mobile communications laboratory had assembled a similar backpack and headgear to create an immersive experience of place-specific information.

Fisher's "Wearable Environmental Media" platform is what led me to walk around the Keio University campus with a headful of gear and a heavy backpack.[32] Precise visual co-registration of virtual images on the physical world requires knowing not only where the user is located to within a few millimeters but also where the user's eyes are directed. This makes for a complicated and heavy prototype. It's a strange experience the first time you put on a helmet that covers your eyes and then watch the world around you through binocular television screens. I took a step, and the co-registration wasn't millimeter-perfect, so the lawn I saw wasn't exactly where my foot felt it to be. The sense of encapsulation, of being able to see the world well enough to navigate it, but viewing it only through the intermediation of cameras, is key to the experience of wearable computers.

If a user doesn't require magical glasses but accesses WorldBoard or CoolTown by glancing at the screen of a handheld device, prototypes can be built from off-the-shelf components today. Without the requirement that the experience of information in places be immersive, the investigation shades into the slightly different research field of context-aware mobile phones. Context-aware device research is part of a multi-industry effort to anticipate a market for location-based services via mobile telephones. We begin to move out of the world of dreamy-eyed futurizers and into the product cycle.

Location, Location, Location

Knowing our exact geographic location is one form of context awareness in which machines are better than humans. Location-aware services have been growing since NTT launched DoCo-Navi in 1999, providing real-time maps and directions on handheld devices. By mid-2001, DoCo-Navi users in Japan were generating between 500,000 and 800,000 daily mapping requests.[33] As for location services in the United States, according to an August 2001 story in the *Washington Post,* twenty-year-old Joe Remuzzi has a global positioning system (GPS) with 2 million points of interest programmed into it, which not only lets him check restaurants in his vicinity but groups them by cuisine: "Especially when I'm going to concerts far, far away, I'm almost like a local," Remuzzi said. "Like it shows where the Cajun restaurants are."[34] GPS navigators also became available in most high-end U.S. rental cars by 2002.

A form of location awareness is built into cellular phone systems. When you turn on your mobile telephone, it transmits a radio signal with an identifier. Cellular antennae located every few miles listen for these signals and thus are able to relay calls to the proper recipients. When you move out of range of one cell, your call is transferred to the control of another cell. By triangulating the signals from nearby cells, it is possible to locate a telephone within a few hundred feet in cities. In other words, every cell phone generates a record of where it has been.

More accurate positioning than cell triangulation is possible, to a range of ten to fifteen meters, through the use of global positioning system chips. The U.S. government developed GPS, which triangulates radio signals from twenty-nine orbiting satellites. Until recently, the U.S. military introduced errors into the data to prevent anyone but U.S. military from using GPS to obtain locations closer than one hundred meters. In May 2000, the U.S. government ended GPS scrambling, and a civilian market for GPS started to blossom. The U.S. government has ordered all telephones sold in the United States to become location-aware by 2005, for the purpose of improving emergency services. In 2002, Japan's KDDI and Okinawa Cellular announced plans to market a GPS-equipped telephone that can sense which direction the device is being pointed, as well as its location.[35]

When I zoom back to a wide view of an urban area in the age of mobile and pervasive technology, I can envision meshes of private and public devices, beacons, kiosks, appliances, place-based information sources and bulletin boards, traffic sensors, and transit services—citywide systems, some designed from the top down, others grown from the bottom up. Cities are places of massive information flows, networks, and conduits and myriad transitory information exchanges. Enthusiasts of "digital cities" are trying to understand the dynamics of computationally pervasive cities populated by mobile communicators in order to consciously design architectures that promote conviviality as well as safety and convenience.[36]

I came across several different flavors of urban virtualization in Helsinki: the grassroots, open-source-oriented Helsinki Arena 2000, the top-down Helsinki Virtual Village, and the social networks of four Internet dudes who called their project Aula. Risto Linturi described a project supported by HP Bristol Labs, Helsinki Telephone, and a company called Arcus, a system to integrate mobile location data in real time. The system is envisioned as

> a distributed messaging environment where all moving vehicles such as buses and taxis could be shown as corresponding avatars with their links in the model. . . . In the virtual Helsinki you can meet your friends as avatars just as you meet them in the real Helsinki. In the virtual world you just do not have to leave home when it is raining or snowing heavily. You can use the same popular meeting points, such as in front of Stockman's warehouse or at the Lasipalatsi Clock Tower. You may even experience the same crowds together and possibly get to know some other people in these crowds.[37]

More recently, the state of California created the Center for Information Technology Research in the Interest of Society (CITRIS) to design "pervasive, secure, energy-efficient, and disaster-proof information systems, delivering new kinds of vital data that people put to use quickly . . . , highly distributed, reliable, and secure information systems that can evolve and adapt to radical changes in their environment, delivering information services that adapt to the people and organizations that need them. . . . We call such systems Societal scale Information Systems."[38]

The attacks of September 11, 2001, stimulated new directions in "intelligent city" design:

> The key lies in developing and deploying technologies that will tie infrastructure components together into a system that's far smarter and more self-aware than anything we have today. Engineers, security consultants and authorities on counterterrorism are working hard to weave together the threads of this technological fabric, which will be pervaded by instruments that can sense harmful chemicals in a reservoir, relay critical data about a damaged building's structural integrity to rescue workers, help map escape routes or streamline the flow of electricity in a crisis. These high-tech networks— joined with simulation tools, enhanced communications channels, and safer building designs—could go a long way toward creating an "intelligent city," where danger can be pinpointed and emergency response directed.[39]

To get a sense of the scope of smart mob infrastructure, zoom from the citywide view to a close-up of the objects, buildings, and vehicles in the city. The growing ability of mobile devices to read barcodes and to communicate with the coming generations of radio chips that will replace barcodes is making it possible to click on the real world and expect something to happen.

The Marriage of Bits and Atoms

The barcode—that enigmatic band of stripes printed on most manufactured products—was an early bridge between physical and virtual worlds. The idea originated in the 1930s with a Harvard business student who invented an "automated grocery system" using punch cards. His idea did not catch on.[40] The modern barcode dates to 1949 and was developed by Norman Woodland, a graduate student and teacher at the Drexel Institute of Technology. The technology lay dormant until 1973, when Norman Woodland's design for IBM corporation was chosen by the grocery store industry and later named the Universal Product Code. In 1981, the U.S. Army began using it to label its equipment. Today, Federal Express is the world's largest user of the barcode. Five billion codes are scanned every day in 140 countries.[41]

Among the many changes made possible by barcodes was a transformation of manufacturing worldwide from a warehouse system to a "just-in-time" system; as automobiles and other component-based systems (including grocery store inventories) are assembled, barcodes and data networks coordinate the manufacture and shipment of future components in tightly synchronized streams. Wal-Mart achieved dominance largely through its global, instantaneous inventory management system.

When you add a barcode scanner or a radio frequency identity tag reader to a handheld device, it becomes easy to link a Web page or other online process to a tag that is physically associated with a place or object. Today, people can point a reader at an object and view relevant content on the screen of a pocket computer or hear spoken information by means of text-to-speech through a cell phone. A company called Barpoint allows users of existing cell phones, pagers, and wireless computers to swipe a barcode with a portable reader or use a telephone to call an automated service and enter the barcode of any item through the keypad.[42] The Barpoint service then provides pricing information and offers to complete an electronic order for the item. This simple capacity might set the stage for significant shifts in power between consumers, retailers, manufacturers, and online merchants. For example, widespread use of wireless handheld devices could turn every bookstore on earth into a showroom for Amazon.com.

Barcodes require line of sight for laser readers, must be read one at a time, and the information they encode cannot be changed dynamically. In the 1980s, researchers started looking at radio frequency identity (RFID) tags as electronic successors to the barcode. RFID tags store, send, and receive information through weak radio signals. Active tags contain tiny batteries and send signals up to more than one hundred feet, depending on power and radio frequency. Because of the batteries, active tags are the more expensive kind and are used today for tracking cattle, merchandise in stores (those bulky plastic anti-theft devices contain small RFID tags, and the gates near store exits are tag readers), and in automatic toll systems for automobiles.

It isn't feasible to put expensive RFID tags on the wide variety of objects that barcodes track. The less expensive passive tag contains a tiny coil of printed conductive ink. When the tag passes through the magnetic field of a reading device, the coil generates just enough electricity to transmit a signal a short distance—moving a coil of conductive wire through a magnetic field is precisely how a generator works. Manufacturers and others who have looked at the advantages of RFID tags believe that they will replace barcodes and revolutionize the way objects are tracked only when the price falls to around one cent, the fabled "penny tag." At the time of this writing, the price has dropped to around fifteen cents. Vivik Subramanian at the University of California claimed to have achieved a breakthrough in the spring of 2002, involving ink-jet printer technology and electronic inks that could print sub-penny smart tags on paper, plastic, or cloth: "Can we print a circuit on a package that when you ping it with a radio signal, it'll reply 'Hey, I'm a can of soup'? Just as importantly, can we do it very inexpensively?"[43] The Auto-ID Center at MIT, sponsored by Procter & Gamble, UPS, the U.S. Postal System, Gillette, Johnson & Johnson, International Paper, and others for whom smart tags could mean huge cost savings is the focus of a major interdisciplinary R&D effort.[44]

Used together, wireless network connections, portable computation, and tag readers make possible new applications that could change the nature of products, places, and social action. For a consumer society, the transformation of consumption may be profound. Changes in the most mundane but essential element of shopping, the label, raise political issues. Opponents of genetically engineered foods and pesticides, for example, have lobbied to require identification of those foods on their labels. Labor-rights activists have called for clothing labels that include a rating of the labor conditions of the manufacturing company or nation that produced the good. In the early days of American trade unions, battles were fought and songs were sung about "wearing the union label." With wireless devices that can read object tags, Web services that offer particular kinds of description and warning information can be created fairly easily. When people find out how the Christian Coalition or Greenpeace rates a product or a place, the collective political power of consumers could shift in unpredictable ways.

Could penny tags be used to promote social capital as well as consumption? Digital annotations of physical objects and places could catalyze interconnection between groups of people within a locality. Imagine a neighborhood bus stop where a number of people wait during the day but often at different times. These people may share a good deal in common but lack effective methods of communicating with one another. Associating discussion boards or Web pages with the bus stop could allow more flexible ways for people to connect with one another. A range of services like news, help wanted listings, discussions, reports of damage or crime, and goods and services for barter or sale could be provided to people while they are present in the space. Entertainment applications, including games, are easy to imagine.

Perhaps the most intrusive near-term application of RFID tags would be "smart money" that could record where it came from, who has owned it, and what it has bought. In December 2001, the European Central Bank was reported to be working on embedding RFID tags in currency by 2005.[45] Although prevention of counterfeiting is the bank's overt motivation, the same technology could afford surveillance of individual behaviors at a scale never before imagined. American civil libertarians assert that sentient currency would violate the U.S. constitutional prohibition against unlawful search and seizure.[46] In July 2001, Hitachi announced that its mu-chip, a square with sides no larger than four-tenths of a millimeter, with a radio transmitter and 128 bits of read-only memory—small enough to embed in paper money without being damaged by folding—will go on the market at around 20 yen each, or approximately 15 cents.[47]

After computers disappear into the walls, they might start floating in the air. The mu-chip is approaching the size of "smart dust," a kind of sentient object that doesn't exist yet. Researchers at the University of California, funded by Defense Advanced Research Projects Agency (DARPA) grants, combine chips that manipulate information with "microelectromechanical systems" that can perform physical activities.[48] Each "mote" combines a sensor (for pollution or nerve gas, for example) with optical transceivers that can communicate via laser beams for miles, sometimes with wings.[49] The first prototype, the size of a matchbox, contained temperature, barometric pressure, and humidity sensors and more computing power than the Apollo moon lander. "There's nothing in this thing that we can't shrink down and put into a cubic millimeter of volume," said UC professor Kristofer Pister.[50] When motes grow small enough, they can fly or float. Flying motes might be taught to flock and swarm.

Smart dust, like digital computers and computer networks, is a brainchild of the Pentagon, whose DARPA sponsors undoubtedly see this technology as the ultimate in invisible combat surveillance devices. Spin offs materialize unpredictably; swarming sensors could be employed in weather prediction, nuclear reactor safety, environmental monitoring, inventory control, and food and water quality control. I wouldn't be surprised if people found ways to turn swarming sentient micromechanical motes into cosmetics, entertainment, or pornography. People for whom pervasive computing is an abstraction will understand very clearly that the traditional barriers between information and material have changed when the air they breathe might be watching them. Computers were room-sized in the 1950s, then desktop-sized in the 1980s. Today, we're holding powerful computing and communication systems in our hands. Next, we'll lose sight of them if we drop them on the rug. The border between bits and atoms is where all the different disciplines of virtual reality, augmented reality, smart rooms, tangible interfaces, and wearable computing seem to be converging.

As Neil Gershenfeld explained it to me, the first epoch of MIT's Media Laboratory, from its foundation in 1980 to the end of the twentieth century, was about "freeing bits" from their different formats as text or audio or video or software and converging them into one digital form. The next epoch, Gershenfeld predicted, will be about "merging bits and atoms." When I first got wind of this notion a few years ago, I didn't connect it with the Internet or pervasive computing. I had been dropping in on Professor Hiroshi Ishii's group for a few years. When I visited Ishii at Media Lab in 1997, he was working on something called tangible bits. Ishii was enthusiastic in 1997 about abandoning traditional ways of operating computers, such as manipulating icons on a screen, in favor of manipulating tangible objects. He called these physical-virtual objects "phicons" for physical icons. That was the first time I had observed the inclusion of part of the physical world within a virtual world.

Media Lab is, above all, a place where people build working models of wild ideas like phicons. Ishii led me to a wide, blank table surface. At the edge of the table were several wooden objects the size of large alphabet blocks. One of them was a model of MIT's landmark dome. I picked up the dome and put it on the table. The blank table turned into a map of the MIT campus. I moved the phicon, and the map moved. I rotated the phicon, and the map rotated. Ishii handed me a second object, which was recognizable as a model of the I. M. Pei–designed Media Lab building. I put it down on the table, and the map shifted so that both the dome and the lab were in their proper places. I shifted one, then the other phicon; the map shifted to adjust, so that both buildings were always in correct juxtaposition to the rest of the landscape.

Media Lab research tends to aim at the technologies people will use in ten or twenty years. Sony's Computer Science Laboratories, located off Sony Street in Sony City in Tokyo, tends to work on projects that are closer to becoming products. I visited Jun Rekimoto, the young director of the Interaction Lab, a group of forty researchers. One can carry a NaviCam handheld device around the Interaction Lab, point it at the door of a researcher's office, and see a presentation about that researcher's work.[51] Rekimoto calls NaviCam a "magnifying glass for augmented reality." Instead of wearing cumbersome headgear, simply point a device at an RFID-augmented object and see or hear the information linked to the object.

Rekimoto invited me to try the "pick and drop" method for moving data and media from one computer to another by using a chip-enhanced pen to "pick up" a virtual object from a screen and then "drop" it onto the screen of a different computer. I picked up a depiction of a Monet painting from a handheld device and dropped it onto a wall display, which displayed it at highest resolution. Rekimoto called this "the chopstick metaphor," to contrast it with the traditional "desktop metaphor" of graphical representations of files and folders.

Rekimoto is "interested in designing a new human computer interaction style for highly portable computers, that will be situation-aware and assistance-oriented rather than command-oriented. Using this style, a user will be able to interact with a real world that is augmented by the computer's synthetic information. The user's situation will be automatically recognized by applying a range of recognition methods, allowing the computer to assist the user without having to be directly instructed. Before the end of the decade, I expect that such computers will be as commonplace as today's Walkmans, electronic hearing aids, and wristwatches."[52] Think of picking and dropping sounds, pictures, and videos among Sony cameras, MP3 players, and PCs.

Perhaps the ultimate bits-and-atoms laboratory at MIT Media Lab is the Physics and Media Group, directed by Professor Neil Gershenfeld. Gershenfeld published a book in 1999 titled *When Things Start to Think*, an allusion to a Media Lab research consortium named Things That Think.[53] He had stepped off a plane from India the morning we met. He had been there as part of MIT's Digital Nations effort to apply technology to problems in the developing world. He wore scuffed white track shoes, chinos, horn-rimmed glasses, and his face seemed younger than the gray in his curly hair suggested.

His frequent travel to India and the entire Digital Nations consortium is based on a belief that pervasive computation can provide relief to some of the more urgent problems in the world's poorest countries. "Much of our work in India is aimed at reversing urbanization by moving opportunity closer to villages. Computers and networks can help make a difference in governance, health care, disaster recovery, educational infrastructure, and land use. But the computers need to cost less than ten dollars and should not require an electrical grid or expert support."

I had been eager to talk about the penny tags, but Gershenfeld wanted to talk about paintable computing. "We're in the endgame of penny tags," he said. "It's now becoming an industrial problem." He now pursues a vision of self-organizing networks of sensors and computers so inexpensive that people could literally paint them on surfaces. One of Gershenfeld's students, William Butera, described a prototype as "an instance of several thousand copies of a single integrated circuit (IC), each the size of a large sand kernel, uniformly distributed in a semi-viscous medium and applied to a surface like paint. Each IC contains an embedded microprocessor, memory, and a wireless transceiver in a 4 mm square package, is internally clocked, and communicates locally. . . . A programming model employing a self-organizing ecology of mobile code fragments supports a variety of useful applications."[54] Imagine smart dust that knows how to organize into ad hoc networks that solve computing problems, configure the painted surfaces as supercomputers, display screens, distributed microphones or speakers, or wireless transceivers.

Gershenfeld's computer screen was projected onto a large white table. He rubbed his hand lovingly across the part of the table's surface where he projected a model of the new Media Lab building while he described how the building itself is an experiment. Gershenfeld will head the Center for Bits and Atoms to be housed in the new building, in which every switch and thermostat will have an Internet address. Paintable computing is a natural extension of Gershenfeld's long-standing belief that "the real promise of connecting computers is to free people, by embedding the means to solve problems in the things around us."[55]

Zoom to yet another level, from the scale of the smart room, with its computationally painted walls, to the scale of the individual human body. The political implications of technical design choices stand out more clearly when computers colonize our most intimate technology—clothing and jewelry—and when people don't sit at computers, hold technology in their hands, or even walk around inside it, but wear it. Issues arising from the design and use of wearable computing bring into high technopolitical contrast the distinctions among virtual reality, augmented reality, and mediated reality, and between smart rooms and personal sentient infomediaries.

Wearable Computers: The Political Battleground of Pervasive Technology

Like most of the wired world, I learned about Steve Mann, the first cyborg online, when he started webcasting everything he saw. Mann, who had been tinkering with wearable computers since he was a child, had ended up at MIT, where he had equipped himself with a helmet that enclosed his head and showed him the world through video cameras. The video feed was filtered through computers that enabled Mann to add and subtract features from the world he saw around him. Starting in 1994, wireless communications gear enabled him to beam everything he saw to a Web page. Mann's wearable computer had many features, including access to his email and the Web, but what was remarkable was his commitment to wearing his wearable computer all the time. By now, he's been mediating reality for most of his life.

Mann, now a professor at the University of Toronto, has wanted to be a cyborg since he was a teen. "Cyborg" stands for "cybernetic organism," a word coined by Manfred Clynes and Nathan Kline and popularized by the inventor of cybernetics, Norbert Wiener, to represent a merger of human and synthetic components. To many, the word and all it evokes is a chilly vision, mechanical and dehumanized, the ultimate bitter victory of technophilia at the expense of all that is humane about humans. Mann has always thought differently, and he wrote a passionate manifesto in 2001 that struck a chord with me after I had spent a year tasting augmented realities:

> Rather than smart rooms, smart cars, smart toilets, etc., I would like to put forward the notion of smart people.
>
> In an HI [humanistic intelligence] framework, the goal is to enhance the intelligence of the race, not just its tools. Smart people means, simply, that we should rely on human intelligence in our development of technological infrastructure rather than attempt to take the human being out of the equation. An important goal of HI is to take a first step toward a foremost principle of the Enlightenment, that of the dignity of the individual. This is accomplished, metaphorically and actually, through a prosthetic transformation of the body into a sovereign space, in effect allowing each and every one of us to control the environment that surrounds us. . . . One of the founding principles of developing technology under the HI system is that the user must be an integral part of the discourse loop. The wearable computer allows for new ways to be, not just do.[56]

As a teenager in Canada, Mann talked his way into a job at a television repair shop and started wiring up portable cameras and screens. Mann's first prototype, WearComp0, was bulky, but it quickly began to evolve into his next version, WearComp1. He took apart game machines to add joysticks, swapped in better batteries, improved the audio-video recorders and displays, and kludged together a wireless data connection. In 1982, Mann started building components and circuits in clothing. By his early twenties, cyborg wasn't something Mann did; it was something he was. He found supportive professors at McMaster University, where he worked toward his master's degree, perfected WearComp, and continued to live as a cyborg through the 1980s.

In 1989, the Private Eye eyeglass display became available, projecting a virtual image onto one eye that appeared to float in space as a fifteen-inch display positioned eighteen inches away.[57] In 1990, Gerald Maguire and John Ioannidis at Columbia plugged the Private Eye into a portable computer and a wireless Internet connection to create a mobile "student note-book."[58] Also in 1990, Andy Hopper at Olivetti's laboratory in Cambridge, England, used infrared sensors to locate the "active badges" of users.[59]

Although MIT has been the site of a great deal of work and has been the center of attention, it can be argued that the field of wearable computing is rooted in Pittsburgh, where "in 1991, 25 participants in a summer rapid prototyping course offered by the Carnegie Bosch Institute were tasked with the following problem: within one semester, design and build a functional computer which could be worn on the body. The resulting system, Vu·Man, became the first of more than a dozen wearable computers to emerge from the project in the subsequent decade."[60]

That same year, Steve Mann moved to MIT as a Ph.D. student at the Media Lab. The first thing he did when he arrived was to sneak up on the roof to install antennae for his radio communications infrastructure. You would think that a person so deeply involved in computers that he had worn them since he was sixteen would find a haven at MIT and the Media Lab, but Mann's beliefs aren't always what you might anticipate in a self-made cyborg. He fears and scorns the motives of military and corporate sponsors:

> The vision of many of those developers working for some of our biggest and most powerful government institutions is in contrast to my original attempts to personalize and humanize technology. Which road will we go down? The road on which wearable computers create and foster independence and community interaction? Or the road on which wearable computers become part of the apparatus of electronic control we are ever more subject to and unaware of?[61]

He makes his position clear regarding some of the fundamental research that Media Lab continues to pursue:

> The smart room is a retrograde concept that empowers the structure over the individual, imbuing our houses, streets and public spaces with the right to constantly observe and monitor us for the purported benefit of ensuring we are never uncomfortable or forced to get up from the armchair to switch on a lamp. Is it any wonder that I first encountered hostility with regard to the direction my research was to take? The very essence of my research was antithetical to the corporate-approved smart room concept. WearComp con-

tests the utility of ubiquitous computing, forcing us to reconsider the current research trend toward cameras and microphones everywhere in the environment watching and listening to us in order to be "helpful.". . . My opposite approach clashed dramatically with MIT's research thrust—a corporate-directed set of priorities that privileges things over people.[62]

Cyborg communities in what Mann calls "cyborgspace" are not, in his view, a dehumanized dystopia but are a defensive strategy against technological tyranny. Mann proposes that citizens can protect themselves against new concentrations of surveillance and control made possible by these technologies only by widely using the self-controlled, technically privatized form of wearable computer. The characteristic of sensory encapsulation is important to Mann. As he navigates the world, he sees *only* the output of his head-mounted cameras, as they are filtered through his wearable computer. Mann can turn the visual background of the world surrounding him into black and white and make his study materials pop up in color when he wants to study in a public place. Mann's reaction to the technologically enhanced Society of the Spectacle that surrounds him is to use WearComp to filter commercial advertisements out of his visual field. The words and pictures on billboards become invisible at his command. Mann concedes that technology has made it possible for commercial interests to bombard modern urbanites with unsolicited sights and sounds designed to nudge them toward consuming a product or service. Mann's radical social proposal is that the encapsulation of humankind in unsolicited commercial messages can only be reversed by using personal mediated-reality technology to filter our informational input and output.

Mann understood that one cyborg would not change society. True democratization would only grow from mass adoption of the technology. The community of cyborgs he had longed for in the lonely early decades of his life slowly began to emerge. A documentary film about Mann, titled *Cyberman,* premiered in March 2002.[63]

Another MIT Media Lab student, Thad Starner, was already engaged in wearable computer research when Mann arrived at MIT. Starner's Ph.D. thesis chronicles his experience of using state-of-the-art wearable computers to remain in touch with his personal communications, the entire Web, and other cyborgs wirelessly linked together into a communal cyborgspace. Starner, now assistant professor and director of the Contextual Computing Group at Georgia Institute of Technology's College of Computing, has worn his wearable computer continually since 1993.[64] Although Mann's on-line presence attracted the most attention, Starner deserves credit as one of the founders of wearable computing. In his thesis, he described the experience of reading email while walking through the halls at MIT. As others started wearing prototype wearable computers, "cyborgspace" started to become a site of social interaction.

Starner reported how he and another cyborg realized that their face-to-face conversations were punctuated by natural breaks that noncyborgs might not understand; each computer wearer in the conversation waited periodically while the other paused to take a note or look up something on-line in the middle of the dialogue. Starner examined his own behavior while brainstorming alone and realized that he used the computer's memory to "hold his place" on certain thoughts. He offered an example of something that happened to him in class:

"What did we say was the importance of deixis?" asked the lecturer. With the end of the term approaching, the class was reviewing their study of discourse analysis.

Volunteering, I said, "We said the importance of deixis is . . . uh . . . uh . . . humph, whoops! Uh, I'll get back to you on that."

The class, most of whom were Media Laboratory graduate students familiar with wearable computing, began to laugh. I had not known the precise wording of the answer and had tried to retrieve my class notes on the topic. Having done this routinely in the past, I had expected to have the information in time to complete my sentence. Due to a complex series of mistaken keystrokes, I had failed so badly that I could not cover my error, much to everyone's amusement.

One of the members of the class leaned over and said, "You actually do that sort of thing all the time, don't you? Now I'm impressed."

The combination of computer messaging tools, wireless connectivity, and a head-up display make such situations possible. In fact, members of the MIT wearable computing community and their colleagues take such an ability for granted. This informal networking can be used to encourage social gatherings, as above. It can also be used to form a type of "intellectual collective."[65]

Starner demonstrated the power of the collective by challenging reporters to ask him questions. Tharner used his handheld keyboard and wireless Net connection to send the question to all the computer users, mobile or stationary, who subscribe to the intellectual collective known as "the help instance." Students doing homework in their dorm room or the library, computer wearers walking across campus, can see the message and respond to it if they know the answer or have access to the appropriate reference.

Mann views the current fashionability of WearComp skeptically: "We cannot assume that all wearable technologies will be empowering. The ease with which researchers, sniffing the winds of technological change, switched from smart rooms to smart clothes (all the while maintaining what can only be described as a corporate ideology) clearly indicates the danger of blanket assumptions concerning the benefits of wearable technology. One can envision many wearable systems that, unfortunately, will take us in the other direction—away from personal freedom."[66] Mann cautions against WearComp that is sold as an individually empowering technology, but which is actually a "double agent" for some other institution or enterprise who wants to control or influence people.[67] The technical question with politically important implications is, Who controls the information that comes into the WearComp and radiates out from the WearComp to sentient devices in the world?

Since Mann left to inspire new generations of wearable computer students at Toronto and Starner started incubating wearable computer research at Georgia Tech, wearable computing has grown to be a major focus at Media Lab. A group at MIT is creating MIThril, the next generation of wearable computer, named after a magical garment in *Lord of the Rings*: "Our goal is to not simply build a platform, but to build a community of researchers, designers, and users."[68]

Perhaps more important than state-of-the-art wearable computer research platforms is the emergence of a hobbyist community similar to the subcultures that preceded and drove the PC and the Web. It didn't take long to find out that cyberspace is full of Web sites and mailing lists devoted to wearable computers. That's how I came to meet a cyborg in the lobby of New York's Roosevelt Hotel. The president of Pakistan was staying at the same hotel that night, so the place was full of Secret Service agents, but Melanie McGee was sitting at a table in black leather and much more: head-mounted display over one eye, wearable computer in a shoulder holster, electrical cables wrapped in black electrical tape linking them, and battery pack on her belt. She composed email with one hand, held a drink in the other. Young men standing around the hotel lobby glanced at her and then talked into their sleeves. She's a programmer and independent software developer when she's not plugging components into her wearable computer. Even though only one of us wore a wearable computer as we walked around Manhattan, I found that the conversation could be augmented by easy access to Google. (Imagine conversations in the days before you could look up the answer to any question.) Melanie is an example of the first wave of enthusiasts, those technically savvy enough to roll their own. The mass market, however, needs a well-designed and affordable plug-and-play system that requires little tinkering.

IBM, Hitachi, and startups are vying to provide the equivalent of the Apple II that kicks the enthusiast community to the next level. Industry analyst Gartner Consulting predicts that 40 percent of adults and 75 percent of teenagers will use wearable computing devices by 2010.[69] Xybernaut sells a voice-activated wearable computer to customers including Bell Canada. The Xybernaut unit, weighing less than two pounds, includes a head-mounted color display, microphone, and optional video camera.[70] IBM and Citizen Watch Company announced WatchPad, a wrist-wearable computer with Bluetooth (a short-range radio technology) and infrared connectivity, speaker, microphone, video display, and fingerprint sensor.[71] In January 2002, Hitachi announced the rollout of their Wearable Internet Appliance, combining a head-mounted display and eleven-ounce computer, running Microsoft's Windows CE operating system, to be supplied to Xybernaut. Initial price for the system was around $2,200.[72] In February 2002, Timex started test-marketing a new watch equipped with a radio frequency transponder that can be linked to a credit or debit card, enabling wearers to pay instantly at Exxon and Mobil gas stations and over 400 McDonald's restaurants in the Chicago metropolitan area—by waving their arms.[73]

Whether it comes through penny chips, wearable computers, geo-coded handheld devices, location-based services, smart rooms, digital cities, or sentient furniture, it seems clear that the next ten years will see more inanimate objects joining the Web and more people linked through mobile group-forming network technologies. The power of individuals to use smart mob media to form beneficial ad-hocracies—the power to solve social dilemmas—depends less on computing power or communication bandwidth and more on trust and willingness to risk the sucker's payoff. That's where reputation could make a crucial difference.

The Evolution of Reputation

I used to live off reputation servers. Let's say you're in the Regulators—
they're a mob that's very big around here. You show up at a Regulator
camp with a trust rep in the high nineties, people will make it their business to look after you. Because they know for a fact that you're a good guy
to have around. You're polite, you don't rob stuff, they can trust you with
their kids, their cars, whatever they got. You're a certified good neighbor.
You always pitch in. You always do people favors. You never sell out the
gang. It's a network gift economy.

—Bruce Sterling, *Distraction, a Novel*

Cooperation Catalysts

You walk into a jewelry store, select a wristwatch, and hand a plastic card to
the proprietor, who slides the card through a small device and waits a few
seconds. You hear the "zip, zip, zip" of a cheap printer. The jeweler accepts
your signature and trades you a valuable timepiece for whatever your card
disclosed to the jeweler's device and whatever you scribbled on the receipt.
You can say the right numbers into a telephone or if you have an Internet
connection and a good credit history, you can buy the same watch by typing
the right numbers on your computer keyboard. Parts of the smart mob infrastructure are in place now, merely lacking a series of software upgrades
already underway. Online credit verification services that have worked for
decades are an ideal carrier for more finely nuanced reputation repositories
capable of forecasting your taste in music, vouching for the trustworthiness

of your computer code, attesting to your ability to evaluate wines, as well as verifying your credit record.

Reputation marks the spot where technology and cooperation converge. The most long-lasting social effects of technology always go beyond the quantitative efficiency of doing old things more quickly or more cheaply. The most profoundly transformative potential of connecting human social proclivities to the efficiency of information technologies is the chance to do new things together, the potential for cooperating on scales and in ways never before possible. Limiting factors in the growth of human social arrangements have always been overcome by the ability to cooperate on larger scales: the emergence of agriculture ten thousand years ago, the origin of the alphabet five thousand years ago, the development of science, the nation-state, the telegraph in recent centuries, did more than accelerate the pace of life and make it possible for the human population to expand. These cultural levers also enlarged the scale of cooperation, radically altering the way people live.

The totalitarian threat posed by the prospect of mobile and pervasive media demands attention. The possibility that breakouts of cooperation could expand liberty is also worthy of attention.

Consider how early versions of "reputation management" or "social filtering" systems currently support new forms of broad-based cooperation:

- Electronic communication networks transformed the centuries-old institutionalized trust system of banking. Today's global institutionalized trust system of credit cards and ATMs, backed up by instantaneously available credit databases, authenticates millions of financial transactions every day.
- eBay, dominant survivor of the e-commerce bubble, uses a reputation system to facilitate billions of dollars worth of transactions for people who don't know each other and who live in different parts of the world.
- Epinions pays contributors of the most popular online reviews of books, movies, appliances, restaurants, and thousands of other items. Epinions's reputation system enables people to rate reviewers and to rate other raters through "webs of trust." The most trusted reviewers are read by more people and therefore make more money.
- Slashdot and other self-organized online forums enable participants to rate the postings of other participants in discussions, caus-

ing the best writing to rise in prominence and most objectionable postings to sink.

- Amazon's online recommendation system tells customers about books and records bought by people whose tastes are similar to their own.
- Google.com, the foremost Internet search engine, lists first those Web sites that have the most links pointing to them—an implicit form of recommendation system.

Hordes of programmers who compete for bragging rights as well as paying work are already driving the evolution of the first-generation reputation systems toward more advanced forms. Upendra Shardanand and Pattie Maes at the MIT Media Lab started something growing on the Net when they introduced Ringo, the "social information filtering" system that recommended music on the basis of shared tastes.[1] The MIT researchers "automated word-of-mouth recommendations" with computational methods. Users were invited to send an email command to the Ringo server. Return email presented a list of 125 musicians. Each user rated the musicians he or she liked. Ringo performed statistical correlations and then suggested new artists to each person—musicians they might not have known about but who were recommended by people with similar musical preferences.

Ringo launched in July 1994 and grew to more than 2,000 users by September. The MIT researchers started a company named Firefly to commercialize Ringo and sold it to Microsoft in 1998. Microsoft eventually implemented its own version of Firefly's "digital passport" technology.[2] Ringo turned out to be the progenitor of an evolutionary lineage.

Finding new books, movies, or music is a popular pursuit, but it represents only one form of the myriad webs of trust that support markets, scientific enterprises, businesses, and communities. Consider the history of online knowledge-sharing economies. One of the most seductive aspects of social cyberspace is the way virtual communities share useful information. I remember how excited I became in the 1980s, when the never-ending "Experts on the Well" discussion inspired people in the Well, a virtual community of a few thousand, to compete for the honor of providing the fastest and most accurate answers online to questions posed by other members of the community.[3] This custom is more sophisticated than automated word-of-mouth systems like Ringo because it requires each human recommender to keep in mind many other people's intellectual preferences, gleaned solely from online conversations.

Trading know-how isn't new. Developing a reputation for distributing high-quality recommendations is one way to accrue social status, and humans have extraordinary talents for social games. Trading know-how with people on six continents in real time, however, is more than just new; it fundamentally transforms knowledge-sharing by drastically lowering the transaction cost of matching questions and answers. While surfing the Web, little extra effort is required to send email to friends with a URL pointing to an interesting page, and little effort is required in finding the right specialized forum to ask a question. More recently, the phenomenon of "weblogging," which enables thousands of Web surfers to publish and update their own lists of favorite Web sites, has tipped online recommendation-sharing into an epidemic.

I stated something long known to Usenet veterans when I wrote in 1988 that one of the most attractive social innovations enabled by virtual communities was the way members could "serve as information hunters and gatherers for each other."[4] Four years later, researchers at Xerox PARC applied a more systematic version of a hunting-and-sharing methodology, introducing the term "collaborative filtering" in 1992 to describe their Information Tapestry. Information Tapestry software enabled researchers to annotate documents as they read them and made it easy for other researchers to use recommendations to find useful documents.[5]

Informal social aggregation of useful knowledge goes back to the lists of frequently asked questions (FAQs) posted to some Usenet newsgroups since the 1980s; these lists of questions and answers, accumulated through years of archived online conversations, were compiled to prevent newcomers from besieging more knowledgeable posters with questions that had already been answered. Telling a newbie to "read the FAQ!" is a way for a group to constrain the overconsumption of a public good; experts contribute knowledge as long as the conversation retains their interest but stop contributing if newbies' questions dominate the conversation. Beyond their defensive function, FAQs constitute a new kind of encyclopedia in themselves, collectively gathered, verified, articulated webs of knowledge about hundreds of topics.[6]

The conversations on Usenet include valuable information in individual postings far beyond the highly distilled information published in FAQs. The problem with Usenet conversations as a repository of knowledge is the difficulty of finding the useful tidbits among the tidal waves of chit-chat and endless flame wars. In 1992 Paul Resnick and his colleagues at the University of Michigan created GroupLens software, which allowed readers to rate Usenet messages and make ratings available to others on request.[7] Resnick, along with many others, has continued to conduct research on reputation systems during the decade since GroupLens.[8] GroupLens continues to provide a free movie recommendation service on the Web.[9]

Automated collaborative filtering systems work best whenever there is a low risk to making a bad decision, such as buying a book or a movie ticket. Amazon.com and other e-commerce sites use collaborative filtering systems to make suggestions to regular customers. Systems that can tell people what they want to buy next are bound to coevolve along with e-commerce. When the risk increases and choices involve larger amounts of money, what happens to trust? eBay's reputation system answers this question with remarkable success. When the currency of a social filtering system changes from knowledge or social recognition to money, the evolution of this social technology forks into lineages of reputation systems that deal with markets and those that deal with recommendations. Later in this chapter I'll return to the role of reputation systems in markets. Both the systems that deal with knowledge and recommendations and those that mediate transactions in financial markets could come into play when future populations of wearable computer users form ad hoc networks around what they know and trust about each other.

Any ways that groups can share knowledge efficiently in the course of online conversation without doing anything beyond having conversation could generate real power in scientific and business communities. Even simple instruments that enable groups to share knowledge online by recommending useful Web sites, without requiring any action by the participants beyond bookmarking them, can multiply the groups' effectiveness.

In 1997, Hui Guo, Thomas Kreifelts, and Angi Voss of the German National Research Center for Information Technology described their "SOaP" social filtering service designed to address several of the problems constraining recommender systems.[10] Guo and his colleagues created software agents, programs that could search, query, gather information, report results, even negotiate and execute transactions with other programs. The SOaP agents could implicitly collect recommendation information by the members of a group and mediate among people, groups, and the Web. At the most implicit level, SOaP agents can collect and cluster URLs that members of the group bookmark in the course of their work. If a member of the group is interested enough to bookmark a site, an implicit recommendation has been made. People who wish to make more explicit annotations are able to do so:

> In our system, information is filtered by communicative social agents which collect human users' assessments and match users' interests to derive recommendations. With agents, it is possible for users to find relevant bookmarks regarding specific topics, find people with similar interests, find groups with similar topics, and also to form groups for direct cooperation.
>
> In order to perform the services, agents in our system use knowledge about users, groups of users, the topics that are relevant to a user, the URLs that a user considers relevant to a topic, and a user's assessments of a URL, e.g., his or her ratings and annotations, in the context of a particular group or in connection with a particular topic. According to our design principle, this knowledge should be obtained without effort on the part of the user, or else it should be optional.[11]

The key to aggregating knowledge through the use of SOaP by a group is social, not technical: The degree of trust among members is determined by each group that uses it. This allows for a variety of communities and degrees of trust. Huge populations of strangers known to one another only by their postings—Usenet, for example—can exchange a rich variety of low-trust recommendations. A smaller invitational network of experts, a self-organized community of interest, or an organizational unit can use the same system to increase their individual and collective knowledge. Individuals are given the power to determine whether their annotations and surfing habits are published, and to whom, but all they need to do at the minimum is surf the Web and bookmark sites that interest them.

Brewster Kahle and Bruce Gilliat created a Web surfers' collaborative filtering system, Alexa Internet, in 1996.[12] Alexa is an implicit filtering system: When a person using it visits a Web site, the person's Web browser provides a menu of Web sites that have been visited by other surfers who have visited the same page. Alexa requires users to install additional software that records their choices as they navigate through the Web and adds data about their choices to the database. Alexa is an instance of a "cornucopia of the commons," which provisions the resource it consumes; users contribute to the database in the act of using it. At the same time it harvests their decisions, the installed software also offers users recommenda-

tions of other sites to investigate. Technology in the Alexa lineage continues to be available as a "related sites" feature for common browsers. Amazon acquired the company in 1999.

Ego Strokes, Opinion Markets, and Bozofilters

During the last months of the twentieth century, a few Internet startups
burned millions of dollars attempting to profit from online knowledge-
sharing communities. Many of these startups succeeded in attracting communities of experts who competed to make the enterprise more valuable
by contributing their knowledge. The volunteer mavens on everything
from hummingbirds to Sumerian antiquities took their payment in pennies
and prestige. The opposite of the free-rider problem emerged in a number
of forms—hordes of compulsive contributors.

The decades-old friendly competitions to provide answers online became a commercial enterprise toward the end of the dotcom era when expert opinion, advice, and recommendation Web sites such as Epinions,
Askme.com, Experts-Exchange, Allexperts.com, ExpertCentral.com, and
Abuzz.com launched. Most of these enterprises failed when Web-based
advertising revenues sank, but many were markedly successful in producing high-quality evaluations about everything from computer program
ming problems to comic book collections. People with expertise contributed answers, tidbits, essays, pages of software code, lore of astonishing
variety. A few contributors earned the kind of currency banks accept. Most
contributed for the social recognition that came with being a top-ranked
reviewer. The "reputation managers" that enabled users and other recom-
menders to rate each other made possible opinion markets that traded almost entirely in ego gratification.

Epinions, launched in September 1999, continued to thrive in 2002, unlike many of its competitors, and it continued to host an active community
of evaluation providers.[13] "Epinionators" are paid between one to three
cents every time another registered member reads and rates their
100–1,000 word reviews. Well-rated reviews rise to the top of their categories' list. A very few contributors even make a living at it, yet hundreds
continue to provide evaluations of thousands of products and services. If
you can use it and pay for it, you can find an Epinion about it. Members
can rate each review as "Highly Recommended," "Recommended,"
"Somewhat Recommended, or "Not Recommended." Members can click a

button next to the name of an Epinionator and add him or her to a personal "web of trust." People who trust each other inherit each other's webs of trust. Although webs of trust are an official feature of Epinions, the first web of *mis*trust appeared spontaneously, created by a user.

Epinions continuously publishes updated ratings for the community to see. This feature is mentioned by some habitual users who joke about their prolific contributions as a compulsion: "I am addicted to a drug called Epinions. I have to keep going back for more," one of the top-rated Epinionators confessed on a message board."[14] Instant social approval can be intoxicating. Science fiction fans of the 1920s who published amateur "fanzines" invented a word for this kind of personal gratification: "egoboo," derived from "ego boost," is the coin of online social prestige in expert opinion communities.[15]

Above all, Epinions is a social network. "Epinions is one of the most active and varied ecosystems on the Web," *Wired* editor Mark Frauenfelder wrote. "It has evolved into a diverse community populated by cliques, clowns, parasites, symbiotes, self-appointed cops, cheaters, flamers, and feuders. It's swarming with people who were English or journalism majors but ended up stuck in other careers. And it has produced member-generated site refinements, such as the Web of Distrust."[16]

The methodology of self-organizing knowledge communities lives on in many forms, although the recommender community industry is a tale of yesteryear. Most self-organizing Web sites now are partially or totally noncommercial. Some self-organizing sites subscribe to the open-source philosophy. Other sites are purely amateur but incorporate quality control. A 2001 story in the *New York Times* spotlighted "The Vines Network," an "Encyclopedia of Everything" written by volunteers for free, in which readers rate content on a 1–10 point scale.[17] Collectively written encyclopedias mushroomed into a genre of its own, including virtual subcultures. Another self-organized encyclopedia, "everything2.com" drew a rich community of regulars organized around a rating system and message boards.[18] At everything2, the contributors of knowledge grow an encyclopedia around conversations about sports, politics, classical history, chihuahuas, or quantum physics.

Another new online subculture has grown out of the self-published Web-surfing diaries known as "blogs," short for "weblogs."[19] Blogging software made it easy for anyone to update a simple Web site frequently. *Wired News* estimated that 500,000 blogs had been created by February 2002.[20] Blogs, sorted by type of content, come in thousands of flavors, but almost all are updated regularly, include links to favorite sites, concentrate on a theme or interest, and include commentary on the mentioned sites. Sometimes blogs are like diaries. Others are like fanzines or indexes to subcultures. Almost every blog includes a list of related or favorite blogs and "discusses" links that enable communities to form. Rings of blogs about similar interests self-organize. Communities of shared affinity emerge spontaneously from discussions. MIT Professor Henry Jenkins describes the power blogging has to reframe issues:

> Imagine a world where there are two kinds of media power: one comes through media concentration, where any message gains authority simply by being broadcast on network television; the other comes through grass-roots intermediaries, where a message gains visibility only if it is deemed relevant to a loose network of diverse publics. Broadcasting will place issues on the national agenda and define core values; bloggers will reframe those issues for different publics and ensure that everyone has a chance to be heard.[21]

The liberating news about virtual communities is that you don't have to be a professional writer, artist, or television journalist in order to express yourself to others. Everyone can be a publisher or a broadcaster now. Many-to-many communications media have proved to be popular and democratic. Evidence: the history of Usenet. The disappointing news about virtual communities is that you don't have to be civil, capable of communicating coherently, or know what you are talking about in order to express yourself to others. Evidence: the history of Usenet. Some people proclaim opinions that are so abhorrent or boring, use such foul language, or are such poor communicators that they sour discussions that would otherwise be valuable to the majority of participants. Some people have a voracious need for attention and don't care whether it is negative attention. Other people use the shield of anonymity to unleash their aggressions, bigotry, and sadistic impulses.

The presence of flamers, bullies, bigots, charlatans, know-nothings, and nuts in online discourse poses a classic tragedy of the commons dilemma. If too many people take advantage of open access to seek other people's attention, the excesses of the free riders drive away the people who make the conversation valuable. Online media that support social communication have a defensive capability that face-to-face socializing lacks: It is possible for civilized conversationalists to tune out those who abuse the conversational commons.

Rules about behavior would be unthinkable to Usenet's anarchic culture. The programmers who populated the early Usenet proclaimed allegiance to "tools, not rules." In the case of conversational noise, Usenet devotees adopted a program known as the "killfile," which enabled people to eliminate from their view (but not that of others) specific words, postings of particular people, or even certain topics of conversations. The words, postings, and topics themselves are unaffected, but killfile users render them invisible to themselves. On the Well, and in other online communities, an equivalent program came to be known as the "bozofilter."

Hiding crap is the easy part. The real achievement is finding quality. The notion that people can use software to filter conversations according to individual preferences has continued to evolve, and other instruments have begun to emerge for enabling both democratic access and tuning out semantic noise. The open source community in particular has been a fertile ground for social reputation systems. Tens of thousands of freelance programmers who work collectively to create and share open source software and who collaborate on paying projects tend to live online. They have a strong ethic of sharing and a strong aversion to censorship. In 1998, an open source programmer, Rob Malda, started a small discussion forum to talk about programming, issues in the news, and pop culture: "News for Nerds, Stuff That Matters," proclaimed the front page. Official editors would select relevant stories every day, post links and commentary, and the Slashdot community around the world added commentary in the form of sequential posts. Malda, who goes by the online handle "Commander Taco," called it "Slashdot," after a commonly used Linux command. Malda later wrote: "We got dozens of posts each day, and it was good. The signal was high, the noise was low."[22]

The time was right for a virtual watering hole to appear as a hangout for the programmers around the world who shared the open source zeitgeist. The Slashdot population grew, and soon there were too many posts to police and too much noise to ignore. Malda chose twenty-five people to help. They deleted spam and awarded points to posts that seemed valuable. Then the Slashdot population grew unmanageable even for twenty-five volunteers. By 1999, if a link to a Web site was posted as a top-level story on Slashdot, that Web site would get so many hits that host servers often crashed, a phenomenon that came to be known Netwide as "being Slashdotted." The original twenty-five moderators chose four hundred more. The Slashdot karma system emerged to filter out noise, point out good postings, and protect against abuse of power from moderators.

When a registered user logs in often enough and reads postings over a sustained period, Slashdot's "Slashcode" software automatically puts that user in a pool of candidates for jury-like service. Randomly selected "moderators" from the pool of regulars are given a limited number of points to use in rating posts of other members, and when they expend those points, their term of service is over until they are selected again. Moderators can use their points to rate postings on a scale of –1 to +5, and they can attach annotations such as "flamebait" or "informative." Posters can choose to remain anonymous, in which case they start with a karma setting of zero and their posts are labeled "Anonymous Coward." Registered posters, who can use pseudonyms, start out with a karma setting of +1. Moderators use their allotment of points to raise or lower the settings of selected posts and hence affect the karma of the selected posters.

Slashdot readers can use a menu to set their "quality filter" reading level. Some readers can choose to read every one of hundreds of posts in a particular discussion; others can set their quality filter to read only those with a rating of 3 or above, usually reducing the number of posts to dozens, or set their quality filter to show only those with the highest rating of five, sometimes reducing a thread of hundreds of posts to a handful.

By 2001, the Slashdot community of registered users exceeded 300,000. At that scale, there was no way to organize except self-organize. Malda and friends tinkered with the reputation system in response to community use and abuse, adhering to four design goals:

- Promote quality, discourage crap.
- Make Slashdot as readable as possible for as many people as possible.
- Do not require a huge amount of time from any single moderator.
- Do not allow a single moderator a "reign of terror."[23]

The Slashdot system evolved several refinements. Moderators cannot post in the same conversations they moderate, and metamoderators are randomly chosen to assign points to the moderators' choices, providing a shield against moderator abuse. Because Slashcode is open source, other groups copied it, set up their own discussions, and began to modify the code to create their own variations.

Reputation is even more important in commerce than it is in conversation. Without some kind of trust metric, e-commerce never would have become possible. Although the number of e-businesses has been reduced from thousands to a smaller number of larger enterprises, eBay, the most successful electronic marketplace, combined e-commerce, online affinity groups, and reputation management.

Restoring the Shadow of the Future

In 1995, Pierre Omidyar created eBay so that his wife could trade Pez dispensers—a form of packaging for candy now valued by collectors. The Omidyars are billionaires now—from creating an electronic marketplace, not from trading Pez dispensers. In 2000, eBay users transacted more than $5 billion in gross merchandise sales. By 2002, eBay had more than 42 million registered users and was the most popular shopping site on the Internet.[24] Millions of items are listed for sale on any given day in thousands of categories. eBay offers no warranty for its auctions; it merely puts buyers and sellers together, gives them a place to display pictures of their wares, automatically manages auctions, provides a reputation management system, and takes a small listing fee.

Omidyar benefited from the power of Reed's Law (Chapter 2). eBay is a "group-forming network" that self-organizes around shared obsessions; all the collectors of Turkish railway tickets, Dickens first editions, Pez dispensers, velvet paintings, and Ming vases find each other at their appropriate auctions and form their own communities. Surprisingly, eBay reported in 1997 that only 27 out of 2 million auctions over a four-month period were considered to involve possible criminal fraud and that 99.99 percent of the auctions attracting bids were successfully completed.[25] "It's almost impossible to believe that random strangers can trade like this without more problems. Retailers have a much higher rate of shoplifting than the fraud that eBay runs into," commented an investment analyst.[26]

The overall rate of fraud is not a reflection of innate human honesty. To the contrary, the smart mobs who use eBay to their advantage are always the target of would-be smarter mobs who try to find loopholes in the system, and the attacks of the would-be smarter mobs spur the efforts of smartest mobs who build improved reputation systems to counter known forms of cheating. eBay looks for evidence of the kind of "shill bidding" that was uncovered when a seller conspired to inflate the price of a painting.[27]

The low rate of fraud on eBay poses a dilemma familiar to students of cooperation. Peter Kollock, a professor at UCLA who had studied virtual communities, has noted that every unsecured financial transaction is a Prisoner's Dilemma in which each party is tempted to benefit by failing to reciprocate:

> The temptation to defect in the exchange has led to a wide range of formal and informal mechanisms for managing this risk. The simple act of meeting face-to-face for the transaction helps reduce the likelihood that one party will end up empty handed. Separating the two sides of the transaction by time or space (such as purchasing something by mail or on credit) introduces greater risks: the party who moves second must be considered trustworthy or have some other form of guarantee. The formal infrastructure that exists to manage these risks is vast and includes such elements as credit card companies, credit rating services, public accounting firms, and—if the exchange goes bad—such services as collection agencies or the court system.[28]

In the Feedback Forum, eBay buyers and sellers can rate each other and comment publicly on the quality of the interaction. Each comment includes one line of text and a rating of +1 (positive), 0 (neutral), or –1 (negative). All feedback comments have to be connected to a transaction; only the seller and winning bidder can leave feedback. Buyers searching for items can see the feedback scores of the sellers. Over time, consistently honest sellers build up substantial reputation scores, which are costly to discard, guarding against the temptation to cheat buyers and adopt a new reputation.

Paul Resnick, whose GroupLens had been a pioneering recommender system in 1992, and Richard Zeckhauser performed empirical studies on "a large data set from 1999" that indicated that despite the lack of physical presence on eBay, "trust has emerged due to the feedback or reputation system."[29] Biological theories of cooperation and experiments in game theory point to the expectation of dealing with others in future interactions— the "shadow of the future" that influences behavior in the present. Resnick et al. assert:

> Reputation systems seek to restore the shadow of the future to each transaction by creating an expectation that other people will look back on it. The connections of such people to each other may be significantly less than is the case with transactions on a town's Main Street, but their numbers are vast in comparison. At eBay, for example, a stream of buyers interacts with the same seller. They may never buy an item from the seller again, but if they share

their opinions about this seller on the Feedback Forum, a meaningful history of the seller will be constructed. . . . Through the mediation of a reputation system, assuming buyers provide and rely upon feedback, isolated interactions take on attributes of a long-term relationship. In terms of building trust, a vast boost in the quantity of information compensates for significant reduction in its quality.[30]

Resnick et al. concluded that reputation systems require three properties in order to function: First, the identities of buyers and sellers must be long-lived, whether or not they are pseudonymous, in order to create an expectation of future interaction. Second, feedback about interactions and translations must be available for future inspection by others. Third, people must pay enough attention to reputation ratings to base their decisions on them. In regard to the third requirement, part of the effectiveness of eBay's reputation system might derive from buyers' and sellers' belief that it works. Reputation, like surveillance, may induce people to police themselves.

Research into reputation management systems stirred up an interdisciplinary vortex, similar to the way that the Prisoner's Dilemma drew together mathematicians, economists, biologists, and sociologists toward a conceptual Schelling point about cooperation.[31] Computer scientists who devise distributed artificial intelligence systems, in which large numbers of intercommunicating dumb units add up to hive-like emergent intelligence, use reputation as a way of controlling the behavior of the distributed agents.[32] Computer security researchers use the term "web of trust" to refer to ways of authenticating people's cryptographic keys by delivering them in person to people who will then certify the keys online by adding their digital signature, thus enabling encrypted communications to take place without a central key-certifying authority.[33]

I visited an economist who is trying to create a discipline of reputation systems research. I had been drawn to the writings of Chrysanthos Dellarocas, formerly of the MIT Sloan School of Management, because he addressed one of the essential questions about the future of smart mobs: Are reputation systems useful tricks for book-buying and online auctions but ultimately incapable of mediating more complex social dilemmas? Or will reputation systems evolve into far more sophisticated social accounting systems?

"Can reputation systems evolve? This question is the center of my research!"[34] Professor Dellarocas received me in his high-rise office in New York University's Stern School of Business. "My aim is to build a foundation in economics for a discipline of designing reputation systems," he added.

Like Resnick and others, Dellarocas recognized that online auctions are Prisoner's Dilemmas: "In transactions where the buyer pays first, the seller is tempted to not provide the agreed upon goods or services or to provide them at a quality which is inferior to what was advertised to the buyer. Unless there are some other guarantees, the buyer would then be tempted to hold back on her side of the exchange as well. In such situations, the trade will never take place, and both parties will end up being worse off."[35]

Dellarocas studied the most frequent methods of cheating reputation systems. Buyers can give unfairly high ratings ("ballot stuffing") and conspire to boost each other's reputations ("shilling"). Buyers can give unfairly low ratings ("bad mouthing"). Sellers can provide good service to everyone except a few specific buyers they dislike or, conversely, can favor other buyers. For these fundamental vulnerabilities, Dellarocas suggests three countermeasures. Controlled anonymity, in which the system reveals reputation information to buyers and sellers but not the identity of either parties, can reduce the possibility of collusion or reprisal. Dropping exceptional scores at the high and low end and discarding scores from the most frequent reviewers can furnish further defenses against cheating.

Although he does believe that reputation systems will grow more capable over time, Dellarocas cautioned, "We are still far from an online reputation marketplace." He pointed out that eBay and Amazon both guard access to their reputation databases and resist attempts to transfer reputation scores from one online marketplace to another. This raises the question of who owns our reputations. Are universal reputations systems possible?

From all the current action in reputation system theory and practice, it isn't hard to predict that scalable, trustable, portable, easy-to-use online reputation systems will continue to evolve. One researcher I'll discuss in Chapter 7 ("Smart Mobs") is even experimenting with distributed reputation systems for ad hoc wearable computer communities. These communities are in such early stages of their development that we can only speculate about how they will fit into mobile and pervasive technologies. Recent scientific discoveries about the role of reputation in evolution, social interaction, and markets offer provocative hints, however.

Mobile, Pervasive, and Reputable

Some of the biological and social research findings I encountered when looking into the nature of cooperation made new sense after I learned about the evolution of online reputation systems. So I went back to the sociologists, the evolutionists, and the game theorists, and lo!—reputation stood out as a single thread connecting the puzzling generosity of hunters in Tanzania, the peculiar pleasure that comes from punishing cheaters, the social function of gossip, the possibility that language evolved from grooming behavior, and the way some communities manage their commons without incurring tragedy. In each of these instances, reputation is the secret ingredient in cooperation.

In Chapter 2, I presented the case that cooperative strategies like TIT-FOR-TAT succeed because they signal a willingness for cooperation but defend themselves against exploitation by retaliating against noncooperation. These two simple strategies, taken together, seem to explain how self-interested individuals can agree to cooperate for common benefit in a wide variety of situations. Organisms that have been observed to cooperate, from stickleback fish to vampire bats, appear to do so on a basis of reciprocation—offering mutually profitable cooperation only to partners who are willing to return the favor, punishing those who have not reciprocated in the past by refusing to cooperate with them now, otherwise known as reciprocal altruism.

In some organisms and some human societies, individuals have been so willing to cooperate that they apparently act against their own self-interest in order to provide benefit to others. Why do antelope hunters in Tanzania and turtle fisherman off Australia expend their energy providing game for tribal feasts, even at the expense of their own families? Biologists think the answer is something called "costly signaling": The hunters are letting others know that they are good citizens and good providers and therefore good husband and partner material.

Anthropologist Kirsten Hawkes concluded that the Hazda hunters of Tanzania spend extra effort and take bigger risks hunting large game like giraffes that can feed the whole tribe instead of going for easier small game that could feed their own families because provisioning big game pays off in prestige, which can be translated into future political power, economic partnership, or sexual attention.[36] Similarly, turtle hunters off the northeast coast of Australia provide feasts for their tribe at the expense of their time and their shares of the catch in order to send a "costly signal" that lets potential mates, allies, competitors, and hunting partners perceive their prowess and willingness to cooperate.[37] Those who receive this information tend to trust it because of the cost the hunters paid to signal it. To biologists Pollock and Dugatkin, reputation evolved as a measure of an individual's willingness to reciprocate, thereby raising the probability that the individual will be chosen as a partner in reciprocally cooperative activities like food-sharing, mating, and hunting together.[38]

Spreading the word about reputation is where gossip comes in. One evolutionary biologist claims that the human brain grew large and language emerged because social grooming—taking turns picking insects out of each other's fur—was inadequate for maintaining social bonds in groups of primates larger than fifty members. Grooming signals willingness to cooperate (literally, "you scratch my back and I'll scratch yours"). In "Why Gossip Is Good for You," Robin Dunbar claims that language grew out of complex social bonding between proto-human females. Whereas simpler signals and smaller brains could have remained adequate for coordinating the males' hunting activities, Dunbar proposes they weren't sufficient for the complicated lists of who did what to whom that could have been the basis for the original proto-human reputation system.[39].

Research reported in 2002 offers provocative theories about how reputation, altruism, and punishment are structured to support human cooperation. A field now known as "experimental economics" has extended game theory to include two specific "minigames": the "Ultimatum Game" and the "Public Goods Game." Research using these games as probes indicate that

- People tend to exhibit more generosity than a strategy of rational self-interest predicts.
- People will penalize cheaters, even at some expense to themselves.
- These tendencies and the emotions that accompany them influence individuals to behave in ways that benefit the group.[40]

The Ultimatum Game takes place between two players who play it once and never again. The players can share the sum of money, but only if they agree on a split. A coin flip gives one player the option of determining how much of the total to keep and how much to offer the other player. The other player, the "responder," can accept the deal and the money is split as proposed, or the second player can refuse the deal and neither player gets any money. The result that is not surprising to people who value fairness but puzzles those who see humans as rational creatures who act in their self-interest is that two-thirds of the experimental subjects offer between $40 and $50 out of $100 total. Only four in one hundred people offer less than 20 percent, and more than half of the responders reject offers smaller than 20 percent of the total.

Why would anyone turn down 20 percent of something in exchange for nothing? Martin A. Nowak, Karl Sigmund, and Karen M. Page of the Institute for Advanced Study at Princeton propose an evolutionary model. Emotions evolved over millions of years of living in small groups. In such groups, gossip distributed information about who accepts unfair treatment and who resists it passionately. If others learn that an individual is willing to meekly settle for smaller than their fair share, they are likely to make lower offers to that individual in the future. If the responder exhibits anger at being treated unfairly (being offered $20 instead of $50, for example), then others will have an incentive to make higher offers in future trades. Reputation for being a sucker is costly, and the emotional response could be an internal model that serves to regulate cheating.

The Public Goods game has provided a window into the role of punishment in managing common resources. Swiss researchers Ernst Fehr and Simon Gachter devised a game in which four anonymous participants had to decide how much to invest in a common pot.[41] They are each given a stake to begin investing, and each can keep what he or she doesn't invest in the pot. The amount invested by the four, each deciding without the knowledge of how the other three are going to respond, is multiplied and then divided equally among the players, with no regard to who was generous (and thus raised the pot for all at their own expense) and who was rationally stingy (and got the divided pot plus all their original stake). This game was then played in rounds, and the amount that each player invested was revealed after each round. In some of the games, players were allowed to spend part of their pool for the privilege of fining each other. In some games, the players were rotated among different groups, so that individuals did not have the opportunity to encounter each other again. Groups in which punishment was allowed resulted in more generous contributions to the common pool, but cooperation deteriorated rapidly in the absence of punishment. Even when there was no possibility of future interaction, many players punished free riders and reported that they did it because they were angry at the cheaters.[42]

Punishment of free riders is "a very important force for establishing large-scale cooperation," Fehr told the *New York Times*, "Every citizen is a little policeman in a sense. There are so many social norms that we follow almost unconsciously, and they are enforced by the moral outrage we expect if we were to violate them."[43] David Sloan Wilson, an evolutionary biologist, told the *New York Times*: "People are used to thinking of social control and moralistic aggression as forms of selfishness, and that you must be punishing someone for your own benefit. But if you look at the sort of punishment that promotes altruistic behavior, you see that it is itself a form of altruism. Once you think of punishment as a form of altruism, then the kind of person who doesn't punish emerges as a kind of freeloader, too."[44]

When Elinor Ostrom looked for common characteristics of communities that managed commons without destroying them, she discovered that imposing sanctions on free riders, but doing it in a graduated manner, is key to cooperation. Self monitoring is part of successful grassroots collaboration, a kind of many-to-many surveillance by mutual consent. If governance is to be democratic rather than Hobbesian, maintenance of social order requires technologies of mutual social control. Marc A. Smith, my cybersociology guru, applied Ostrom's findings to his research on Usenet and speculated about the future of online reputation systems:

> Effective self-regulation relies upon sanctioning, which relies upon monitoring. If it is difficult to identify either the largest contributors or the most egregious free riders, sanctioning, whether in the form of reward or punishment, cannot function effectively. In the physical world, monitoring occurs in many ways. The mutual awareness of coworkers around common coffeepot chores or neighbors around maintaining common spaces is often constructed through casual interaction and fairly cheap monitoring and record keeping. But without the background of a social network of general awareness among neighbors, most neighborhoods become more dangerous and shabby. The widespread use of wireless digital devices means that monitoring the contributions and consumption of a common resource by potentially vast groups can be made fairly cheap and fluid.
>
> The most interesting implications are the ways these tools can allow loosely related people to cooperate and collectively create a range of services that are otherwise costly or impractical. These tools allow groups of unrelated people to cooperate with one another by providing a framework for possible sanctions for misconduct and assurances of prior cooperation. As a

result, matchmaking services supported by reputation services may be one of the most central applications. If people who can provide one another with a needed good or service can easily find one another and get assurances and recourse so that they can trust one another, a wealth of pent-up value can be released.[45]

None of the theories and data gathered by biologists, sociologists, and economists predicts what populations will do in an environment of ad hoc networks, wearable computers, pervasive media, and online reputation systems, but most of the conditions for a phase change in the scale of cooperation could be met by smart mob infrastructure: mutual monitoring, graduated sanctions, widespread dissemination of both positive and negative reputation information, ease of locating and verifying other potential cooperators, and global social networks that cluster people by affinity. In order for such an infrastructure to be everywhere, inexpensive, and always available, it is going to have to complete a passage that is presently underway, the transition to a wireless world.

The build-out of a planetary communication system in the form of wires, satellites, and optical cables took about a century. This build-out was largely a top-down enterprise, organized by telecommunication monopolies and regulated by government bureaucracies. Toward the end of the process, when a sufficient number of people were interconnected, bottom-up grassroots applications transformed the original wired infrastructure into entirely new phenomena like the Web, virtual communities, and p2p networks. The build-out of the wireless infrastructure, now in its final stages, is at present a cacophony of top-down and grassroots movements, standards, and industries. The telecommunications giants of the previous, wired epoch have staked their claims to the future in the form of expensive licenses for slices of the electromagnetic spectrum—the high-stakes, still iffy 3G era of mobile telephony. At the same time that the 3G dinosaur seems stalled in a mire of financial and technical difficulties, a nimble breed of mammal seems to be multiplying rapidly down there in the grassroots—the amateurs who have taken advantage of a loophole in the restrictive regulation of the radio spectrum to create shared wireless networks.

Wireless Quilts

Because nobody controlled what people did with the Internet, millions of people invented new things to do with the Internet. They innovated because they had a guaranteed right to publish web pages or start businesses or create applications like the World Wide Web. This explosive innovation happened because the Internet was held in commons—an innovation commons—instead of auctioned off. Policymakers, faced with the opportunity to create an innovation commons for the wireless Internet, want to sell the right to innovate to the highest bidder. We're at a critical point where we're choosing which path to go down, and the problem is that most people in wireless policymaking are control freaks. They're the Soviets of our time. They think the only way to run an economy is if the government decides who uses spectrum for what purposes. I fear that the Soviet mentality will destroy innovation here. Instead of top-down control, we need radical decentralized opportunity to innovate and create using this medium.

—Lawrence Lessig

Unwiring the World, One Neighborhood at a Time

I had heard übergeek friends rhapsodize about "wireless freenets" and something called "eight oh two dot eleven bee," but I never watched anyone pull an Internet connection out of the air until Lars Aronsson, instigator of Elektrosmog, flipped open his laptop and surfed the Web from a café near Stockholm's Sergel Square. Elektrosmog is one of the groups that materialized in dozens of cities around the world in 2000–2002 around the goal of connecting neighborhood wireless access points into "a cloud of free

Internet connectivity that will cover most inhabited areas."[1] When I returned from Stockholm in June 2001, I walked around San Francisco with a friend who downloaded streaming video to his computer from the atrium inside an office building where unsecured commercial wireless networks inadvertently extended their clouds of connectivity.

While I pursued my investigation of smart mobs, wireless networks were surfacing in places where computer users cluster—coffee shops. Recalling earlier links between smart mob experimentation and caffeinated conviviality, the PARCtab and Cambridge webcam coffeepots, I wasn't surprised to learn that wireless broadband startup MobileStar, in partnership with Microsoft, started installing wireless networks in hundreds of Starbucks coffee shops.[2] By February 2002, wireless access came to the café in my own suburban town, through a commercial enterprise called Surf and Sip.[3] Whether you seek corporate or co-op flavor of wireless broadband, the best way to find public wireless Internet access in a new city these days is to go where expensive coffee is served.

MobileStar's business ran into trouble at the end of 2001 and was purchased by telecommunications giant VoiceStream in 2002.[4] However, mergers and acquisitions in the telecommunications industry are not the only powerful influence on future smart mob infrastructure. While telephone companies eat and digest wireless broadband startups in the commercial arena, gangs of amateurs all over the world are quietly growing ad hoc networks from the neighborhood up.

Waiting for 3G services from the telephone companies of the world isn't the only way to access the Internet wirelessly and at high speeds, claims Lars Aronsson and his confrères in the community wireless movement. The tech news that had my übergeek friends buzzing, known formally as "wireless LANs" (local area networks) and "ad hoc peer-to-peer networks," precipitated a new community of homebrew innovators. Once again, a freemasonry of volunteers has a chance to build a new medium that increases in value when it is shared. This time, the people who use and create the infrastructure have an opportunity to own it.

Recent technical and regulatory events have made it possible for citizens to share wireless Internet access today at speeds higher than expected for 3G in the future. A radio beacon access point costs $100–$500, and a 1.5 megabit per second (T1) leased line to connect the beacon to the Internet costs around $500–$800 per month. Many laptop computers, equipped with easy to install 802.11b (wireless) cards, can use that wireless access point's Net connection simultaneously. More expensive, higher-speed Internet access through T3 lines or coaxial cable can support populations of wireless connections up to 5 megabits per second. (More about what those megabits mean in a moment.) New technology and social contracts make it possible for a relatively small number of people to do what used to require huge corporate monopolies.

Wireless LANs aren't a free lunch, but they make possible an extremely inexpensive lunch, and you can now pack your own lunch instead of buying only the monopoly brand. Someone has to buy a high-speed Internet connection from an existing ("upstream") provider in order to support a ("downstream") wireless community, but now the community of users has the power to do things that only the connection provider could do in the past. One other salient factor is a technique known as "voice over Internet Protocol," which makes it cost-effective to carry voice conversations on user-owned wireless networks.

Whether wireless guerrillas blanket the world with inexpensive high-speed Internet access before the big players crush them remains to be seen. Open wireless cooperatives have the advantage of starting with zero debt (it doesn't cost any more to provide "community" wireless access than it would to provide wireless access for your own home), whereas 3G providers are saddled with billions in startup costs from spectrum licenses to towers to rights-of-way. One thing that nobody disputes is that wireless technologies are a cost-effective way to bring high-speed Internet services to what is known as "the local loop" or "the last mile"—the connection between people's PCs or mobile devices and the fast fiber optic networks that pump data around the world at what are known as "broadband speeds." Wireless is undoubtedly the best way to bring online the majority of the world's population.

Wiring the world over the past century, from the telegraph to the Internet, disrupted old social patterns and led to the creation of new ones. Unwiring the world over the next decades will disrupt existing social arrangements just as profoundly, in several different ways:

- Untethering the Web colonizes the world with computation, pervading environments far from the desktop with networked intelligent devices. Computation, once available only through wired access points, becomes available everywhere.
- Telecommunications networks become available in places where wires weren't previously economically feasible. One in eight peo-

ple in Botswana have a mobile telephone.[5] Some of the most advanced wireless LAN experiments in the United States are on Indian reservations that don't have telephone lines.

- High data-speeds made possible by radio-based technologies are likely to multiply the effects of mobile Internet in unpredictable ways as well. In digital media, quantum leaps in speed often trigger qualitative jumps in the ways people use them.

Just as photography changes to cinema at 24 frames per second, and the Internet changed to the Web at tens of thousands of bits per second, broadband portends a transformation in the nature of the medium of mobile Internet. Broadband is about data transfer rates of tens of millions of bits per second. Combine high transfer rates, yesterday's supercomputer on today's chips, and p2p methodology, and many things presently unimagined become possible.

"802.11b" is a number I hear a lot when wireless freenetters talk. Also known as "WiFi," 802.11b refers to a technical standard, ratified by the FCC's Project 802 committee in 1999, about the way data can be sent via a small slice of the radio spectrum open for unlicensed use.[6] Although the use of most of the electromagnetic spectrum is restricted by governments for military and licensed commercial use, a small amount of available spectrum has been kept open for unlicensed use, which allows garage door openers, cordless telephone receivers, and guerrilla wireless networks to operate. A few visionaries at the FCC had been pushing to open some of the spectrum for experimentation since the early 1980s. A movement initiated by Apple Computer in the 1990s took advantage of this tiny loophole, which made it possible to set up base stations, plug an inexpensive card into a laptop, and provide Internet access at up to 11 megabytes per second (5 times faster than 3G, 150 times faster than a dial-up modem), within a few hundred feet of an access point connected to the Net (and up to tens of miles with inexpensive external antennae).[7] The lobbying process initiated by Apple succeeded in adding more bandwidth to the unlicensed spectrum, and in 1999 Apple introduced its "Airport" 802.11b networking software, which brought the price of an access point down to $300.

The bottom-up force of wireless freenetting and the top-down force of 3G mobile telephony are heading for decisive conflicts over the next five years. An eventual showdown has been inevitable since the U.S. government locked its regulatory framework onto a technical understanding of wireless technologies as it stood in 1912–1934. In response to the sinking of the Titanic, which involved various wireless communication snafus, the United States and other nations began regulating—and leasing—use of the electromagnetic spectrum. The Radio Act of 1927 allocated the radio spectrum to broadcasters through licensing, created a high-level regulatory authority, the Federal Radio Commission, and made unlicensed broadcasting a criminal offense. The Communications Act of 1934 added authority over telephone and telegraph communications and created the Federal Communications Commission.[8] The 1927 and 1934 laws established that airways are public property, that commercial broadcasters must be licensed to use the airways, and that the main condition for use is whether the broadcaster serves "the public interest, convenience, and necessity."[9]

Since only specialists understand (or even hear about) the fine points of wireless technologies and their regulatory implications, the big-boys-only business of selling the spectrum has largely been ignored by the citizens on whose behalf the transactions were executed.[10] Economist Ronald Coase, who later won a Nobel Prize, convinced the FCC that auctioning spectrum was more efficient and inherently more fair than the original license-granting procedure because it eliminated outright granting of licenses as political favors and insured that the owner of a spectrum license, having paid top dollar for it, would be motivated to develop the use of that spectrum allocation.[11] Top dollar in a public auction is indeed more open than political deal making. As a consequence, however, "public interest, convenience, and necessity" have been defined by those with the largest stake in yesteryear's technologies.

Recently, those who are knowledgeable about the law and about the state of the art of radio technologies are challenging the idea that chopping up the frequency bands into specific pieces of property is the most efficient way to use the resource. In a *Foreign Policy* article, Stanford law professor Lawrence Lessig wrote: "Americans are captivated by the idea, as explained by Yale Law School professor Carol Rose, that the world is best managed "when divided among private owners" and when the market perfectly regulates those divided resources. But the Internet took off precisely because core resources were not "divided among private owners." Instead, the core resources of the Internet were left in a "commons."[12] Keep in mind, that a commons in the spectrum would not necessarily replace the ownership of licenses for parts of the spectrum—large parts of the spectrum could be allocated to commons and to auctioned property. And the establishment of a commons doesn't rule out private enterprise. Plenty of private enterprises grew up around the Internet, and unlike the spectrum, no large chunks of the original Internet were sold for the exclusive use of one enterprise.

Telecommunication companies around the world paid more than $150 billion to various governments in the late 1990s for licenses to use portions of the electromagnetic spectrum for future commercial purposes such as broadband access for mobile phones.[13] At the same time that governments were auctioning off the electromagnetic spectrum, rapidly evolving wireless communication technologies started making it possible to treat the spectrum as abundant rather than scarce. Technologies known as "spread spectrum," "wideband," and "software-defined radio" have explosive implications. If the spectrum ceases to be a scarce resource because of technological innovation, then the government doesn't need to regulate its use to protect its owners, the citizens, in the same way it did when the spectrum was first regulated at the beginning of the radio age. The neighborhood wireless activists are up against powerful financial interests and political powers, from AT&T to the FCC. But they have Moore's, Metcalfe's, and Reed's laws on their side.[14]

In 1999 and 2000, geeks around the world started getting the same idea. Matt Westervelt in Seattle, a systems administrator for Real Networks, created a Web site with a map of his neighborhood in Seattle and invited anyone who put up a base station to mark it on the map.[15] In London, James Stevens established "Consume the Net" with the invitation: "Fed up with being held to ransom in the local loop, phased by fees to ISP's, conscious of community? OK so let's build a fresh network, one that is local, global, fast, expanding, public and user-constructed."[16] Instead of a telecommunications corporation, a consumer-owned cooperative corporation could govern these newly possible enterprises.

If all the infrastructure for a grassroots wireless network can be built from inexpensive, easily installable access points that radiate high-speed Internet access within several hundred feet, and if overlapping networks can cooperate in moving bits of data around the way the interconnected networks of the Internet do, then grassroots networks in an urban area could piece together what Lars Aronsson and others call a cloud of wireless Internet access. Usenet also started as a patchworked, peer-to-peer network in which each node paid its own way. Imagine a Usenet of inexpensive, low-power wireless access points that each serves hundreds of mobile devices in its vicinity.

If one thing unites the disparate WiFi activists, it's the conviction that they are asserting a right to a public good. The telephone wires, coaxial cables, satellites, and optical networks that brought us the first, wired phase of the Internet—a physical infrastructure that was created and owned by someone who charges for access to it—is not required for WiFi. Everybody owns the airwaves. You buy a radio or base station, and what you and your neighbors agree to do with them, including creating your own network of contiguous access points, is your business. Elektrosmog, Aaronsson wrote on the organization's Web site, "grew out of a skepticism toward the claims of the telecom industry regarding the usefulness and success of the future 'third-generation mobile telephone systems' (3G) as the only means to implement the wireless Internet."[17] Boston-centered Guerrilla Net's Brian Oblivion foresees a self-sufficient infrastructure that "requires a networking fabric which lies outside of governments, commercial Internet Service Providers, telecommunications companies, and dubious Internet regulatory committees.[18] Or, as WirelessAnarchy puts it: "Cheaply and easily, using off-the-shelf equipment and a little ingenuity, you too can create your own net. It's wireless, it's anarchy, it's your ISP's worst nightmare."[19]

Anthony Townsend, research scientist at New York University's Taub Urban Research Center, takes a more civic than anarchic approach to wireless networking: "We're trying to build a public service," he told me during a 2002 telephone interview.[20] Townsend teamed up with Terry Schmidt to open the first node of their network in May 2001 at a coffee shop near Schmidt's apartment.[21] NYCWireless now provides free broadband wireless access in more than thirty "hotspots" in New York City, including Washington Square Park, Tompkins Square Park, and MacDougal Street in the West Village.[22] As an urban planner, Townsend is particularly interested in the way WiFi affects the way people use public places, and he remains confident that informed designers can nudge the effects of WiFi on cities toward the convivial and away from the alienating.

NYCWireless members realized that Bryant Park would be a perfect place for an experiment in designing public communication infrastructure in "ways that help drive community formation," Townsend told me. Outdoor movies in the summer draw thousands of people. During the daytime in pleasant weather, workers from nearby offices bring their laptops and cell phones and work in the park. NYCWireless, in partnership with the Bryant Park Restoration Corporation, is launching free wireless broadband in the park and designing opt-in "buddy lists" that would enable local people to know when their friends are logged in from the park.

NYCWireless was part of an application for an Urban Empowerment Zone grant to bring wireless broadband and computers to low-income neighborhoods in Yonkers.[23] Townsend sees wireless networks, whether they are financed as cooperatives, nonprofits, or commercial enterprises, as opportunities to "learn how to use technology to create new connections between people, instead of isolating them."[24] NYCWireless is building alliances with community groups and developing an infrastructure "built around certain core values: community oriented, low barrier to entry, privacy conscious and secure, utilize social contract and social expectations, and provide common ground for interactions."[25] Mark Schultz, a senior associate of law firm Baker and McKenzie who works on legal issues pro bono for NYCWireless, says, "You have to wonder whether it's going to be part of the infrastructure of the future, just like the streets or the electricity or the sewers and everything else. Whether Internet access is something we're all just going to have ubiquitous access to. That would be cool. And this may be a first step to that."[26]

After September 11, WiFi performed a service nobody had anticipated. For weeks after the attack on the World Trade Center, businesses in lower Manhattan lacked Internet access, due to the massive destruction of both wired and wireless infrastructure. Then people like Nathaniel Freitas at a company called ThinAirApps started seeking alternatives.[27] Freitas looked out his office window, saw the logo of a dotcom that had recently gone out of business, and out of desperation, sent email to an address listed on the dotcom's Web site. Tristan Stoner, a VP at INTV, the company that had purchased the defunct dotcom's access, offered to share INTV's working business-grade connection. They set up a line of sight WiFi connection, and Freitas's fifty employees were back online. Around the same time, NYCWireless was contacted by Blink.com, another company that had lost Internet access. Townsend posted a plea online and received permission to put an antenna up on a neighborhood building that housed a small Internet Service Provider (ISP). Ricochet, a wireless modem network that had been shut down when its owner, Metricom, filed for bankruptcy protection, temporarily reactivated its network for the use of emergency workers near ground zero.

In the San Francisco Bay Area, a resource center and interest group for wireless activists grew out of PlayaNet—instant broadband infrastructure for a temporary autonomous zone in the middle of nowhere.[28] Every year, 25,000 dionysiac technogeeks gather for a collective art ritual in the Nevada desert, the Burning Man festival, constituting the fifth-largest city in Nevada for a week.[29] Burning Man has dozens of radio stations and its own WiFi network, one of the earliest. PlayaNet gave birth to the Bay Area Wireless Users Group (BAWUG), which maintains a mailing list of over a thousand and sponsors monthly meetings. BAWUG member Cliff Skolnick publishes a map of voluntarily open WiFi networks in the San Francisco area (which is how I discovered that p2p maven Cory Doctorow had moved from Toronto). According to Doctorow, "BAWUG's online how-to is the wireless guerrilla's bible."[30] SFLan's manifesto proclaims: "Imagine a citywide wireless LAN that grows from anarchistic cooperation."[31]

When I started getting up to speed on the WiFi movement, I paid a visit to Tim Pozar, whom I had known since the days he was involved in connecting the grassroots computer bulletin board network Fidonet to the Internet. One of the founders of BAWUG, Pozar is planning what he calls a "Neighborhood Area Network" that could cover a large part of the San Francisco Bay Area; Pozar and his "Sunset Network" colleagues are quietly obtaining rights to place $2,000 high-quality wireless access points on San Francisco hilltops.[32] Directional antennae for longer-range WiFi, it turns out, can be made easily with the right kind of Pringles potato chip can.[33]

Tool-sharing, the fundamental principle of the original ethical hackers, is one of the ways grassroots groups accelerate growth of the movement. Internet technology publisher and conference organizer O'Reilly Associates maintains an online cookbook and published a book on *Building Wireless Community Networks*.[34] The NoCat Community Wireless Network Project in Sonoma County, California, is creating a Linux program and open source "centralized authentication code" that will make it easy for a member of one wireless cooperative to seamlessly use another network's bandwidth. Personal Telco Project in Portland, Oregon, proclaims: "By creating, packaging, and disseminating Open Source tools, documentation, and community support, we are building citywide networks which are open to, and maintained by, the public."[35]

WiFi might thrive as a commercial industry. Sky Dayton, who founded the third most successful ISP, EarthLink, at age twenty-two, announced in December 2001 that he was starting a new business named "Boingo."[36] Boingo bootstrapped itself by aggregating more than 400 existing hotspots.

Boingo provides access to any subscribers of those hotspots who pay up to $75 per month, and Boingo shares the revenues with the ISPs. Dayton is aiming for 5,000 hotspots by the end of 2002. Korea Telecom is planning to roll out 10,000 WiFi Hotspots, and in Japan, one service, WIS-net, signed up 9,000 subscribers the first month.[37] Other wireless ISP aggregators have followed. A report commissioned by IBM in 2002 predicted that the number of North American hotspots will grow to 151,000 sites by 2008.[38]

Whether or not wireless Internet access becomes a profitable business, the success of WiFi as a tool within industries was assured when Federal Express Corporation started equipping its delivery fleet with WiFi networks that transmit encrypted broadband data when a truck nears a terminal and senses a hotspot.[39] UPS is also deploying 802.11b wireless LANs in all its distribution centers worldwide.[40] Ephraim Schwartz, *InfoWorld*'s mobile computing pundit, forecast in December 2001 that "as WiFi gets incorporated into corporate networks, gets deployed in public places, and even becomes part of the design and construction of new homes, VOIP (voice over IP) will become the killer app that closes the deal for WiFi installation."[41] Any lingering doubts that some form of 802.11b would not break out of the homebrew freemasonry were erased when Bill Gates made this pronouncement at a Microsoft developer's conference: "Microsoft expects 802.11b and its supersets to be present in most places that people spend time. In corporate offices it will be pervasive. In campuses, hotels, convention centers, airports, shopping centers; virtually everywhere this 11 megabit and up capability will be there."[42]

WiFi technology and its regulation have problems, serious ones, that must be overcome if it is to break out of the homebrew hobbyist world and become a mass medium. The fact that my friend could download streaming video in the atrium of San Francisco office buildings highlights one of the barriers to commercial WiFi success. So many businesses have installed unsecured, wide-open wireless networks that the name "war driving" has been adopted to describe the practice of roaming with a laptop and antenna in search of open networks (the name comes from "war dialing," a hacker practice of dialing random numbers in search of unsecured dial-up systems).[43] Computer security consultant Peter Shipley identified eighty open networks by driving around downtown San Francisco for an hour.[44] A member of NYCWireless found 1,400 open networks in a portion of midtown Manhattan.[45] Not only are such networks open to "borrowing" or monitoring by unauthorized users, but the confidential information communicated on those networks is crackable, too. Data communications security implemented in the first versions of WiFi software was proven insecure in 2001; software available on the Internet named "AirSnort" made it possible even for technical novices to engage in "whacking"—wireless hacking.[46]

Grassroots networks face another barrier. Users who share their Internet connectivity might be violating the user's agreement with their provider. "This would be akin to stealing cable," said an AT&T Broadband representative, and sharing a Time-Warner cable Internet account through WiFi "would be a violation of the agreement . . . and might subject that customer to federal and state penalties," said a Time-Warner representative.[47] However, one hundred people can share a commercial-grade Internet connection and divide the cost among themselves. NYCWireless and others work with upstream providers who are happy to sell them high-speed Internet access for redistribution. The very inexpensive lunch comes in with the dramatically lower costs of redistributing bandwidth once it is available from the upstream service provider. It's as if the telephone wires between your local telephone switching center and your home became obsolete.

Electromagnetic frequency interference is another technical matter that carries political consequences. When the United States began regulating radio, the radio receivers of the time lacked the capabilities available today. If two broadcasters in the same region use frequencies that are close together, receivers have trouble distinguishing the two broadcasters. Careful regulation of radio and television broadcasters was necessary to make sure that no more than one had a license to broadcast at a given frequency in a geographic region. However, the entire basis of frequency regulation was called into question when "smart radios" came along and suddenly millions of broadcasters became possible in the space where only one could exist before. (More about this technology in a minute.) Another barrier to WiFi (and one that the 3G interests are likely to use against it) is that under FCC regulations, the modification of unlicensed equipment (like adding a Pringles can) is illegal.

Finally, one key public health matter that WiFi designers must address if the technology is to be widely adopted is radio frequency radiation. The radios operate on the same frequencies as microwave ovens, and a powerful access point emits as much radiation, within one or two feet, as a microwave oven.[48]

WiFi security, radiation, and interference problems might be solvable, or WiFi might be a dead end or transitional technology. In any case, the companies that paid $150 billion for licenses to use the spectrum in the old way are not strongly motivated to come up with an entirely new way to allocate spectrum. Technical and regulatory barriers have one weakness, however: They attract people who like to break through barriers.

Tonga, Mongolia, the Rez, and Wales: The New Electronic Frontiers

Colonel Dave Hughes, USA, Ret., is the only character who has popped up in the plot every time I've investigated the roots of a technology revolution. In 1983, exploring the brave new world of the 300 bit per second modem, I encountered him on the Source, a pre-Internet online meeting place. A West Point graduate who had commanded combat troops in Korea and Vietnam, Hughes retired to Colorado and became fired up about the democratic potential of personal computers and modems.[49] In 1992, when I was documenting the world of virtual communities, I learned that Hughes was introducing the Internet to Indian reservations and the Big Sky Telegraph system in rural Montana, so I made a pilgrimage to Hughes's Internet-equipped booth in Rogers' Bar in Old Colorado City to interview him.[50] I have seen Dave Hughes a dozen times, and I've never seen him without his Stetson. He has a twinkle in his eye and a wicked grin when you see him face to face, but otherwise, Hughes is as take-no-prisoners pugnacious offline as he is notorious for being online. I offer these details in support of my suspicion that if anyone can mount a frontal assault on or outflank the FCC, it's Hughes.

In 2002, I learned that Hughes was involved in wireless broadband on Indian reservations, in Mongolia, and in Wales. In a documented and thoroughly public scheme with wireless activist and entrepreneur Dewayne Hendricks, distinguished law professor and activist Lawrence Lessig, the National Science Foundation, and several sovereign Indian reservations, Hughes just might force the FCC to change the way the electromagnetic spectrum is regulated.

I telephoned Hughes in 2002 and asked him why he started experimenting with wireless. "From the beginning, I've looked for ways to make grassroots communications affordable in rural communities," he answered.[51] Community was always central to Hughes's schemes. As he told Lawrence

Lessig, his motivation was "community—not politics, not business, not government—community in all its parts."[52] And the telephone-based business model wouldn't work for the rural communities that concerned Hughes. "Telephone-based dial-up modem access to the Net is too expensive if you have to dial in from a hundred miles away. I started looking at packet radio as a way to get around these costs," Hughes recalled in our telephone conversation. As a way around the problem, he found a radio technology called "spread spectrum," which is used in the industrial, scientific, and medical portion of the spectrum where people can operate without a license—802.11b territory. He started connecting rural schools with wireless, saving them thousands of dollars per month in "local loop" costs.

When Hughes told me that the idea of "frequency-hopping, spread-spectrum" radio first occurred to actress Hedy Lamarr while she played four-handed piano, I knew I was in for a tale. Sure enough, Lamarr was born Hedwig Maria Eva Kiesler, an Austrian aristocrat, famous as a teenager for being "the most beautiful girl in the world."[53] She was married to an Austrian arms merchant who did business with the German government prior to World War II. Her husband was so possessive that he forced her to attend his technical meetings with the German military. Unhappy with her marriage and the Nazi regime, Hedwig drugged her maid, escaped to England and then to Hollywood, where she became Hedy Lamarr. One night, while playing four-handed piano with avant garde composer George Antheil, she thought of a way to solve the problem of radio-guided torpedoes.

Lamarr recalled from her ex-husband's meetings that the Germans were unable to guide torpedoes with radio signals because the target ship could jam the signals by broadcasting on the same frequency. Lamarr suddenly wondered if there was a way to send a chunk of your signal on one frequency and then hop to a completely different frequency for the next part of the signal. With both the transmitter and the receiver synchronized regarding which frequencies to hop to next—a little like playing four-handed piano—the signal would resist jamming. She thought the transmitter and receiver could be synchronized mechanically, using something like a piano roll. On August 11, 1942, Lamarr and Antheil were awarded U.S. Patent Number 2,292,387 for the Secret Communications System.[54] The U.S. Navy tried to make it work, but mechanical controls using paper tape were inadequate. In 1958, the Navy pulled out the old patent and used electronics to synchronize the frequency hopping. By the 1960s, spread-spectrum radio communications of several different kinds, starting with Lamarr and Antheil's frequency-hopping patent, formed the basis for U.S. military communications.

The military reserved the right to spread-spectrum applications. GPS satellites, another smart mob–enabling technology that originated with the U.S. military, use spread-spectrum (but not frequency-hopping) technology.[55] In 1985, the military allowed the FCC to open up spread-spectrum radio manufacturing for use in specific frequency ranges ("bands"). In broader and different bands of frequencies than WiFi is permitted, spread-spectrum radio technology became the basis for many cellular telephone systems. By the end of the 1990s, the necessary equipment grew affordable by hobbyists.

I remember seeing Hughes and wireless pioneer Dewayne Hendricks at a meeting at Apple Computer in the early 1990s. The meeting was sponsored by Steve Cisler, Apple's evangelist to libraries and the public service community. Cisler brought together the people from around the world who were trying to combine virtual communities and local civic institutions to create "community networks." Although community networkers were working with the pre-Web wired Internet and slow modems, Cisler invited Hendricks, who had started a wireless networking company, Tetherless Access, a good ten years before 802.11b opened up wireless networking. Hendricks and Hughes were both exploring radio-based means of providing Internet access to remote areas, following some of the work pioneered by amateur radio ("ham") operators. In 2002, Hendricks reminded me in personal communication that "hams picked up a lot of the DARPA research in survivable packet radio networks and turned it into a device that allowed a radio and computer to be connected in an affordable fashion, enabling amateurs to construct self-routing packet radio networks. Hams were the first to show the value and utility of wireless community networking."[56] Hendricks pointed out in our recent communications that ham radio operators have had a little-publicized global wireless data communication network running for some time—which came into play after the terrorist events of September 11 to support emergency communications in lower Manhattan.

In 1996, the U.S. State Department and the National Science Foundation, seeking to promote democracy and a good business climate in Mongolia as it emerged from communist rule, heard about Hughes's experiments with wireless Internet access in rural Colorado and asked him to

bring wireless broadband to Ulan Bator. Hughes knew just who to contact—Dewayne Hendricks, who went to Mongolia and networked seven
institutions, up to ten kilometers away from the country's sole Internet
feed, in ten days.

His experience in Mongolia gave Hendricks the idea that he could experiment with new technologies that could provide even higher bandwidth
and greater distances by finding sympathetic partners outside the FCC's
jurisdiction. In 1998, Hendricks was introduced to the Crown Prince of
Tonga. Because the policy regarding use of the electromagnetic spectrum
in Tonga is whatever the Crown Prince says it is, Hendricks's Tonga company, licensed in Tonga as a common carrier, will be free to experiment
with technologies and power levels prohibited by FCC regulation. Then, as
Hendricks told a *Wired* magazine writer, "I learned about an FCC initiative to improve communications services on Indian reservations, and it
dawned on me that 551 sovereign nations were close at hand."[57]

While Hendricks was unwiring North American Indian reservations,
Hughes paid a visit to the land of "nine generations of rebellious Welsh
minister" forebears. At a New Year's Eve celebration in a pub, Hughes recalled, "I realized that most of the Welsh population lived within wireless
range of a pub. A couple of hundred dollars per pub, easy install, and you
have instant national broadband infrastructure for a country 50 miles wide
by 150 miles long."[58] An activist from Wales came to Old Colorado City to
videotape Hughes proclaiming his vision for the future of Welsh telecommunications. The video is online—a remarkable combination of tour,
demo, how-to, and polemic.[59] In the activist's video, Hughes emphasizes
the same benefit to local small businesses he pushes in rural Colorado:
Wireless broadband isn't just bringing more things to consume and buy but
offers a channel to create, sell, and promote their local point of view to the
rest of the world. Hughes returned to Wales in February 2002, as a guest
of the Welsh Digital College, to evangelize Welsh movers and shakers.
While the United States and other nations tie up the development of their
communication systems because of the investment by telephone companies in 3G licenses, watch places like Wales to see the future media sphere
emerge first. Or visit Okinawa, which some policy analysts in Japan are
pushing to become a "radio haven" for the development and deployment
of advanced wireless technologies.[60]

Under National Science Foundation sponsorship, Hendricks is attempting to bring wireless broadband access to the Turtle Mountain, Fort

Berthold, Fort Peck, and Sitting Bull community colleges.[61] In these communities, basic voice communication infrastructure is nonexistent. Wireless broadband can bring telephony to the reservation along with high-speed Internet access to its educational institutions at a fraction of the cost of "wireline" telephones alone. Hendricks is collaborating with researchers at the University of California, San Diego, who have deployed solar-powered relays to bring wireless broadband to the La Jolla and Pala Native American reservations.[62] Investigators reported that the high-speed wireless network using 802.11b access points "proved to be very cost effective and relatively easy to install when compared to wireline options. For one thing, installation took months instead of years and a few hundred thousand dollars instead of a few million dollars."[63]

Because Hendricks intends to use new technologies that are currently prohibited at higher power levels and in wide bands of the spectrum, his partners on the reservations are prepared for possible conflict with the FCC. One of these technologies, "wideband," doesn't focus on a single frequency but transmits encoded pulses, each a billionth of a second long, across the entire spectrum, at extremely low power levels—literally in the background noise of radio technologies that concentrate on specific frequency bands. If each transmitting device can share the common resource of spectrum by transmitting during a billionth of a second when no other device is using it, and the receivers are smart about what to listen for, a gargantuan amount of spectrum room becomes available for sharing bandwidth. Some researchers believe ultrawideband data transmission could achieve gigabit speeds—a billion bits per second.[64] Gigabit wireless would turn the present technological, regulatory, and economic regime of networked communications upside down. Today, a T1 line is 1.5 megabits per second—1/666 of 1 gigabit per second—and costs $1,000 a month or more.

The FCC, the military, and emergency services fear that a major potential problem with the new wireless technologies is "interference"—the danger that multiple broadcasters on the same frequency could make it difficult for receivers to distinguish one competing signal from another. As I'll discuss, this fear is based in part on the limitations of radio technology of the early twentieth century. However, caution is clearly in order when it comes to fire department, ambulance, military, and police communications and GPS devices. The FCC is properly worried that the noise from too many spread-spectrum users could interfere with emergency communications and threaten public safety. Technologists counter that the answer is not in regulation of spectrum but in improving the devices used to broadcast and receive signals. National security interests are also concerned that wideband technologies are difficult to intercept and easy to encrypt.

Hendricks, Hughes, David Reed, and Lawrence Lessig are part of a growing movement of advocates who would like to see much more of the spectrum opened, far beyond today's tiny experimental loopholes. Another technology that David Reed and Hendricks both mentioned to me, "dense-packet radio networks," has the valuable property of automatically growing carrying capacity as use expands, accommodating, potentially, billions of simultaneous transmissions in the same region. Indeed, an MIT student's doctoral thesis proved that efficiency of spectrum use can increase as the number of devices increases, provided they are smart devices that cooperate electronically to use the spectrum efficiently.[65] If you could buy a dense-packet radio receiver and turn it on, not only would you be turning on access to the Internet for you and your local network, but your receiver would serve as a relay for other nearby, similarly equipped transceivers. Your radio would act as a "router," picking those bits that are meant for it out of the stream and passing along all the others to the nearest other radio. The network's carrying capacity grows more plentiful and each radio needs to use less power as more people join the network, provided that each user serves as a relay for nearby routers—one of those "sheep shit grass" situations that economists describe more decorously as "the law of increasing returns."[66]

Within ten years, Intel intends to integrate "software-configurable radios" in every chip it manufactures; the way a software-configurable radio uses spectrum can be changed on the fly by the computer, so a single PC add-on could switch from being an FM radio tuner to a cell phone to an 802.11b card.[67]

Spread spectrum, wideband, software-configurable radios, and dense-packet radio networks don't exhaust the list of technologies competing to make traditional spectrum allocation obsolete. We're accustomed to thinking of our telephones, for example, as devices that plug into the telephone or cable company's network. What if the devices themselves could become the network? Dense-packet radio networks and other state-of-the-art but ahead-of-the-regulatory-structure technologies make possible fully ad-hoc, self-organizing, multi-hop mesh networks. Imagine telephones that directly communicate with each other, relaying signals from device to device the way Usenet nodes do, without using any other communication network other than the telephones that happen to be nearby.

Yet another new technology is known as "ad-hoc peer-to-peer networking." If any one node of what is also called a "mesh" network has a fat enough pipeline to the Internet, then the network of devices can cooperatively distribute the bandwidth. In a mesh network, each node also can serve other users simultaneously as infrastructure, like a cellular system without fixed cells that relays messages among telephones.

A company called MeshNetworks was funded by DARPA (today's successor to ARPA) to make it possible to "parachute two or three thousand soldiers in the middle of nowhere and have them instantaneously form an ad-hoc peer-to-peer network and communicate."[68] The company is planning a $35 chip that could serve as a wireless access point; telephones equipped with such chips could serve as relay stations for other nearby telephones. Imagine those 1,500 people in Shibuya Crossing, and the people within range of them, rippling out through Tokyo, using their telephones as the routers in an ad hoc communication network. Mesh technologies can transmit data at 6 million bits per second, enough for data, voice, Internet, audio, and video. In February 2002, the FCC granted MeshNetworks an experimental license to test their technology in limited frequency bands.[69] Nokia markets "wireless routers" based on mesh network technology in the unlicensed bands.[70] Strange as the notion seems, population densities and mobile telephone penetration in major metropolitan areas make self-sufficient peer-to-peer networks entirely possible.[71]

I wasn't surprised to discover teenagers growing mesh networks by putting their toys together. The "Cybiko handheld" is an inexpensive device for the youth market, created by a Russian company. Priced at around $100, Cybiko (Japanese for "cyber girl") devices combine a walkie-talkie, texting terminal, FM radio player, voice recorder, game and music player, email, and organizer.[72] Cybiko base stations can provide up to 200 Cybiko users with wireless Internet access, email, and instant messaging. America Online is one of the investors. As of this writing, over half a million first-generation devices are in circulation. The next generation incorporates protocols for ad hoc peer-to-peer networks.

Hidekazu Umeda created mobile peer-to-peer software protocols that DoCoMo and other traditional wireless service providers can't be happy about, since his mobile p2p software could turn all the mobile telephones, personal digital assistants, Cybikos, and other wireless devices in Tokyo into one giant ad-hoc network that moves voice and data around without the intermediation of the traditional telecommunication networks.[73] I met with Umeda and his colleague, Yuichi Kawasaki, after normal office hours in the Web design firm that employed them during the day. There was a slight irony to convening a discussion with hard-core digital revolutionaries in the rosewood-paneled presentation room on the seventeenth floor of Tokyo's posh Cerulean Tower. Kawasaki dreams of a mobile gift economy: "I'd like to see people able to use their mobile devices to swap data/games/music completely outside of centralized control. With technologies like Bluetooth, virtual communities could be formed purely by the exchange of data between mobile devices." In other words, they want to enable smart mob formation.

"Bluetooth" is the name of a standard for short-range radio communication chips that can link the broadband Internet to the ad hoc networks of devices in a computation-pervaded environment. It won't be a technology most people will use, but it will be inside devices most people will use. In 1994, Ericsson Mobile Communications started studying low-power, low-cost radio devices as a way to eliminate cables connecting mobile telephones, headsets, PCs, and printers.[74] The Bluetooth Special Interest Group, founded in 1998 by Ericsson, Nokia, Intel, IBM, and Toshiba, was joined by Microsoft and Motorola—almost everybody in telecommunications.[75] Whenever two devices equipped with Bluetooth chips are within ten meters of each other, they automatically open communication; each Bluetooth chip periodically broadcasts a query for other devices in the area. Just as boxy cathode ray tube computer displays are being replaced by flat-panel liquid crystal screens, cables will give way to short-range wireless chips over the next ten years. As a side-effect of replacing cables, Bluetooth chips enable the creation of local ad-hoc networks—the kind that pervasive computing devices will use.

The industry heavy-hitters who back Bluetooth anticipate widespread adoption of Bluetooth when the price per chip drops to $5. Like WiFi, Bluetooth technology must solve existing security and interference problems. Nevertheless, UPS plans to deploy Bluetooth, along with 802.11b LANs, in its worldwide distribution hubs.[76] Forrester Research analyst Lars Godell forecasts "235 million Bluetooth-enabled mobile phones, PDAs and laptops, versus 22 million WLAN-enabled devices" by 2006.[77] Bluetooth is the immediate-vicinity link connecting mobile devices and roaming people in a computation-pervaded environment, from your telephone to your PC to your printer to your MP3 player, to a vending machine. WiFi is the broadband zone at home, work, or the café where you can plug into the worldwide Net.

When it comes to wireless communications, however, politics is as important as technology.

Open Spectrum versus the Good Old Boys

Law professor and activist Lawrence Lessig has prepared a pro bono legal defense team for Dewayne Hendricks. They intend to challenge the legal basis of current spectrum regulation. Tribal colleges were informed by the project administrators that "Wireless technology raises questions about who controls the spectrum on reservations. Campuses that are interested in participating in the project need to demonstrate awareness that there could be problems with the Federal Communications Commission, local telephone companies, and others."[78] The early skirmishes in the battle for the electromagnetic spectrum have been joined.

One new radical idea is backed up by solid science: Abandon the idea of a regulated spectrum and dumb devices, say the advocates of "open spectrum," and turn the spectrum into a commons anyone can use as long as they use a broadcasting or receiving device that is smart enough to cooperate with all the other devices. Why not? That's exactly how, and why, the Internet worked so well. There is no central regulation of how the Internet's communication bandwidth is used, just a standard protocol for connecting.[79]

Regulate the devices, not the spectrum, say open-spectrum advocates, and create conditions for entrepreneurial innovation and broad economic benefits that extend far beyond the existing large corporations that now are the sole beneficiaries of spectrum regulation. To some, this position sounds vaguely communistic. "Are you a communist when you use your cordless phone? Because the unlicensed band your cordless phone uses is a little commons," retorts Dave Hughes, the last guy you'd want to call a communist to his face.[80] To complicate the issue, advocates of "open-source software-defined radio" are designing radios that can transmit and receive on any frequency and modulate with any scheme (i.e., AM, FM, spread spectrum), making it far more difficult to regulate devices, since modifications take place only in the software.[81]

During my journeys into cybersociology, I had discovered Elinor Ostrom's studies of commons that were not tragically mismanaged and encountered the notion of "public goods" in the experimental economics games probing cooperation. And Lawrence Lessig had referred to an "innovation commons" built into the Internet's end-to-end architecture. When the same notion showed up in the hot center of policy debate concerning wireless Internet regulation, another conceptual Schelling point in the smart mobs literature revealed itself. The commons is where smart mobs could gather; commons are what smart mobs have the potential to create and what they have to be careful not to overconsume.

I asked Lessig to explain what he meant when he said that the Internet was a public resource "held in common," rather than divided up among private owners. Lessig pointed to the difference between railroad and highway regulation. In a railroad, the individual cars have no intelligence, and only one train can be on a specific stretch of track at a time, so railroads must be carefully centrally coordinated. Automobiles, however, presumably have intelligent drivers who can figure out how to get where they need to go without colliding with other vehicles. Central coordination is no longer required. "The highway is a commons," Lessig explained. Everybody has access to the highway, nobody needs permission to use the highway system, anyone can start a trucking company and use the system. The devices that you can use on the highway commons are regulated—you can't drive a tank, and if you have no lights, you'll be pulled over. Lessig noted, in light of the railroad/highway comparison, "Regulation of spectrum could move from the world of railroads, where central coordinators have to figure out who uses the track when, to the world of highways, where smart devices figure out how to use their common resource as they actually want."[82]

New York University law professor Yochai Benkler proposed in a 1998 article that current technology puts the present rationale for licensing spectrum into question.

> The central institutional choice regarding wireless communications is whether to rely on centralized control by identifiable organizations, or on multilateral coordination among numerous users. On the one hand, it is possible to treat spectrum as a resource whose use must be centrally determined by someone with the power to decide how wireless communications equipment will be used in a given spectrum unit. That entity can either be "the owner" of the defined spectrum unit, if privatization is chosen, or the licensee operating within parameters set by the regulator, if licensing contin-

ues to be the rule. On the other hand, it is now technically possible to rely on standards and protocols to enable multilateral coordination of transmissions among equipment owners, without identifying any person whose choices trump those of all other potential users. The central question then is no longer how to allocate spectrum channels—how to decide who makes unilateral decisions about who may communicate using a frequency band and for what types of communications—but whether to coordinate by defining channel allocations. While the answer may be that we should permit a commons to develop alongside proprietary allocations, we will fail to permit that development if we continue to misperceive the choice at hand as one between licensing and exhaustive privatization.[83]

Benkler used the term "open spectrum" in the summer of 2001, and analyst Kevin Werbach, former counsel for New Technology Policy at the Federal Communications Commission, publicized it in Esther Dyson's influential *Release 1.0,* describing the coalition of technologists, academics, and legal activists emerging around the idea of deregulating spectrum.[84] The idea is not to do away with auctions but to mix several ways of allocating spectrum and then see which works best. Big players will be able to buy pieces of spectrum at auction, and other large amounts of spectrum will be held as a commons.

The regulatory aspects of WiFi are coming under pressure as Moore's Law reveals itself in the industry: Over the past thirty months, Intel has increased the communication capacity of its WiFi chip by 5,400 percent and dropped the price by 82 percent.[85] Sony is planning to put WiFi chips in every TV set and PC it sells in Japan, and Microsoft is planning a launch in the fall of 2003 for Mira, a wireless computer tablet with a WiFi Internet connection built in.

Lessig believes that WiFi is a sound start for a wireless commons, even with its imperfections. "People who say that 802.11b is an imperfect technology forget that it's always imperfect technologies that get people into this radical destabilizing mode of operation that eventually takes down the Goliaths of the era," he told me.[86] "Who said that modems crossing telephone lines to get access to computer networks were perfect technologies? They were slow and unreliable. But what that did, because it was not controlled, was create strong demand for much higher quality connections which drove adoption of the Internet. Imperfect but decentralized and free technologies are a critical way to induce innovation and grow the network."[87]

David Reed, during our lunchtime conversation at MIT in 2001, emphasized that "this is the worst time to allocate property rights to spectrum in ways that block others from using it."[88] Reed told me then that "ad-hoc wireless networks now can be designed so that capacity grows as the number of stations increases, and each station uses less power as the stations get closer together—a virtuous circle. Physics meets cooperation." Reed, who played an important part in facilitating innovation through the end-to-end architectural principle underlying the Internet, told Werbach, "We could have the greatest wave of innovation since the Internet (and probably bigger in impact, because more pervasive) if we could unlock the spectrum to explore the new possibilities."[89]

New technologies have a history of destroying the dominance of prior technologies or making them obsolete. Joseph Schumpeter claimed that "this process of Creative Destruction is the essential fact about capitalism."[90] Lessig reminded me of Machiavelli's counterpoint to Schumpeter: "Innovation makes enemies of all those who prospered under the old regime, and only lukewarm support is forthcoming from those who would prosper under the new."[91] Those who created an infrastructure in which the devices (telephones, televisions, and radios) are inexpensive and dumb, the network that connects the devices is highly specialized and expensive to install, and the service is sold on a metered basis (telephony, cable TV, and wired Internet access) are challenged by new enterprises in which cheap devices *are* the network, and no private enterprise owns the medium that carries their messages. The old telecommunications regime, if it is to survive, must either block challenging innovations politically, acquire the companies that challenge them, or change into different kinds of enterprises themselves. The market and the consumer have no obligation to remain loyal to obsolete technologies when something better comes along; just because Western Union had a large investment in telegraphy doesn't mean that telephony should have been prevented through regulation or legislation.

In his 2001 book, *The Future of Ideas,* Lessig proposed a mixed regulatory regime:

> The ideal mix in the short term would be a regime that had both a commons and a property component, with the property component subject to an important caveat. There would be broad swaths of spectrum left in the commons; there would be broad swaths that would be sold as [economist

Thomas] Hazlett proposes. But in light of the emerging technologies for sharing, even the spectrum sold as property would be subject to an important qualification: Other users would be free to "share" that spectrum if they followed a "listen first" protocol—the technology would listen to see whether a certain chunk of spectrum were being used at a particular time, and if it weren't it would be free for the taking.[92]

The regulatory regime that will shape the future of wireless technology is not the only crucial unsettled policy issue. Who will have control over the use of the cloud of personal information smart mob technologies transmit, as mobile and pervasive communications evolve and merge? In each of the converging technologies that constitute smart mobs, issues of control remain to be resolved.

- Many-to-many mobile communications, such as texting, empower cooperative bands of intercommunicants in urban spaces, whether they are teenagers in Tokyo or Helsinki, or as we'll see in the next chapter, political activists in Manila and Seattle.
- Wearable computing, open-source software, and encrypted communication provide a means of giving individuals more control over their personal data clouds.
- Tactics of distributed control, lateral cooperation, and governance through reputation create leverage in several different realms, from human communities sharing irrigation resources to super-computer swarms attacking diseases.
- The Internet, highways, public streets, parks, beaches, scientific findings, works in the public domain, and the electromagnetic spectrum produce more value for more people when they are held in commons and self-managed to prevent tragedy than when they are divided as private property and managed by Hobbesian authority.

Only the earliest signs of future smart mob behavior are observable as the constituent technologies leave the laboratory and enter the product cycle, but important clues to the future of political action can be found in what happened in Manila and Seattle in 2001.

Smart Mobs:
The Power of the Mobile Many

Bypassing the complex of broadcasting media, cell phone users themselves became broadcasters, receiving and transmitting both news and gossip and often confounding the two. Indeed, one could imagine each user becoming a broadcasting station unto him or herself, a node in a wider network of communication that the state could not possibly even begin to monitor, much less control. Hence, once the call was made for people to mass at Edsa, cell phone users readily forwarded messages they received, even as they followed what was asked of them.

Cell phones then were invested not only with the power to surpass crowded conditions and congested surroundings brought about by the state's inability to order everyday life. They were also seen to bring a new kind of crowd about, one that was thoroughly conscious of itself as a movement headed towards a common goal.

**—Vicente Rafael, "The Cell Phone and the Crowd:
Messianic Politics in Recent Philippine History"**

Netwar—Dark and Light

On January 20, 2001, President Joseph Estrada of the Philippines became the first head of state in history to lose power to a smart mob. More than 1 million Manila residents, mobilized and coordinated by waves of text messages, assembled at the site of the 1986 "People Power" peaceful demonstrations that had toppled the Marcos regime.[1] Tens of thousands of Filipinos converged on Epifanio de los Santas Avenue, known as "Edsa," within an hour of the first text message volleys: "Go 2EDSA, Wear blck."[2] Over four days, more than a million citizens showed up, mostly dressed in black. Estrada fell. The legend of "Generation Txt" was born.

Bringing down a government without firing a shot was a momentous early eruption of smart mob behavior. It wasn't, however, the only one.

- On November 30, 1999, autonomous but internetworked squads of demonstrators protesting the meeting of the World Trade Organization used "swarming" tactics, mobile phones, Web sites, laptops, and handheld computers to win the "Battle of Seattle."[3]
- In September 2000, thousands of citizens in Britain, outraged by a sudden rise in gasoline prices, used mobile phones, SMS, email from laptop PCs, and CB radios in taxicabs to coordinate dispersed groups that blocked fuel delivery at selected service stations in a wildcat political protest.[4]
- A violent political demonstration in Toronto in the spring of 2000 was chronicled by a group of roving journalist-researchers who webcast digital video of everything they saw.[5]
- Since 1992, thousands of bicycle activists have assembled monthly for "Critical Mass" moving demonstrations, weaving through San Francisco streets en masse. Critical Mass operates through loosely linked networks, alerted by mobile phone and email trees, and breaks up into smaller, tele-coordinated groups when appropriate.[6]

Filipinos were veteran texters long before they toppled Estrada. Short Message Service (SMS) messaging was introduced in 1995 as a promotional gimmick.[7] SMS messaging, free at first, remained inexpensive. Wireline telephone service is more costly than mobile service, and in a country where 40 percent of the population lives on one dollar a day, the fact that text messages are one-tenth the price of a voice call is significant.[8] A personal computer costs twenty times as much as a mobile telephone; only 1 percent of the Philippines' population own PCs, although many more use them in Internet cafés.[9] By 2001, however, 5 million Filipinos owned cell phones out of a total population of 70 million.[10]

Filipinos took to SMS messaging with a uniquely intense fervor. By 2001, more than 70 million text messages were being transmitted among

Filipinos every day.[11] The word "mania" was used in the Manila press. The *New York Times* reported in 2001:

> Malls are infested with shoppers who appear to be navigating by cellular compass. Groups of diners sit ignoring one another, staring down at their phones as if fumbling with rosaries. Commuters, jaywalkers, even mourners—everyone in the Philippines seems to be texting over the phone . . . . Faye Slytangco, a 23-year-old airline sales representative, was not surprised when at the wake for a friend's father she saw people bowing their heads and gazing toward folded hands. But when their hands started beeping and their thumbs began to move, she realized to her astonishment that they were not in fact praying. "People were actually sitting there and texting," Slytangco said. "Filipinos don't see it as rude any more."[12]

Like the thumb tribes of Tokyo and youth cultures in Scandinavia, Filipino texters took advantage of one of the unique features of texting technology—the ease of forwarding jokes, rumors, and chain letters. Although it requires effort to compose messages on mobile telephone keypads, only a few thumb strokes are required to forward a message to four friends or everybody in your telephone's address book. Filipino texting culture led to a national panic when a false rumor claimed that Pope John Paul II had died.[13]

Many Filipino text message jokes and rumors were political. Vicente Rafael, professor at the University of California, San Diego, sees Filipino texting culture as inherently subversive:

> Like many third world countries recently opened to more liberal trade policies, the Philippines shares in the paradox of being awash in the latest technologies of communication such as the cell phone while mired in deteriorating infrastructures such as roads, postal services, railroads, power generators and land lines. With the cell phone, one appears to be able to pass beyond these obstacles. And inasmuch as such infrastructures are state run so that their breakdown and inefficiencies are a direct function of governmental ineptitude, passing beyond them also feels like overcoming the state, which to begin with is already overcome by corruption. It is small wonder then that cell phones could prove literally handy in spreading rumors, jokes, and information that steadily eroded whatever legitimacy President Estrada still had.[14]

The "People Power II" demonstrations of 2001 broke out when the impeachment trial of President Estrada was suddenly ended by senators linked to Estrada. Opposition leaders broadcast text messages, and within seventy-five minutes of the abrupt halt of the impeachment proceedings, 20,000 people converged on Edsa.[15] Over four days, more than a million people showed up. The military withdrew support from the regime; the Estrada government fell, as the Marcos regime had fallen a decade previously, largely as a result of massive nonviolent demonstrations.[16] The rapid assembly of the anti-Estrada crowd was a hallmark of early smart mob technology, and the millions of text messages exchanged by the demonstrators in 2001 was, by all accounts, a key to the crowd's esprit de corps.

Professor Rafael sees the SMS-linked crowd that assembled in Manila as the manifestation of a phenomenon that was enabled by a technical infrastructure but that is best understood as a social instrument:

> The power of the crowd thus comes across in its capacity to overwhelm the physical constraints of urban planning in the same way that it tends to blur social distinctions by provoking a sense of estrangement. Its authority rests on its ability to promote restlessness and movement, thereby undermining the pressure from state technocrats, church authorities and corporate interests to regulate and contain such movements. In this sense, the crowd is a sort of medium if by that word one means the means for gathering and transforming elements, objects, people and things. As a medium, the crowd is also the site for the generation of expectations and the circulation of messages. It is in this sense that we might also think of the crowd not merely as an effect of technological devices, but as a kind of technology itself. . . . Centralized urban planning and technologies of policing seek to routinize the sense of contingency generated in crowding. But at moments and in areas where such planning chronically fails, routine can at times give way to the epochal. At such moments, the crowd . . . takes on a kind of telecommunicative power, serving up channels for sending messages at a distance and bringing distances up close. Enmeshed in a crowd, one feels the potential for reaching out across social space and temporal divides.[17]

The Battle of Seattle saw a more deliberate and tactically focused use of wireless communications and mobile social networks in urban political conflict, more than a year before texting mobs assembled in Manila. A broad coalition of demonstrators who represented different interests but were united in opposition to the views of the World Trade Organization planned to disrupt the WTO's 1999 meeting in Seattle. The demonstrators included a wide range of different "affinity groups" who loosely coordinated their actions around their shared objective. The Direct Action Network enabled autonomous groups to choose which levels of action to participate in, from nonviolent support to civil disobedience to joining mass arrests—a kind of dynamic ad hoc alliance that wouldn't have been possible without a mobile, many-to-many, real-time communication network. According to a report dramatically titled, "Black Flag Over Seattle," by Paul de Armond:

> The cohesion of the Direct Action Network was partly due to their improvised communications network assembled out of cell phones, radios, police scanners and portable computers. Protesters in the street with wireless Palm Pilots were able to link into continuously updated web pages giving reports from the streets. Police scanners monitored transmissions and provided some warning of changing police tactics. Cell phones were widely used.
>
> Kelly Quirke, Executive Director of the Rainforest Action Network, reports that early Tuesday, "the authorities had successfully squashed DAN's communications system." The solution to the infrastructure attack was quickly resolved by purchasing new Nextel cell phones. According to Han Shan, the Ruckus Society's WTO action coordinator, his organization and other protest groups that formed the Direct Action Network used the Nextel system to create a cellular grid over the city. They broke into talk groups of eight people each. One of the eight overlapped with another talk group, helping to quickly communicate through the ranks.
>
> In addition to the organizers' all-points network, protest communications were leavened with individual protesters using cell phones, direct transmissions from roving independent media feeding directly onto the Internet, personal computers with wireless modems broadcasting live video, and a variety of other networked communications. Floating above the tear gas was a pulsing infosphere of enormous bandwidth, reaching around the planet via the Internet.[18]

From Seattle to Manila, the first "netwars" have already broken out. The term "netwar" was coined by John Arquilla and David Ronfeldt, two analysts for the RAND corporation (birthplace of game theory and experimental economics), who noticed that the same combination of social networks, sophisticated communication technologies, and decentralized organizational structure was surfacing as an effective force in very different kinds of political conflict:

> Netwar is an emerging mode of conflict in which the protagonists—ranging from terrorist and criminal organizations on the dark side, to militant social activists on the bright side—use network forms of organization, doctrine, strategy, and technology attuned to the information age. The practice of netwar is well ahead of theory, as both civil and uncivil society actors are increasingly engaging in this new way of fighting.
>
> From the Battle of Seattle to the "attack on America," these networks are proving very hard to deal with; some are winning. What all have in common is that they operate in small, dispersed units that can deploy nimbly—anywhere, anytime. All feature network forms of organization, doctrine, strategy, and technology attuned to the information age. They know how to swarm and disperse, penetrate and disrupt, as well as elude and evade. The tactics they use range from battles of ideas to acts of sabotage—and many tactics involve the Internet.[19]

The "swarming" strategies noted by Arquilla and Ronfeldt rely on many small units like the affinity groups in the Battle of Seattle. Individual members of each group remained dispersed until mobile communications drew them to converge on a specific location from all directions simultaneously, in coordination with other groups. Manila, Seattle, San Francisco, Senegal, and Britain were sites of nonviolent political swarming. Arquilla and Ronfeldt cited the nongovernmental organizations associated with the Zapatista movement in Mexico, which mobilized world opinion in support of Indian peasants, and the Nobel Prize–winning effort to enact an anti-landmine treaty as examples of nonviolent netwar actions. Armed and violent swarms are another matter.

The Chechen rebels in Russia, soccer hooligans in Britain, and the FARC guerrillas in Colombia also have used netwar strategy and swarming tactics.[20] The U.S. military is in the forefront of smart mob technology development. The Land Warrior experiment is scheduled to field-test wearable computers with GPS and wireless communications by 2003.[21] The Joint Expeditionary Digital Information (JEDI) program links troops on the ground directly to satellite communications. JEDI handheld devices combine laser range-finding, GPS location awareness, direct satellite telephone, and encrypted text messaging.[22] Remember the DARPA-funded startup MeshNetworks from Chapter 6, the company whose technology enables military swarms to parachute onto a battlefield and self-organize an ad hoc peer-to-peer wireless network? Small teams of special forces, wirelessly networked and capable of calling in aircraft or missile strikes with increasing accuracy, were introduced by the United States and its allies in Afghanistan: netwar.

Examples later in this chapter demonstrate that smart mobs engaging in either violent or nonviolent netwar represent only a few of the many possible varieties of smart mob. Netwars do share similar technical infrastructure with other smart mobs. More importantly, however, they are both animated by a new form of social organization, the network. Networks include nodes and links, use many possible paths to distribute information from any link to any other, and are self-regulated through flat governance hierarchies and distributed power. Arquilla and Ronfeldt are among many who believe networks constitute the newest major social organizational form, after tribes, hierarchies, and markets. Although network-structured communications hold real potential for enabling democratic forms of decision-making and beneficial instances of collective action, that doesn't mean that the transition to networked forms of social organization will be a pleasant one with uniformly benevolent outcomes. Arquilla and Ronfeldt note the potential for cooperation in examples like the nongovernmental organizations that use netwar tactics for public benefit, but they also articulated a strong caution, worth keeping in mind when contemplating the future of smart mobs:

> Most people might hope for the emergence of a new form of organization to be led by "good guys" who do "the right thing" and grow stronger because of it. But history does not support this contention. The cutting edge in the early rise of a new form may be found equally among malcontents, ne'er-do-wells, and clever opportunists eager to take advantage of new ways to maneuver, exploit, and dominate. Many centuries ago, for example, the rise of hierarchical forms of organization, which displaced traditional, consultative, tribal forms, was initially attended, in parts of the world, by the appearance of ferocious chieftains bent on military conquest and of violent secret societies run according to rank—long before the hierarchical form matured through the institutionalization of states, empires, and professional administrative and bureaucratic systems. In like manner, the early spread of the market form, only a few centuries ago, was accompanied by a spawn of usurers, pirates, smugglers, and monopolists, all seeking to elude state controls over their earnings and enterprises.[23]

In light of the military applications of netwar tactics, it would be foolish to presume that only benign outcomes should be expected from smart mobs. But any observer who focuses exclusively on the potential for violence would miss evidence of perhaps an even more profoundly disruptive potential—for beneficial as well as malign purposes—of smart mob technologies and techniques. Could cooperation epidemics break out if smart mob media spread beyond warriors—to citizens, journalists, scientists, people looking for fun, friends, mates, customers, or trading partners?

Substitute the word "computers" for the words "smart mobs" in the previous paragraph, and you'll recapitulate the history of computation since its birth in World War II.

Lovegety and p2p Journalism

Organized conflict is undoubtedly a site of intensive cooperation. Humans enjoy cooperating to each other's benefit, as well, given the right conditions and payoff. Alexis de Tocqueville made an important observation in regard to early-nineteenth-century America:

> The best-informed inhabitants of each district constantly use their information to discover new truths which may augment the general prosperity; and, if they have made any such discoveries, they eagerly surrender them to the mass of the people. . . . Men attend to the interests of the public, first by necessity, afterwards by choice: what was intentional becomes an instinct; and by dint of working for the good of one's fellow-citizens, the habit and the taste for serving them is at length acquired.[24]

Elinor Ostrom and other students of common pool resource management (discussed in Chapter 2) have detailed the ways farmers, fishers, and foresters around the world devise ingenious social arrangements to balance cooperation and self-interest.[25]

Consider a few experiments on the fringes of mobile communications that might point toward a wide variety of nonviolent smart mobs in the future:

- "Interpersonal awareness devices" have been evolving for several years.[26] Since 1998, hundreds of thousands of Japanese have used Lovegety keychain devices, which signal when another Lovegety owner of the opposite sex and a compatible profile is within fifteen feet.[27] In 2000, a similar technology for same-sex seekers, the "Gaydar" device, was marketed in North America.[28] Hong Kong's "Mobile Cupid service" (www.sunday.com) sends a text description of potential matches who are nearby at the moment.[29]

- ImaHima ("are you free now?") enables hundreds of thousands of Tokyo i-mode users to alert buddies who are in their vicinity at the moment.[30]
- Upoc ("universal point of contact") in Manhattan sponsors mobile communities of interest; any member of "manhattan celebrity watch," "nyc terrorism alert," "prayer of the day," or "The Resistance," for example, can broadcast text messages to and receive messages from all the other members.[31]
- Phones that make it easy to send digital video directly to the Web make it possible for "peer-to-peer journalism" networks to emerge;[32] Steve Mann's students in Toronto have chronicled newsworthy events by webcasting everything their wearable cameras and microphones capture.[33]
- Researchers in Oregon have constructed "social middleware," which enables wearable computer users to form ad-hoc communities, using distributed reputation systems, privacy and knowledge-sharing agents, and wireless networks.[34]

In the fall of 2001, I visited the office of ImaHima in Tokyo's ultra-modern Ebisu Garden Place Tower. ImaHima founder, Neeraj Jhanji, was the only person in the office on a Saturday morning. The DoCoMo skyscraper I had visited the day before was visible through the window. Neeraj, twenty-nine, a native of India, remained in Tokyo after a stint with an international consulting firm. One sunny Saturday, walking alone in one of Tokyo's most popular and crowded districts, he wondered if any of his friends were nearby. "I looked at my phone and the answer seemed obvious," he told me.[35] Even without GPS location awareness, it would be possible to use the Internet to coordinate locations. At the time I spoke to Jhanji, ImaHima had won the prestigious Prix Ars Electronica, had been adopted as an official i-mode site, and had gained 250,000 users with a median age of twenty-five. ImaHima was planning to launch in European markets by 2002.[36]

Jhanji showed me how the service works. When you join, you fill out a profile and set up a buddy list similar to the kind used with Internet instant messaging; each person must give permission before someone else can know automatically where they are. You also list your favorite places. When you select the "update" link on your mobile's ImaHima menu, everyone on your buddy list knows, for example, that you are within a few blocks of Shibuya station and are free for lunch.

The just-in-time, just-in-place matchmaking service for strangers, an intriguing aspect of ImaHima, is also where the most caution is required. With young women in Tokyo being targeted on the street by solicitors for "hostess bars," no service could hope to attract any females without strict controls—nor would DoCoMo's strict policies allow a service to become a lucrative official i-mode site. "You can search through the list of your friends," Jhanji told me, "or you can ask permission to contact a stranger whose profile matches your request and who is nearby. But if you request permission to communicate and the other person denies your request, the system blocks you from communicating with that person again."

The ambience of the Manhattan location of Upoc differs sharply from the milieu of Ebisu Garden Tower. Upoc's building on lower Broadway is close enough to ground zero for the lingering stench to have been strong outside the building when I visited Upoc in November 2001. Upoc had used its own service as a virtual office in the days after the September attack. Upoc employee Alex LeVine sent a group SMS message to three dozen others employees immediately after he saw the second plane crash: "Do not go to work. Stand by for more directions."[37] Then he messaged nine employees already at work, telling them to evacuate. Although wireline telephone, cellular telephone, and email were all down, Upoc employees discovered that their text messaging service, based out of a server safely in New Jersey, stayed up and enabled them to regroup.

I met LeVine, Andrew Pimentel, and Upoc founder Gordon Gould in their office, a standard open-plan geek farm. It was heartening to see that at least a few rooms full of twenty-somethings in Aeron chairs still existed. Gould had been an enthusiastic participant in virtual communities. He knew the power of online social networks and noticed how today's teens have taken to mobile phones and pagers the way his generation had taken to computer keyboards. Upoc provides instant infrastructure for a smart mob, whether it is a group of shopping buddies, fans, families, political street theater, or affinities as yet undefined. The confusing clash of standards and services that has slowed the adoption of SMS services in the United States created an opportunity to provide a platform for mobile communities among users of different services. Register for Upoc on the Web, join an existing group, or start one of your own and invite your friends and family, and suddenly you can receive and broadcast text messages to your group, no matter what mobile telephone service they use or where they are located. Link up to your roving tribe from your desktop email and vice versa. More than 100,000 users have registered for hundreds of groups.[38]

I registered for an Upoc account and observed from afar for two weeks before I visited New York. I joined "nyc celebrity sightings," a mobile community of celebrity stalkers, and "nyc terror alert," which promised immediate messages in the case of terrorist attack. I also joined the "channel" for a youth entertainer named "lil bowwow" and received offers of tickets and opportunities to download lil bowwow's latest ringtone. After an afternoon of buzzing around California, feeling my phone buzz, and noting that Julia Roberts had been spotted in midtown Manhattan or that a fifteen-year-old lil bowwow fan in Brooklyn just got out of school, I switched to receiving my messages as email until I went to New York in person. Scanning the scores of messages exchanged every day in just a few groups made it clear that some kind of community ferment was underway.

"Communities started forming from the week we started testing the service," Gould told me.[39] Andrew Pimental, who had conducted Upoc's marketing research, added, "There are virtual cliques, groups of friends, enemies, grudges, gangs, fights, and double agents with multiple handles who spy in groups to make sure nobody is badmouthing them or their clique." Upoc members can set up groups in any of three ways—secret, private, or public. Anyone can join a public group. Private groups are listed in the directory, but people join by applying and can be expelled by the founder. Secret groups are not listed and are known only to their members.

I unexpectedly experienced the "nyc terror alert" in action. The next to last day of my stay in Manhattan, walking up Fifth Avenue toward a morning meeting, my pocket started buzzing. I looked at the screen of my mobile and learned that two minutes earlier, American Airlines flight 587 had crashed after takeoff from JFK. I immediately reserved a train ticket to Boston for the next day, in case the airports remained closed. It was another one of those living-in-the-future moments. I had become one of those people I had first observed at Shibuya Crossing a year and a half earlier. My pocket buzzed again. Another plane crash? No. A celebrity spotted in an upscale deli downtown.

What if smart mobs could empower entire populations to engage in peer-to-peer journalism? Imagine the impact of the Rodney King video multiplied by the people power of Napster. What if people beamed WearComp video to the Web, offering continuous views of breaking events that hitherto have been available only from Newscorp, AOL-Time-Warner, and Disney? Would it be possible to turn the table on the surveillance society and counter the media monopolies? What would be the effect on public opinion if thousands of WearComp-equipped citizens webcast all they saw and heard? Wild as it sounds, mobile squads of citizen telejournalists have already surfaced. Whether today's experiments will even make it onto the radar of the media giants remains to be seen, but the first stirrings of p2p journalism have already been reported in Toronto and Tokyo.

In 2000, WearComp researcher, innovator, and evangelist Steve Mann launched "ENGwear, an experiment in wearable news-gathering systems conducted by students and researchers at the Humanistic Intelligence Lab at the University of Toronto."[40] In the spring of 2000, Mann and a group of his students, all wearing computers equipped with "EyeTaps," which broadcast everything they saw and heard to the Web, showed up at a demonstration in Toronto called by the Ontario Coalition Against Poverty (OCAP). Violence broke out. Mann reported, "We, along with the journalists and various television crews, ran for cover. However, unlike the reporters, my students and I were still broadcasting, capturing almost by accident the entire event. Whatever we saw before us was captured and sent instantly in real time to the World Wide Web, without our conscious thought or effort."[41]

Mann claims that the WearComp journalist-researchers who made their first appearance at the OCAP demonstration could be a model for a wider movement, which could influence as well as chronicle events:

> WearComp represents a solution to this legacy of suppressed creativity and confining imagination in an age where ever-fewer sources of information seem to reach us, even as the conduits of information grow exponentially. What my students and I undertook in deciding to "cover" the OCAP protest was an experiment in media diversification. This is the process by which we merge our cyborg narratives with the demands of a growing cyberspace that we should, and one day will, be able to interact with and control. Facilitating

the individual's creation and broadcast of their own narratives and perspectives is an important part of wearable computing technology. . . .

What my students and I did—and continue to do—is something far more important than just providing "home movies" and "alternative" images for viewing on the Internet. We are also engaging in a process of cultural reclamation, where the individual is put back into the loop of information production and dispensation.[42]

Justin Hall, the journalist who helped me interview Shibuya youth, recently reported that Tokyo's G3 videophones, like the one I carried around Tokyo, make it possible to send video to a Web site in real time: "With the technology in place," wrote Hall, "it's only a matter of time before an important amateur news video is directly distributed to the web, or to ten friends with video-mail in a news chain letter. When that happens, this new form of news distribution will become the news, and then ultimately, it will be no big deal."[43]

Hall reported that some of the videophones offered digital editing capabilities and that a new service in Japan made it possible to post photos and text on the Web directly from a mobile phone. People already use weblogging software to "blog" in real-time from conferences and conventions (Chapter 5), continuously updating their Web pages through 802.11b connections.[44] Putting cameras and high-speed Net connections into telephones, however, moves blogging to the streets. By the time this book is published, I'm confident that street bloggers will have constructed a worldwide culture.

Mobile Ad Hoc Social Networks

Imagine my excitement, many months into my smart mob odyssey, when I came across a research report titled "When Peer-to-Peer Comes Face-to-Face: Collaborative Peer-to-Peer Computing in Mobile Ad Hoc Networks," from the "Wearable Computing Group" at the University of Oregon.[45] The Oregon group, assembled by Professor Zary Segall and led by Gerd Kortuem, had designed a test bed for smart mobs around the same time I began to believe such a development was possible.

"Mobile ad hoc social network" is a longer, more technical term than "smart mob." Both terms describe the new social form made possible by the combination of computation, communication, reputation, and location awareness. The *mobile* aspect is already self-evident to urbanites who see the early effects of mobile phones and SMS. *Ad hoc* means that the organizing among people and their devices is done informally and on the fly, the way texting youth everywhere coordinate meetings after school. *Social network* means that every individual in a smart mob is a "node" in the jargon of social network analysis, with social "links" (channels of communication and social bonds) to other individuals. Nodes and links, the elements of social networks made by humans, are also the fundamental elements of communication networks constructed from optical cables and wireless devices—one reason why new communication technologies make possible profound social changes.

The Wearable Computing Group specializes in exploring the community aspects of wireless, wearable, and peer-to-peer technologies. Kortuem agreed with my assessment when I called him to talk about the research at the University of Oregon. "When I talk about community," he told me, "I mean both the users who form social networks when they interact personally and communities of developers, like the open source community, where each member shares ideas and contributes to building something larger."[46] In Oregon, Toronto, Pittsburgh, Atlanta, Palo Alto, and Tokyo, small bands of researchers are beginning to walk around the same geographic neighborhoods while wearing intercommunicating computers.

Kortuem and colleagues realized that p2p computing and wireless networking technologies made it possible to design ad hoc networks of mobile devices to support the ad hoc social networks of the people who wear them. The fundamental technical unit cited by Kortuem and other wearable computing researchers has come to be known as the "personal area network," an interconnected network of devices worn or carried by the user. The concept was first described by Tom Zimmerman, now at IBM's Almaden Research Center, who had invented the VR "dataglove" while he was an MIT student.[47]

Kortuem and colleagues treat the personal area networks as building blocks of a dynamic community of networks with emergent capabilities of its own. The research is as much behavioral as it is computational, beginning with simple experiments matching properties of mobile computing networks with the needs of social networks. The community of personal area network users within geographic proximity, for example, could serve as a wireless mesh network, dynamically self-organizing a cloud of broadband connectivity as nodes came in and out of physical proximity, providing always-on Internet connections to members. Using Bluetooth and other short-range wireless technologies such as very-low-power wideband radio, individual members of the community could engage in more intimate and timely information exchanges when face to face, whereas WiFi technologies could provide the infrastructure for neighborhood-wide and Internet-wide communication:

> Mobile ad hoc systems provide opportunities for ad hoc meetings, mobile patient monitoring, distributed command and control systems and ubiquitous computing. In particular, personal area networks enable the creation of proximity-aware applications in support of face-to-face collaboration.
>
> Mobile devices like cell phones, PDAs and wearable computers have become our constant companions and are available wherever we go. . . . Personal area networks open the opportunity for these devices to take part in our everyday social interactions with people. Their ability to establish communication links among devices during face-to-face encounters can be used to facilitate, augment or even promote human social interactions.
>
> In some sense, an ad hoc mobile information system is the ultimate peer-to-peer system. It is self-organizing, fully decentralized, and highly dynamic.[48]

Short-range radio frequency links such as those used by Bluetooth chips and wearable computers create a sphere of connectivity within the immediate vicinity of the wearer. Paul Rankin, at Philips Research laboratory in England, wrote about the need for intermediary agents to negotiate transactions between the "aura" of one person and radio beacons in the environment, or another person's aura.[49] "Auranet" is what Jay Schneider, Kortuem, and colleagues named their "framework for structuring encounters in social space based on reputations and trust."[50] The wireless instantiation of a 12-foot information bubble around wearable computer users is a physical model of what sociologist Erving Goffman calls the "Interaction Order," the part of social life where face-to-face and spoken interactions occur.[51] Goffman claimed that the mundane world of everyday interactions involves complex symbolic exchanges, visible but rarely consciously noticed, which enable groups to negotiate movement through public spaces. Although people use the ways they present themselves to "give" information they want others to believe about themselves, Goffman noted that people also "give off" information, leaking true but uncontrolled information along with their more deliberate performance.

One form of information that people give off, called "stigma" by Goffman, is markings or behaviors that locate individuals in a particular social status. Although many stigma can have negative connotations, stigma can also mark positive social status. The information we give off by the way we behave and dress helps us coordinate social interaction and identify likely interaction partners. When the Interaction Order is formalized and modeled automatically in an Auranet, the social network and the technological network meet in a way that makes possible new capabilities such as automated webs of trust for ad hoc interactions—for example, assembling a carpool of trustworthy strangers when you drive downtown or seek a ride.

Kortuem et al., noting the lack of fully embodied "human moments" in purely virtual worlds, concentrated on ways to enhance the most basic sphere of human social behavior, the face-to-face encounters of everyday life. Indeed, the primary question asked by the Oregon researchers is the primary question regarding smart mobs: What can communities of wearable computer users do in their face-to-face encounters? At a technical level, the wearable devices can share bandwidth by acting as nodes in an ad hoc wireless network. The devices could exchange media and messages, similar to the way Napster and Usenet use links between individual nodes to pass data around. However, as soon as the members of the community allow their computers to exchange data automatically, without human intervention, complex issues of trust and privacy intervene—the unspoken norms of the interaction order. Kortuem et al. explored the social and technical implications of personal agent software, which filters, shields, and acts as a go-between for their users.

A number of social and technical barriers must be overcome in order for mobile ad hoc communities to self-organize cooperatively. Nobody is going to contribute their personal area network to a community internetwork unless they feel secure about privacy and trust—who snoops whom, and who can be counted on to deal honestly? Privacy requires data security, and security is complicated by wireless communications. Encryption techniques make secure wearable community infrastructure possible, but someone has to figure out how to build them. Trust means a distributed reputation system, which the Oregon group has prototyped. When you break down the interesting idea of mobile, ad hoc social networks into the elements needed to make it work in practice, a rich and largely undeveloped field for research opens.

Another experiment by the Eugene group mediates social encounters by comparing personal profiles automatically and alerting participants in a face-to-face encounter of mutual interests or common friends that they might not know about (a recommendation system for strangers).[52] Each social encounter of wearable computer users involving automatic exchanges of personal data, sharing of bandwidth, or passing of messages from others would necessarily involve individual computations of where each participant's self-interest lies in relation to a computation of the other party's trustworthiness. Kortuem et al. recognized this complex weighing of trust versus self-interest as an example of our old friend, the Prisoner's Dilemma, and designed an experimental system called WALID to test some of these issues, taking advantage of the fact that the Oregon wearable computing researchers lived and worked in the same general neighborhood in Eugene, Oregon:

> WALID implements a digitized version of the timeworn tradition of borrowing butter from your neighbor. You do a favor for others because you know that one day they will do it for you.
>
> With WALID two individuals use their mobile devices to negotiate about and to exchange real world tasks: dropping off someone's dry cleaning, buying a book of stamps at the post office, or returning a book to the local library.
>
> WALID employs personal agent software to find close-by community members and to negotiate the exchange of tasks. The agents maintain a user's task list, become fully aware of the locations and activities involved. When an encounter occurs, the agents produce a negotiation. If both users approve, a deal is struck.
>
> The role of the agent in a negotiation is to evaluate the value of favors and to keep scores. Having to run across town just to drop off someone's mail compares unfavorably with buying milk for someone if the grocery store is just a block away. Agents employ ideas from game theory to ensure that results of negotiations are mutually beneficial; they cooperate only if there is the opportunity to enhance the user's goals.[53]

In our telephone conversation, Kortuem noted that at the beginning of wearable computing research, the main goals involved either creating tools for professionals, such as maintenance and repair specialists, or creating tools to augment individuals, in the manner promoted by Steve Mann. "I came to realize," Kortuem told me, "that what is really interesting is not the technology of a specialized application at a job site, but what happens if ordinary people are empowered to use this technology and what effects might emerge when technology penetrates society."[54] These words will be worth remembering when millions of people carry devices that invisibly probe and cloak, reach out, evaluate, interconnect, negotiate, exchange, and coordinate invisible acts of ad hoc cooperation that create wealth, democracy, education, surveillance, and weaponry from pure mind-stuff, the way the alchemy of inscribing ever-tinier patterns on purified sand invokes the same forces from the same place.

Swarm Intelligence and the Social Mind

Massive outbreaks of cooperation precipitated the collapse of communism. In city after city, huge crowds assembled in nonviolent street demonstrations, despite decades of well-founded fear of political assembly. Although common sense leads to the conclusion that unanimity of opinion among the demonstrators explained the change of behavior, Natalie Glance and Bernardo Huberman, Xerox PARC researchers who have studied the dynamics of social systems, noted that a *diversity* of cooperation thresholds among the individuals can tip a crowd into a sudden epidemic of cooperation. Glance and Huberman pointed out that a minority of extremists can choose to act first, and if the conditions are right, their actions can trigger actions by others who needed to see somebody make the first move before acting themselves—at which point the bandwagon-jumpers follow the early adopters who followed the first actors:

> Those transitions can trigger a cascade of further cooperation until the whole group is cooperating.
>
> The events that led to the mass protests in Leipzig and Berlin and to the subsequent downfall of the East German government in November 1989 vividly illustrate the impact of such diversity on the resolution of social dilemmas. . . . The citizens of Leipzig who desired a change of government faced a dilemma. They could stay home in safety or demonstrate against the government and risk arrest—knowing that as the number of demonstrators rose, the risk declined and the potential for overthrowing the regime increased.
>
> A conservative person would demonstrate against the government only if thousands were already committed; a revolutionary might join at the slightest sign of unrest. That variation in threshold is one form of diversity. People also differed in their estimates of the duration of a demonstration as well as

in the amount of risk they were willing to take. Bernhardt Prosch and Martin Abram, two sociologists from Erlangen University who studied the Leipzig demonstrations, claim that the diversity in thresholds was important in triggering the mass demonstrations.[55]

Sudden epidemics of cooperation aren't necessarily pleasant experiences. Lynch mobs and entire nations cooperate to perpetrate atrocities. Decades before the fall of communism, sociologist Mark Granovetter examined radical collective behavior of both positive and negative kinds and proposed a "threshold model of collective behavior." I recognized Granovetter's model as a crucial conceptual bridge that connects intelligent (smart mob) cooperation with "emergent" behaviors of unintelligent actors, such as hives, flocks, and swarms.

Granovetter studied situations in which individuals were faced with either-or decisions regarding their relationship to a group—whether or not to join a riot or strike, adopt an innovation, spread a rumor, sell a stock, leave a social gathering, migrate to a different country. He identified the pivotal statistic as the proportion of *other* people who have to act before an individual decides to join them. Thresholds appear to be an individual reaction to the dynamics of a group.

One of Granovetter's statements yielded a clue to smart mob dynamics: "By explaining paradoxical outcomes as the result of aggregation processes, threshold models take the 'strangeness' often associated with collective behavior out of the heads of actors and put it into the dynamics of situations."[56] Smart mobs might also involve yet-unknown properties deriving from the dynamics of situations, not the heads of actors. Goffman's Interaction Order, the social sphere in which complex verbal and nonverbal communications are exchanged among individuals in real time, is precisely where individual actions can influence the action thresholds of crowds. Mobile media that can augment the informal, mostly unconscious information exchanges that take place within the Interaction Order, or affect the size or location of the audience for these exchanges, have the potential to change the threshold for collective action.

I started looking for ways to connect these congruent ideas operationally. How would they map onto an ad hoc social network of wearable computer users, for example? When my idea hunting brought me to "the coordination problem," a social dilemma that is *not* a Prisoner's Dilemma, separate ideas began to fit together into a larger pattern.

A coordination problem does not involve the Prisoner's Dilemma zero-sum game between self-interest and common resources but instead represents the quandary that confronts individuals who are ready to cooperate, but whose cooperation is contingent on the prior cooperation of others. Monitoring and sanctioning are important not simply as a way of punishing rule breakers but also as a way of assuring members that others are using common resources wisely. That is, many people are contingent cooperators, willing to cooperate as long as most others do (what Ostrom referred to as a "commitment problem"). Thus, monitoring and sanctioning serve the important function of providing information about others' actions and levels of commitment.

In *Rational Ritual: Culture, Coordination, and Common Knowledge,* Michael Suk-Young Chwe claims that public rituals are "social practices that generate common knowledge," which enables groups to solve coordination problems. Suk-Young Chwe writes: "A public ritual is not just about the transmission of meaning from a central source to each member of an audience; it is also about letting audience members know what other audience members know."[57] Everyone in a group has to know who else is contributing, free riding, and sanctioning in order to solve both free rider and coordination problems on the fly with maximum trust and minimum friction. This is the key to the group-cooperation leverage bestowed by reputation systems and many-to-many communications media.

Threshold models of collective action and the role of the Interaction Order are both about media for exchange of coordinating knowledge. Understanding this made it possible to see something I had not noticed clearly enough before—a possible connection between computer-wearing social networks of thinking, communicating humans and the swarm intelligence of unthinking (but also communicating) ants, bees, fish, and birds. Individual ants leave chemical trail markers, and the entire nest calculates the most efficient route to a food source from a hundred aggregated trails without direction from any central brain. Individual fish and birds (and tight-formation fighter pilots) school and flock simply by paying attention to what their nearest neighbors do. The coordinated movements of schools and flocks is a dynamically shifting aggregation of individual decisions. Even if there were a central tuna or pigeon who could issue orders, no system of propagating orders from a central source can operate swiftly enough to avoid being eaten by sharks or slamming into trees. When it comes to hives and swarms, the emergent capabilities of decentralized self-organization can be surprisingly intelligent.

What happens when the individuals in a tightly coordinated group are more highly intelligent creatures rather than simpler organisms like insects or birds? How do humans exhibit emergent behavior? As soon as this question occurred to me, I immediately recalled the story Kevin Kelly told at the beginning of *Out of Control,* his 1994 book about the emergent behaviors in biology, machinery, and human affairs.[58] He described an event at an annual film show for computer graphics professionals. A small paddle was attached to each seat in the auditorium, with reflective material of contrasting colors on each side of the paddle. The screen in the auditorium displayed a high-contrast, real-time video view of the audience. The person leading the exercise, computer graphics wizard Loren Carpenter, asked those on one side of the auditorium aisle to hold the paddles with one color showing and asked the other half of the audience to hold up the opposite color. Then, following Carpenter's suggestions, the audience self-organized a dot that moved around the screen, added a couple of paddles on the screen, and began to play a giant game of self-organized video Pong, finally creating a graphical representation of an airplane and flying it around the screen. Like flocks, there was no central control of the exercise after Carpenter made a suggestion. Members of the audience paid attention to what their neighbors were doing and what was happening on the screen. Kelly used this as an example of a self-conscious version of flocking behavior.[59]

Musician and cognitive scientist William Benzon believes that the graphical coordination exercise led by Carpenter and described by Kelly is similar to what happens when musicians "jam" and that it involves a yet unexplored synchronization of brain processes among the people involved:[60]

The group in Carpenter's story is controlling what appears on the screen. Everyone can see it all, but each can directly affect only the part of the display they control with his or her paddle. In jamming, everyone hears everything but can affect only that part of the collective sound that they create (or withhold).

Now consider a different example. One of the standard scenes in prison movies goes like this: We're in a cell block or in the mess hall. One prisoner starts banging his cup on the table (or on one of the bars to his cell). Another joins in, then another, and another, until everyone's banging away and shouting some slogan in unison. This is a simple example of emergent behavior.

But it's one that you won't find in chimpanzees. Yes, you will find them involved in group displays where they're all hooting and hollering and stomping. But the synchrony isn't as precise as it is in the human case.

And that precision is critical to my argument. That precision allows me to treat the human group as a collection of coupled oscillators. Oscillation is one of the standard and simplest emergent phenomena. Once a group has become coupled in oscillation, we can treat the group as a single entity. To be sure, there's more to music than simple oscillation. But oscillation is the foundation, the starting point, and all the elaboration and complexities take place within this framework.

In effect, in musical performance (and in dance), communication between individuals is pretty much the same as communication between components of a single nervous system. It's continuous and two-way, and it does not involve symbolic mediation. Think of Goffman's interaction order, but drop verbal communication from it. It is a public space that is physically external to the brains of participating individuals, but it is functionally internal to those brains.[61]

Kevin Kelly traced back the new theories regarding emergent properties to William Morton Wheeler, an expert in the behavior of ants.[62] Wheeler called insect colonies "superorganisms" and defined the ability of the hive to accomplish tasks that no individual ant or bee is intelligent enough to do on its own as "emergent properties" of the superorganism. Kelly drew parallels between the ways both biological and artificial "vivisystems" exhibit the same four characteristics of what he called "swarm systems":

- the absence of imposed centralized control
- the autonomous nature of subunits
- the high connectivity between the subunits
- the webby nonlinear causality of peers influencing peers[63]

Steven Johnson's 2001 book, *Emergence,* shows how the principles that Kelly extrapolated from biological to technological networks also apply to cities and Amazon.com's recommendation system: "In these systems, agents residing on one scale start producing behavior that lies on one scale above them: ants create colonies; urbanites create neighborhoods; simple pattern-recognition software learns how to recommend new books. The movement from low-level rules to higher level sophistication is what we call emergence."[64] In the case of cities, although the emergent intelligence resembles the ant-mind, the individual units, humans, possess extraordinary onboard intelligence—or at least the capacity for it.

At this point, connections between the behavior of smart mobs and the behavior of swarm systems must be tentative, yet several of the earliest investigations have shown that the right kinds of online social networks know more than the sum of their parts: Connected and communicating in the right ways, populations of humans can exhibit a kind of "collective intelligence." In the summer between my smart mob inquiries in Scandinavia and my expedition to Tokyo, my inquiries brought me to a fellow who seems to have discovered the underpinnings of group intelligence. Bernardo Huberman, formerly at Xerox PARC, now scientific director of Hewlett-Packard's Information Dynamics research laboratory, was doing intriguing research on the emergence of primitive forms of collective intelligence.

I visited Huberman in his office, located in the same Palo Alto complex as the CoolTown laboratory. Huberman is a master of thinking of new ways of looking at familiar phenomena, seeing computer networks as ecologies, markets as social computers, and online communities as social minds. Originally a physicist, Huberman presents his findings in pages of mathematical equations. When I visited him in his office, he seriously agreed that "the Internet enables us to building collective intelligence."[65] At PARC, he had directed investigations of "the ecology of computation." As soon as I told him about smart mobs, he jumped up and exclaimed, "The social mind!" And he dug out a chapter on "The Social Mind" that he had published in 1995. Huberman thought it useful to think of emergent intelligence as a social computation:

> Intelligence is not restricted to single brains; it also appears in groups, such as insect colonies, social and economic behavior in human societies, and scientific and professional communities. In all these cases, large numbers of agents capable of local tasks that can be conceived of as computations, engage in collective behavior which successfully deals with a number of problems that transcend the capacity of any individual to solve. . . . When large numbers of agents capable of symbolic-processing interact with each other, new universal regularities in their overall behavior appear. Furthermore, these regularities are quantifiable and can be experimentally tested.[66]

The interesting statement is the last one. There have been varieties of theories about the Internet as the nervous system of a global brain, but Huberman and colleagues have made clever use of markets and game simulations as computational test beds for experiments with emergent group intelligence. The fall that I visited Huberman, he and his colleagues had used "information markets" to perform experiments in emergent social intelligence and found that group forecasts were more accurate than those of any of the individual participants' forecasts.[67] In information markets, members trade symbolic currency representing predictions of public information. The Hollywood Stock Exchange, for example, uses the market that emerges from the trading of symbolic shares to predict box office revenues and Oscar winners. The HP research team makes the extraordinary claim that they have created a mathematically verifiable methodology for extracting emergent intelligence from a group and using the group's knowledge to predict the future in a limited but useful realm: "One can take past predictive performance of participants in information markets and create weighting schemes that will predict future events, even if they are not the same event on which the performance was measured."[68]

Decades ago, computer scientists thought that someday there would be forms of "artificial intelligence," but with the exception of a few visionaries, they never thought in terms of computer-equipped humans as a kind of social intelligence. Although everyone who understands the use of statistical techniques to make predictions hastens to add the disclaimer that surprises are inevitable, and one of the fundamental characteristics of complex adaptive systems is their unpredictability, the initial findings that internetworked groups of humans can exhibit emergent prediction capabilities are potentially profound.

Another research group that takes emergent group intelligence seriously is the laboratory at Los Alamos, where a group of "artificial life" researchers issued a report in 1998, "Symbiotic Intelligence: Self-Organizing Knowledge on Distributed Networks, Driven by Human Interaction."[69] The premise of this interdisciplinary team is based on the view proposed by some in recent years that human society is an adaptive collective organism and that social evolution parallels and unfolds according to the same dynamics as biological evolution.[70] According to this theory, which I will revisit in the next chapter, new knowledge and new technologies have made possible the evolution of the maximum size of the functioning social group from tribes to nations to global coalitions. The knowledge and technologies that triggered the jump from clan to tribe to nation to market to network all shared one characteristic: They each amplified the way individual humans think and communicate, and magnified their ability to share what they know.

The Los Alamos team, looking at some of the same characteristics of the Internet that Huberman and his colleagues investigated and citing a range of research that has only recently begun to emerge as a discipline, claim that "self-organizing social dynamics has been an unappreciated positive force in our social development and has been significantly extended, at least in scope, by new technologies."[71] The Los Alamos group cited evidence for their hypothesis that the self-organizing social systems that have driven human social evolution will be enhanced by self-organized, distributed, information and communication systems. The research conducted directly by the Los Alamos researchers reinforced Huberman et al.'s claim that groups of humans, linked through online networks, can make collective decisions that prove more accurate than the performance of the best individual predictors in the group. If it isn't a dead end, the lines of research opened by Huberman's team, the Los Alamos researchers, and others could amplify the powers of smart mobs into entirely new dimensions of possibility, the way Moore's Law amplified the powers of computer users.

Will self-organized, ad hoc networks of computer wearers, mediated by privacy-protecting agents, blossom into a renaissance of new wealth, knowledge, and revitalized civil society, or will the same technological-social regime provide nothing more than yet another revenue stream for Disinfotainment, Inc?

Or is that the wrong question? Given the direction of the technological, economic, and political changes I have touched on so far, I propose the following questions:

- What do we know now about the emergent properties of ad hoc mobile computing networks, and what do we need to know in the future?
- What are the central issues for individuals in a world pervaded by surveillance devices—in terms of what we can *do* about it?
- What are the long-term consequences of near-term political decisions on the way we'll use and be affected by mobile, pervasive, always-on media?

I hope that the understandings I've shared from my investigations of the past two years make it clear that smart mobs aren't a "thing" that you can point to with one finger or describe with two words, any more than "the Internet" was a "thing" you could point to. The Internet is what happened when a lot of computers started communicating. The computer and the Internet were designed, but the ways people used them were not designed into either technology, nor were the most world-shifting uses of these tools anticipated by their designers or vendors. Word processing and virtual communities, eBay and e-commerce, Google and weblogs and reputation systems *emerged*. Smart mobs are an unpredictable but at least partially describable emergent property that I see surfacing as more people use mobile telephones, more chips communicate with each other, more computers know where they are located, more technology becomes wearable, more people start using these new media to invent new forms of sex, commerce, entertainment, communion, and, as always, conflict.

Always-On Panopticon . . . or Cooperation Amplifier?

There is need to reflect upon and discuss which social practices and relationships need to be sheltered from the pressure effects of global, commercial networking. At a time in which people are frantically trying to get connected, we would do well to ask: when and where does it make sense to remain unconnected? While leaving intact many of the burdens of the industrial/automotive era, we have come perilously close to achieving complete slavery to email, digital work, and the wired and wireless apparatus that surrounds us.

—Langdon Winner, "Whatever Happened to the Electronic Cottage?"

New technologies arise that permit or encourage new, richer forms of non-zero-sum interaction; then (for intelligible reasons grounded ultimately in human nature) social structures evolve that realize this rich potential—that convert non-zero-sum situations into positive sums. Thus does social complexity grow in scope and size.

—Robert Wright, "Nonzero: The Logic of Human Destiny"

Maybe You Should Refuse It

If the citizens of the early twentieth century had paid more attention to the ways horseless carriages were changing their lives, could they have found ways to embrace the freedom, power, and convenience of automobiles without reordering their grandchildren's habitat in ugly ways? Before we start wearing our computers and digitizing our cities, can the generations of the early twenty-first century imagine what questions our grandchildren will wish we had asked today? Technology practices that might change the way we think are particularly worthy of critical scrutiny: High-resolution screens and broadband communication channels aren't widget-making machinery but sense-capturing, imagination-stimulating, opinion-shaping machinery. I begin this concluding chapter with critical perspectives on smart mobs because uncritical acceptance puts us at risk of hypnotizing ourselves with the assistance of the technology we're attempting to evaluate.

I've described teenage technology enthusiasts in Shibuya, Manila, and Stockholm. Evidence of early *non*adopters among younger generations is also a valuable clue. Social norms regarding technology practices might subdivide into multiple subcultures in the future, segmented according to members' moral stance toward mobile media. Rich Ling and Per Helmerson's study of Norwegian teens revealed that "a certain percent of all teens, about 10%–15%, have resisted adoption of the mobile telephone. Like those adults who do not purchase a television, these teens often have clear ideologies against ownership and use."[1] Nicola Green's research in the United Kingdom revealed that the college students she studied categorized mobile telephone users as "good users," those who adjusted their use of the phone to their physical and social context; "bad users," those who acted inconsiderately of others in hearing range; and "incompetent users" ("most often described as 'parents'"), those who simply don't know how to use mobile media.[2]

"Maybe you should refuse it" is a good place to start thinking about what we need to do—but not, I believe, the place to stop thinking. For some people, refusing to buy the latest gadget is the healthiest response. For most people, individual decisions about the roles of mobile and pervasive technologies in our lives are more likely to involve matters of degree than crisply binary choices. I suspect that thoughtful technology usage in the future will require each person and family to decide which settings and which times should be sequestered from the reach of communication media. Will we be wiser in our choices of how to use the small screen in our hand than we were with the TV screen in what used to be the family room? When you or your children demand the latest sport shoe that doesn't just flash lights but receives purchase recommendations from Bluetooth beacons at the mall, keep in mind what an Amish gentlemen told me:

"It's not just how we use the technology that concerns us. We're also concerned about what kind of people we become when we use it."[3]

Before plunging into the darker scenarios about the ways smart mob technologies could pose threats, I will declare my personal biases: I believe we can understand how smart mob media could threaten us and how they could benefit us. We have a lot to learn about technologies of cooperation. I believe that people could use this knowledge to construct democratic power. How we use smart mob technologies and what we know about how to use it could make a decisive difference.

Smart mob technologies pose at least three kinds of potential threats:

- Threats to liberty: Pervasive computing is converging with ubiquitous surveillance, providing the totalitarian snoop power depicted in Orwell's *1984*.
- Threats to quality of life: From individual angst to deteriorating communities, it isn't clear whether life in the infomated society delivers convenience faster than it erodes sanity and civility.
- Threats to human dignity: As more people turn more aspects of their lives over to symbiotic interaction with machines, the more mechanical and less humane we become.

Can Discipline Evolve?

In 2002, BBC News reported that the image of the average urbanite is caught on closed-circuit television cameras three hundred times a day.[4] In 2001, Virgin Mobile admitted that they had stored the location records of every mobile call made by each one of its 1 million customers since the service launched in 1999.[5] During Super Bowl XXXV, seven months *before* the terrorist attacks on the United States made high-tech surveillance checkpoints a part of daily American life, the face of every person who entered the stadium was captured by digital video cameras and compared computationally to a database of wanted criminals.[6] In March 2002, Motorola and Visionics, the company that created the Super Bowl facial recognition system, announced their intention to market mobile telephones that include real-time facial recognition capabilities to law enforcement personnel.[7]

Every telephone call, credit card transaction, mouse-click, email, automatic bridge toll collection, convenience market video camera, and hotel room electronic key collects and broadcasts personal information that is increasingly compiled, compared, sorted and stored by an unknown and possibly unknowable assortment of state security agencies and people who want to sell something. Context-aware, location-based, and agent-mediated services will multiply the amount of information that citizens will broadcast in the near future. The amount of information that comes back at us is multiplying at an alarming rate as well, as everyone who spends time clearing unsolicited commercial email ("spam") from their inboxes knows.

Although state-sponsored surveillance and much commercially motivated data collection is conducted for the most part without the consent or knowledge of the surveillant, issues of privacy today are complicated by the voluntary adoption of technologies that disclose private information to others. How many mobile telephone users know that they don't have to make a call for others to triangulate their location? They only need to switch on the device. Will users of mobile and pervasive technologies have the power to cloak, give away, or sell their personal data clouds—or to know who is inspecting them?

For decades, people have feared the use of surveillance technology as a tool of repressive social control by a totalitarian state—Orwell's "Big Brother."[8] Orwell didn't take into account the possibility that computing and communication technologies would seduce consumers into voluntarily trading privacy for convenience. David Lyon, an astute analyst of the surveillance society, made this observation about the effect of consumerism on contemporary surveillance:

> Things have changed since Orwell's time, and consumption, for the masses, has emerged as the new inclusionary reality. Only the minority, the so-called underclass, whose position prevents them from participating so freely in consumption, now experience the hard edge of exclusionary and punitive surveillance. Anyone wishing to grasp the nature of contemporary surveillance must reckon with this fact. Whereas the major threat, for Orwell, came from the state, today consumer surveillance poses a series of novel questions which have yet to find adequate analytical and political answers. A perfectly plausible view is that in contemporary conditions consumerism acts in its own right as a significant means of maintaining social order, leaving older forms of surveillance and control to cope with the non-consuming residue.[9]

Remember the point of sale display at the IBM Almaden Research Center (Chapter 4) that observes consumers and tailors its message to what it learns about them? Increasingly, the most sophisticated privacy intrusions are instigated by merchants, not secret police. Merchants want personal information about people in order to tailor their products and pitches, and they are willing to spend money to gain customers. Smart mob technologies, because they sense and communicate what users/wearers transact and experience, greatly increase the chances that consumers will voluntarily trade their privacy for various enticements from merchants, from money to bargains to the latest, coolest, algorithmically recommended identity-signifiers.

If the day comes when millions of people go about their lives while wearing sensor-equipped wearable computers, the population itself could become a collective surveillant: Big Everybody. Steve Mann proposed that communities of wearable computer users will monitor, warn, and aid each other, creating virtual "safety nets" for voluntary affinity groups.[10] Steven Feiner, who has pioneered "wearable augmented reality systems" at Columbia University, has proposed a chilling counter-scenario. Feiner asks what might happen in a future world of wearable computer communities if some organization offers individuals a small payment for continuous real-time access to their digital experience-stream.[11] Individuals in Feiner's scenario would have the power to protect their own personal privacy while displaying what they see of the rest of the world. Feiner conjectures that the enabling technology for peer-to-peer journalism also enables many-to-many surveillance.

> Massively parallel image and audio processing could make it possible to reconstruct a selected person's activities from material recorded by others who have merely seen or heard that person in passing. Imagine a private two-person conversation, recorded by neither participant. That conversation might be reassembled in its entirety from information obtained from passersby, who each overheard small snippets and who willingly provided inexpensive access to their recordings. The price paid for such material, and the particular users to whom that price is offered, might even change dynamically, based on a user's proximity to events or people of interest to the buyer at that time. This could make it possible to enlist temporarily a well-situated user who may normally refuse access at the regular price, or to engage a user's wearable computer in a "bidding war" among competing organizations, performed without any need for the user's attention.[12]

The Osaka police took the first steps toward Feiner's scenario in April 2002, when they opened a call-in line for citizens with 3G phones to send video of crimes they might witness.[13]

Sociologist Gary Marx was the first to describe a "surveillance society," in which, "with computer technology, one of the final barriers to total control is crumbling."[14] Marx noted that the growing ability of computers to compile dossiers about individuals by piecing together countless tiny, otherwise harmless shards of information about transactions, medical conditions, buying habits, and demographic characteristics constituted a distinct class of "dataveillance," distinguished from traditional snooping methodologies of audio or visual recording by its ease of computer automation: "Computers qualitatively alter the nature of surveillance—routinizing, broadening, and deepening it."[15]

Surveillance technologies become a threat to liberty as well as dignity when they give one person or group power to constrain the behavior of others. Any inquiry into the relationship between social control, surveillance, power, and knowledge must contend with the historian-philosopher-psychologist-sociologist Michel Foucault, a fiercely cross-disciplinary thinker who was to surveillance what Darwin was to evolutionary biology. Foucault's fundamental insight was that power not only belongs to the powerful but permeates the social world. He wrote that power "reaches into the very grain of individuals, touches their bodies and inserts itself into their actions and attitudes, their discourses, learning processes and everyday lives."[16]

As Einstein showed that space and time could be understood only in relation to each other, Foucault revealed the reciprocal connections between knowledge and power. In Foucault's view, power is so strongly connected to knowledge that he often wrote them this way: "power/knowledge." About the relationship of the two, Foucault stated: "Knowledge, once used to regulate the conduct of others, entails constraint, regulation and the disciplining of practice. Thus, there is no power relation without the correlative constitution of a field of knowledge, nor any knowledge that does not presuppose and constitute at the same time, power relations."[17]

Examining the history of punishment, Foucault focused on a change over recent centuries in the way societies treat criminals and the mentally ill. The age-old techniques of torture and execution or consignment to dungeons were replaced by more subtle and effective methods. Rational institutions and authoritative specialists—modern prisons and police, hospitals, asylums, psychiatrists, and doctors—helped order society more effectively than the threat of physical punishment.

"Discipline" was Foucault's term for a mode of power/knowledge that included social welfare bureaucracy, armies and police forces, public education, and other practices that impose regular patterns on behavior and relationships. Foucault uses the word "discipline" to refer both to methods of control and to different branches of knowledge, for he saw knowledge specialization and social control as part of the same power/knowledge matrix.

As an example of discipline and power/knowledge, Foucault cited the Panopticon ("all-seeing place"), an architectural design put forth by Jeremy Bentham in the mid-nineteenth century for prisons, insane asylums, schools, hospitals, and factories. Instead of employing the brutal and spectacular means used to control individuals under a monarchial state, the modern state needed a different sort of system to regulate its citizens. The Panopticon applied a form of mental, knowledge-based power through the constant observation of prisoners, each separated from the other and allowed no interaction. The Panoptic structure would allow guards to continually see inside each cell from their vantage point in a high central tower, unseen themselves. The system of unobserved observation created a kind of knowledge in the mind of the inmate that was in itself a form of power. It isn't necessary to constantly surveil people who believe they are under constant surveillance:

> The major effect of the Panopticon: to induce in the inmate a state of conscious and permanent visibility that assures the automatic functioning of power. So to arrange things that the surveillance is permanent in its effects, even if it is discontinuous in action; that the perfection of power should tend to render its actual exercise unnecessary; that this architectural apparatus should be a machine for creating and sustaining a power relation independent of the person who exercises it; in short, that the inmates should be caught up in a power situation of which they are themselves the bearers.[18]

The emergence of surveillance and social control institutions marked a historical transition to a system of disciplinary power in which every movement is supervised and all events recorded. The result of this surveillance of every part of life, by parents, teachers, employers, police, doctors, accountants, is acceptance of regulations and docility as part of the way every "normal" person thinks and behaves. Disciplinary methods systematically isolated and neutralized "the effects of counter-power that spring from [an organized group] and which form a resistance to the power that wishes to dominate it: agitations, revolts, spontaneous organizations, coalitions— anything that may establish horizontal conjunctions."[19] For Foucault, the real danger was not necessarily that individuals are repressed by this form of social order but that they are "carefully fabricated in it."[20]

Power and counter-power sometimes combine with the human talent for cooperation rituals to create significant benefits. The rule of law, governance through social contracts, protection of civil rights, expansion of political enfranchisement, and evolution of cooperative enterprises (think of the Red Cross) demonstrate how power that goes around in the right circles can work to common advantage. Social communication—what people in cities, on the Internet, in smart mobs do—is the means by which power and counter-power coevolve. Since we climbed down from the trees and started hunting together, human groups have found numerous ways to cooperate for mutual benefit. We do so in the face of significant challenges, and when we succeed, we do so with the help of mutual monitoring and sanctioning. When I encountered Foucault's attention to mutual monitoring and sanctioning as a way in which groups self-enforce conformity and suppress potential rebellion, I recalled how Ostrom and others highlighted mutual monitoring and sanctioning in communities that solve collective action dilemmas.

Every social order, not just repressive ones, requires methods of mutual social control. The key question is whether populations of users can use what we now know about cooperation to drive power/knowledge to a higher level of democracy. Isn't that exactly what happened when printing made literacy available to entire populations, not just to a tiny elite? If discipline did not include the capacity for changing itself, the cooperation and democracy that exist today would not have come into being after millennia of slavery, tyranny, and feudalism. More to the point is a question for the present generations: Can discipline change in the future? Can people use mobile communication, peer-to-peer and pervasive computing, location awareness, and social accounting systems to evolve a higher form of discipline, transforming the forces revealed by Foucault according to the principles revealed by Ostrom and Axelrod?

Softened Time, Blurred Places, Colonized Lives

In addition to threats against liberty and privacy, critical questions about smart mobs arise in regard to the quality of life in an always-on, hyper-connected culture. A few of the most important questions about quality of life address ways that mobile and pervasive technology usage affects interpersonal relationships, the way individuals experience time, and the vitality of public spaces.

Technology critic Langdon Winner challenges the image of the "electronic cottage" that was promoted twenty years ago, at the dawn of the PC era.[21] Although Winner accurately points out that progress in personal information technology has not alleviated traffic jams or emptied office buildings, I must note that I am sitting in my garden at this moment, typing these words on my laptop computer, connecting to the Internet by way of a wireless network. The lawn as floor and sky as ceiling definitely improve *my* life—and you don't find me contributing to rush hour traffic. I agree with Winner that infogadgetry has made possible a way of life that seems the very opposite of pastoral knowledge work, whereby telecommuters log in from their electronic cottages. Winner cited an anthropological study of Silicon Valley culture that concentrated on 450 people who "employ complex ecologies of electronic devices—cell phones, beepers, laptops, personal digital assistants, voice mail, personal Web pages," noting:

> Preliminary findings reveal a world in which work has become everything, with electronic devices the glue that holds it all together. The people interviewed report that they are always on call. Through phone, beepers, email and the like, their time is totally interruptible. In the office, in their cars, and in their houses, the demands of work come pouring in. Work is so pervasive that conventional boundaries between work and home have all but collapsed.[22]

Winner observed that a "gnawing dilemma" in the lives of the hyper-infomated Silicon Valleyites studied by the anthropologists was constant negotiation of communication access—seeking to maximize access to others while controlling the access others have to them.

The intervention of digital technology into social relationships carries another danger: People may start reacting to mechanical artifacts as if they were reacting to people, and badly designed communication devices may cause people to blame each other for the shortcomings of their machines. These psychological reactions, closely tied to the way the input and output aspects of devices (the "user interface") are designed, are part of a discipline known as "social interface theory." When I first heard about the findings of Stanford Professor Byron Reeves and Associate Professor Clifford Nass, I visited Nass at Stanford, who explained his findings over lunch. Using experimental methods that have been developed to study the ways people react to one another, Reeves and Nass substituted automatic devices such as computers, or even representations of people such as video images, for one of the parties in classic two-person social psychology experiments. They found that although people claim that they know the difference between humans and machines, their cognitive, emotional, and behavioral responses to artificial representations of humans are identical to the reactions they have to real people.[23] Humans evolved over a long time to pay close attention to other people, to the way people treat us, to facial expressions and tone of voice. We make social decisions and life and death decisions based on this human-centered response system we've evolved. Artificial representations of people or electronic mediators have only come along in the past one hundred years. Our artifacts might be in the information age, but our biology is still prehistoric.

I was reminded of what Jim Spohrer had told me of his experiences with pervasive computing, when I visited him at IBM's Almaden Research Center (Chapter 4): "Something startling happens when technology acts as if it is aware of the human user and responds to human behavior in context. Suddenly, magically, without artificial intelligence, things start seeming intelligent!" Other IBM researchers have noted the role of "social attribution errors" in the design of devices that mediate social interactions. If the social interfaces of the devices are not carefully designed, people mistake mechanical errors for human errors, falsely influencing their assessment of other people or social situations.[24] The same researchers who noted "social attribution errors" also pointed out that head-mounted displays, even Steve Mann's sleek sunglasses, interfere with a key element of human social communication—eye contact.

Human discourse without eye contact has its dangers. Anyone who has experienced a misunderstanding via email or witnessed a flame war in an online discussion knows that mediated communications, lacking the nuances carried by eye contact, facial expression, or tone of voice, increase the possibility of conflicts erupting from misunderstandings. Between social interface theory, social attribution errors, and the possibility of miscommunication, at the very least the designers of smart mob technologies must focus heightened attention on the potential social side effects of their design decisions. And those who shape the norms of wearable communities by virtue of being the first generations of users must keep in mind that artificial mediation brings hazards as well as advantages to social communication.

Carried to its extreme, the experience of living in a world pervaded by context-aware devices could lead to what researcher Mark Pesce calls "technoanimism," a "very dynamic relationship to the material world that to our eyes is going to look almost sacrilegious or profane."[25] Given Nass and Reeves's discovery that our long evolution in the ages before movies and talking computers has not prepared us to react differentially to real humans and human simulations, we should prepare for startling emergent social behaviors when mobile communicators grow context aware and billboards customize their displays according to the demographics of the people who look at it. Widespread popular beliefs that computationally colonized objects are intelligent, even if they aren't, could lead to unpleasant unintended consequences. If pervasive computation devices and anthropomorphic software agents lead people to confuse machines with humans, will people grow *less* friendly, less trusting, and less prepared to cooperate with one another? Or is it possible for informed designers to account for social attribution errors to create cooperation-amplifying technologies? Even if the potential design flaws of technoanimistic devices are overcome, especially if they are overcome, what do we do about the way we spend more and more time interacting with devices?

Many of the threats to quality of life posed by mobile communications and pervasive computing seem to be linked to changes in the way people experience time. Leslie Haddon wrote: "Researchers examining changing time patterns have noted the paradox that while time budgets show that on average the amount of leisure time has increased, many people perceive that their lives have become busier."[26] Leopoldina Fortunati of the University of Trieste, analyzing the spread of mobile telephony and texting in Italy, observed: "Time is socially perceived as something that must be filled up to the very smallest folds," thus eliminating "the positive aspects of lost time" that "could also fill up with reflection, possible adventures, observing events, reducing the uniformity of our existence, and so on."[27] While the Internet competes with television and with face-to-face communications in the home and workplace, smart mob technologies compete with attention to other people who are present in public places and with the users' own idle time between home and work.

Mizuko Ito and her graduate students had noticed that the expected times of appointments for Tokyo youth had become fluid, and Norwegian researcher Rich Ling had observed a "softening of time" among texting youth in his part of the world.[28] Ling and Yttri called the new way of arranging appointments "hyper-coordination."[29] Finnish researcher Pasi Mäenpää made the same forecast in writing that Kenny Hirschhorn, the futurist at European telecommunication giant Orange, and Natsuno-san at DoCoMo had made in conversation: The mobile telephone is evolving into a kind of remote control for people's lives. Our technology-assisted and hyper-informed pace of living apparently now requires further technology, in order for the hyper-informed to control our own lives. And controlling our lives through mobile devices involves scheduling future activities:

> In the mobile culture one lives with the other foot permanently planted in the future, using the mobile to administer and manage his or her future meetings and affairs. Places and times are not planned in advance; rather people agree (or just understand without further mention) to call "when they get there." This makes life less bound, since it is possible to arrange each day according to the events it brings about.
>
> The mobile maintains a readiness for flexible meetings and for arranging them as befits the day. . . . The mobile blurs the previously organized everyday structure and shifts it to a more flexible direction. This brings about a change in our perception of time, so that the notion of a previously produced, organized future is replaced by a sliding sense of time which is constantly tilted towards the future. The future is no longer conceived as something consisting of exact moments as much as of approximate places-in-time which are open to negotiation according to the situation.[30]

Another characteristic of a changing sense of time that Mäenpää observed among Finnish youth was their use of texting to share experiences in real time, to go through parts of the day simultaneously exchanging their thoughts and observations with a small group of friends, each of whom was located in a different place. Sociologist Barry Wellman, extending his studies of online social networks to include users of mobile devices, concluded that the ability to be in immediate contact with one's social network even if they are in different places, enables several broad kinds of social changes.[31] When the social networking capabilities of the desk-bound Internet go mobile, according to Wellman,

The shift to a personalized, wireless world affords networked individualism, with each person switching between ties and networks. People remain connected, but as individuals rather than being rooted in the home bases of work unit and household. Individuals switch rapidly between their social networks. Each person separately operates his networks to obtain information, collaboration, orders, support, sociability, and a sense of belonging.[32]

According to Wellman, it is easier for individuals to connect with multiple social milieux, with limited involvement in each one, which in turn diminishes the control each milieu exercises over the individual and decreases its commitment to the individual's welfare. People switch fluidly from network to network, using their communication media to contact the social network needed for each moment. This means that *network capital*—the ability to use the technological network to contact social networks and to make use of them to one's benefit—becomes important in a mobile and pervasive world, along with financial capital and social capital. Those who know how to tap into smart mob social network capital will gain advantages. Those who know not, have not.

Smart mob technologies already seem to be changing some people's sense of place as well as their experience of time, with visible effects on public spaces such as sidewalks, parks, squares, and markets, where more and more of the physically co-present population are communicating with people far away. Leopoldina Fortunati has conjectured that the many Italians now seen talking or texting with their mobiles have "stolen" communication from public to private spheres.[33] Fortunati claims that by taking their attention back into the private sphere, Italians have devalued the unspoken rules regarding participation in public communication space.

Wellman shares Fortunati's fear that the privatization of communications will lead to public spaces where "people pass each other unsmiling."[34] Haddon has noted that over half of those surveyed in Italy, the United Kingdom, and Germany had a negative reaction to the use of mobile phones in public, and other observers in Scandinavia noted similar reactions. Haddon attributes this social friction to the "way that mobile telephony disrupts the constructed spheres of privacy of others in those public spaces."[35] Fortunati believes that "the ambiguous dimension of presence/absence in space also means the restructuring of the sense of belonging to a place, one of the four classic poles of the sense of belonging (apart from belonging to the family, one's country, and one's race). It is actually transformed into the sense of belonging to one's communicative network."[36] Fortunati's conjecture echoed Mizuko Ito's observation that Tokyo thumb tribes consider themselves "present" at a gathering if they are in touch via texting.

Now in its earliest stages, the "presence of those who are absent" is found by many to be a disturbing new development in a longer-term degeneration of civility in human communication. In Fortunati's words:

> How is it that artificial communication can have the better over natural communication? We can find an answer to this question. With the advent of the small screen, we had already shifted attention away from natural communication, fragmenting it with TV consumption. And so initially we learned to talk while we were watching TV at home; later, we learned to answer a call, brusquely interrupting an already ongoing conversation with somebody. That is, what we do in this case is divert attention from interpersonal communication in favour of a virtual conversation, over a distance. In the same way as we hushed our family members to be able to follow the TV program, in the same way in the case of the mobile, we make our flesh and blood interlocutor helpless while we talk into the mobile and give the person at the other end more importance than the person in front of us. So, it is the previous devaluation of natural communication that is the element that has implicitly permitted the emptying out of our presence in space, both as standers-by and as users of the mobile.[37]

One category of critique contends that electronic communication media have created an artificial world in which people spend most of their waking hours, a hyper-real amusement park of pixels, slogans, sitcoms, spam, and advertisements designed to maximize consumer spending and minimize resistance to consumption. In the 2000 edition of *The Virtual Community,* I discussed the "Frankfurt School" philosophers Adorno and Horkheimer who saw mass media as a weapon of psychological manipulation of the consumer by a culture industry that eats everything authentic, privatizes everything public, and feeds it back to people as pay-as-you-go fables.[38] An even more extreme position was taken by Jean Baudrillard, whose descriptions of the "hyperreal" portray a world in which everyone is so mesmerized that they have forgotten that their environment is no longer real.[39] Hyperreal media, Baudrillard proposed, are the ultimate refinement of capitalism, generating desire for consumption simply by manipulating the simulation of the moment. Selling people beliefs, hopes, and distractions generates profits at the same time it pacifies and neutralizes possible resistance from consumers. There are only a few necessities of life to turn into products, but an infinity of symbols, and a pacified population of symbol-consumers, in hyperreality.

It's hard not to think of Baudrillard in Times Square or Shibuya Crossing, or driving through any suburb in the world at night, the curtains of every house lit by the blue glow of cathode tubes. I started using the word "disinfotainment" about ten years ago to describe the combination of increasingly spectacular media with the ownership and reshaping of journalism by entertainment interests.[40] Who would deny that there is some degree of truth to this most cynical viewpoint, given the growing consolidation of mass media ownership, the capture of much of the Internet by large commercial interests that now move to enclose it, the trivialization of journalism by the entertainment companies that now own broadcasting networks and newspapers?[41] Yet many-to-many media confer a power on consumers that mass media never did: the power to create, publish, broadcast, and debate their own point of view. Newspaper, radio, and television audiences were consumers, but Internet audiences were "users" with powers of their own. The most important question about this new wrinkle in power/knowledge is whether it sets the stage for counter-power that would surprise Adorno, Horkheimer, and Baudrillard, or whether it is yet another simulacrum, a simulation of counter-power that really doesn't change who has all the chips.

Many-to-many media cannot survive if too many free riders take advantage of universal access to other people's attention. Ironically, the democratization of publishing power afforded by many-to-many networks could spell the death of social cyberspace through a form of informational littering. When i-mode users were hit by "mobile spam" sent to their telephones by computerized autodialers, DoCoMo paid out a staggering $217 million in refunds.[42] The lack of a "shadow of the future" creates a vulnerability for hit-and-run artists. At least the big global disinformation factories have an incentive to maintain a relationship with their customers. Spam, a classic tragedy of the commons problem, wastes every Internet user's time and attention. People who care more about their personal gain than the value of the network or other people's time broadcast commercial solicitations, many of them indecent, to hundreds of millions of people at a time. Spam is growing because the selfish solicitors are rewarded by a miniscule percentage of clue-impaired victims who respond to the solicitations. The Net's immune system has been fighting back, and several varieties of legislation have been proposed, but spam technology seems to be keeping a step ahead of countermeasures. The irony would be painful if the advanced cooperation machinery of many-to-many media is rendered unusable by chronic noncooperation.

The most profound category of threat posed by smart mobs is the threat to human dignity. Our marvelous information technology, claim a number of thoughtful critics, externalizes only one part of human nature, the part that grasps and exploits, the part that harvests efficiency by treating humans like components. Another school of critics warns that the enthusiastic embrace of our muscle-multiplying, brain-extending artificial creations could lead to an abandonment of the biological body—the "posthuman" era.

Symbiosis or Abomination?

Jacques Ellul wrote his bleak and prescient book, *The Technological Society*, in 1954, when there were no more than a dozen computers in the world. Ellul addressed the seductive danger he perceived in a way of thinking and doing. This way of thinking is necessary for what most of us think of as technology, but it is invisible and not always connected to physical machines. *Technique* applies to governments as well as artifacts: "the ensemble of practices by which one uses available resources in order to achieve certain valued ends."[43] Slavery is technique. The alphabet is technique. Government is technique. Steam power is technique. Ellul claims the key characteristics of technique are rationality, artificiality, automatism of technical choice, self-augmentation, monism, universalism, and autonomy. A community of computer-wearers who cooperate through a computerized reputation system would seem to fit those criteria.

To Ellul, technique is in the process of rearranging the world and the way humans act in the world. He warned that "human life as a whole is not inundated by technique. It has room for activities that are not rationally or systematically ordered. But the collision between technique and spontaneous activities that are not rationally or systematically ordered is catastrophic for the spontaneous activities."[44] Ellul could have been describing the hyper-coordinated teens of Scandinavia or the hyper-informated households of Silicon Valley—except he wrote those words more than half a century ago.

Like Foucault after him, Ellul was deeply concerned about the way humans were internalizing technique and remaking ourselves in its image, were educating and regulating ourselves to conform to technique's latest shape, for in that way, technique has proved successful in assimilating everything in its path: "Technique can leave nothing untouched in a civilization. Everything is its concern. Technique, which is destroying all other civilizations, is more than a simple mechanism: it's a whole civilization in itself."[45]

To Ellul, technique is not a malevolent force but a blind force, which by its nature encourages humans to mobilize more and more resources to perfect ever more efficient and powerful techniques. The original "enclosure of the commons," which started in England around 1730, Ellul pointed out, was the result of the application of technique to both agriculture and ownership. The peasants who had never owned anything but a few animals had been able to graze and cultivate common lands in return for providing labor, a part of their herds and harvests, and fighting men when necessary, to the local lord. The ancient hierarchies of feudalism began to transform into something less hierarchical but radically more dynamic with the advent of a new organizational form, the market. Peasants were fenced out of what used to be the commons when large landowners, the commercial successors to the feudal elite, applied new scientific techniques of agriculture and began to accumulate the new metatechnology, capital. The uprooted peasants fled to the cities, where they served as a workforce for the application of technique to manufacture, first in the textile industry, and then everywhere. Technique reorders human affairs toward more efficient technique, from the "satanic mills" of industrial England to the wearable media of Silicon Valley.

If he were alive today, I suspect Ellul would call the microchip "distilled technique," and he would declare that the implantation of chips in everything everywhere represents the final, concrete triumph of technique over all human values that can't be measured, ordered, and mechanized. The problem that would concern Ellul most acutely would not be technique itself but the historic human inability to protect valued qualities of life from technique's relentless quantification, mechanization, and digitization of everything—including, but not limited to, the very codes of life and processes of biological evolution, the biochemistry of thought and emotion, and the creation of artificial life-forms totally divorced from the realm of flesh. Technique has enabled humans to attain powers we attributed only to the gods a few generations ago. The question is whether we have the wisdom to use our power-tools without amputating something vital.

In 1967, Lewis Mumford, in *The Myth of the Machine*, proposed that the most powerful and dehumanizing invention was not a visible machine but a social machine in which humans were treated as components in a massive hierarchical system for building pyramids and skyscrapers, empires and civilizations.[46] Mumford conjectured origins for what he sometimes called "the megamachine" in a prehistoric arrangement that maps perfectly onto Foucault. Mumford proposed that leaders of the people with muscle, the hunter-kings who had conquered the other local bands of armed men, teamed up with the leaders of the people who had tamed the magic of symbols. The astrologer-priest would anoint the guy with the most loyal spear-carriers as a god, and the god-king would elevate the priest to the leadership of a cult that ordered the lives of their subjects— power/knowledge put in action.

By organizing workforces and military forces hierarchically and breaking their tasks into component parts, entire populations could organize into social machines to build pyramids and conquer empires. By freeing a priestly elite for intellectual training, the administration of empire became possible, and the tools of imperial administrators—numbers and alphabets—set the stage for more efficient organization (what Foucault would call discipline) and the power/knowledge that literacy enabled. Are networked thumb tribes playing with a form of counter-power to hierarchical megamachines? We've considered what tyrannies smart mobs might enable. And we've seen that the alphabetic weapon of Mesopotamian despots became the foundations of democracies. What liberties might the intelligent use of mobile and pervasive media make possible?

One of the first pioneers of artificial intelligence research, an MIT researcher named Joseph Weizenbaum, applied the arguments posed by Ellul and Mumford directly to the future of computing, a field he knew well. In *Computer Power and Human Reason*, published in 1976, Weizenbaum emphasized that the aspect of human nature that computers externalize is our most machine-like aspect.[47] He called this "the tyranny of instrumental reasoning," building on Heidegger's view of technology as the result of a human tendency to "enframe" the world by converting it into a resource to be used to some end.[48] Weizenbaum warned that it would be a terrible mistake to believe all human problems are computable. Anticipating the voluntary cyborgs of future decades, Weizenbaum declared that it would be an abomination to start connecting the nervous tissue of living creatures to future computers. Considering that part of Steve Mann's WearComp involves a number of electrodes affixed to his body to monitor his heart rhythm and other bodily processes, the era of the cyborg ceased to be a future development a few years back.

"Cyborg," or "cybernetic organism," is a term that Mann and other wearable computer enthusiasts use proudly to describe their technically augmented capabilities, and they say it with no more sense of shame than they would exhibit when saying that they wear eyeglasses or look through a microscope. As medical technology provides more and more intimately bioconnected mechanical life-support systems, and more people spend more time in communication with mechanical thinking aids, an entire literature of cyborg criticism has grown up.[49] One critic, Mark Dery, argued in his 1996 book, *Escape Velocity: Cyberculture at the End of the Century*, that certain cyborg subcultures who call themselves "extropians" or "transhumanists" actively seek to transcend the flesh, projecting a quasi-mystical faith onto the scientific whiz-bangery of technology.[50] These extreme technophiles ask why we should put up with the messiness, mortality, limitations in intelligence and physical power that accompany the human body as it evolved biologically, now that we seem to be on the verge of building more effective substitutes for vital organs. Isn't it foolish, they propose, to refuse to research technologies of immortality when eternal life might be within the grasp of modern science?[51] Dery warns that transhumanism might be leading us away from humanity as we know it and into something Ellul might have predicted—a world in which we become fine-tuned down to our DNA as components in ever consuming, ever expanding, profit-generating machinery.

I am attracted to Steve Mann's vision of cyborg communities as alliances of individuals who have taken charge of their technological extensions, but the pace and invasiveness of prosthetic engineering development cry out for a cautionary approach to the future of embodiment. In March 2002, British robotics scientist Kevin Warwick, hoping to perfect techniques for curing spinal cord injuries in the future, implanted several hundred tiny sensors into the main nerve in his left arm, connected to a radio transceiver that can exchange signals with a remote computer.[52] Ellul would say that technique would not stop its incursion when spinal cord injuries are cured but would continue to invade human organs and more closely mesh the human nervous system with the technical exoskeleton of networked computers. Do we have to give up part of our humanity to enable the paralyzed to walk? Didn't Faust face a similar decision in Goethe's parable about the price of the power of modernism?[53]

Which characteristics of the flesh should and could be sequestered from the attractions and colonizations of technique? If some people live in smart mobs as cyborgs, how will that change those people who remain embodied in the traditional manner, and how will the two groups negotiate coexistence? Twentieth-century science fiction explored many of these questions. In the twenty-first century, the cyborgs are no longer fictional. It's not too outlandish, given the direction of scientific development, to ask how human our grandchildren are likely to be—and how decisions we make now will affect our descendants.

What Do We Need to Know?

Before anyone can make intelligent decisions about what to do with smart mob technologies, more people need more reliable, practical knowledge about the following issues:

- How to regulate the mobile Internet in ways that free innovation and promote competition without undermining the foundations of democratic societies
- The interdisciplinary dynamics of cooperation systems, natural and artificial
- The cognitive, interpersonal, and social effects of mobile, pervasive, always-on media
- How ubiquitous mobile Internet access and information embedded in places might reshape cities

New laws and regulations are attempting to turn Internet "users" into passive "consumers." Recent political decisions are locking onto the familiar model of traditional broadcast-era mass media—"content" fed through monopoly-controlled, metered, one-way pipelines to passive consumers. The Internet grew and innovated explosively because every node that can receive content can also send content through an unfenced, any-to-any network in which large commercial enterprises coexist with millions of noncommercial or small commercial operators. Internet users were not passive consumers but the "prosumers" the Tofflers had predicted in the 1980s.[54] Just because the new medium has come from an innovation-rich and universally accessible commons doesn't guarantee that it will remain that way; radio and television were tamed in their day.

The U.S. Congress's and FCC's laws and rulings over the next few years will make the difference between a traditional broadcast model and a peer-to-peer model for wireless Internet. In the future, U.S. policies favoring multinational corporations probably will be incorporated in the international intellectual property treaty frameworks that are being put into place around the world. So far, decisions have favored large intellectual property owners, removed common carriage and public access responsibilities from cable and telephone companies, and confined new wireless technologies to tiny sectors of spectrum, reserving the rest for the exclusive use of license-holders invested in established technologies.[55] Indeed, the most realistic prediction is that unless some new pressures are brought to bear and the U.S. and global regulatory process changes its present course, mobile and pervasive technologies won't be used by smart mobs at all but will be more aptly described by the science fiction story *The Marching Morons*.[56]

The telecommunications industry is not the only group of vested interests who have attempted to prevent innovation and to turn active technology users into passive consumers of prepackaged content. Hollywood studios were concerned that the advent of television would render movies obsolete and sought to crush the emerging medium; the studios were thwarted by Walt Disney, who needed to put his movies on TV in order to raise money to build Disneyland.[57] The Motion Picture Association of America's chief lobbyist in Washington, D.C., Jack Valenti, fought to prevent the sale of video cassette recorders to consumers, testifying before Congress that the "VCR is to the American film industry as the Boston Strangler is to a woman alone"; electronics manufacturers such as Sony successfully opposed Valenti's efforts.[58] With digital television broadcasts on the horizon, Hollywood lobbyists (again led by Valenti) have formed the Broadcast Protection Discussion Group to lobby for legislation that casts a dark shadow on future innovation in the telecommunication, computer hardware, and open source software industries.[59] I turned to Cory Doctorow, who now works for the Electronic Frontier Foundation, a public-interest organization working on behalf of citizens, to explain the recent underpublicized but potentially damaging lobbying campaign:

> Despite the fact that VCRs did not kill movies and in fact became a major
> revenue source for Hollywood studios, the studios fear that digital TV will

make it too easy to trade movies via the Internet. The BPDG is asking the U.S. Congress to create a mandatory standard that would give Hollywood veto power over any future technology capable of interacting with DTV.[60] This means that any future inventor of a technology that could be used with DTV will have to promise that the invention won't be used in a computer unless the computer is also approved by Hollywood; if they don't make this legally binding promise, the inventor won't be allowed to license the device for manufacture. DTV devices and computers share the same technologies, so a law to protect DTV could give Hollywood total control over the design specifications of future computers. Hollywood doesn't want any open source software interacting with DTV, because DTV can be modified by users. Effectively, this would amount to a ban on open source software. Hollywood was unsuccessful in shutting down previous technologies because technology companies fought their attempts to do so, but this time, technology companies are cooperating.

The mandatory standard proposed by BPDG is only the first regulatory step. DTV receivers will also have analog outputs, to which one could connect analog-to-digital converters and effectively remove all such protection, which led the Motion Picture Association of America to ask the Senate Judiciary Committee for a second mandate requiring all analog-to-digital converters to be equipped with a "cop chip" that will check for digital watermarks indicating that the converter is being used to digitize copyrighted work.[61] The cop chip would have the power to shut down the offending device. If you video record your child's first steps, and a Mickey Mouse cartoon is playing on a TV in the background, the cop chip will shut down your recorder. If you talk on your mobile phone while walking down the street and somebody drives by with their window open and their car radio is playing a copyrighted song, the cop chip will shut down your phone.

Finally, Hollywood is calling for a redesign of the Internet to stop p2p file sharing, which amounts to a proposed ban on decentralized packet switching in favor of centralized networks that can be monitored for acts of infringement.[62]

Recent legal and regulatory actions are the first moves of a thus far successful campaign to lock down the formerly freewheeling Internet and return to the days of three television networks and one telephone company, when customers were consumers and no one sliced into profits with their own businesses or challenged old technologies with new ones.[63] This time, the dinosaurs are well aware of the dangers from the mammals and are taking big thumping steps to protect themselves. Most people aren't clear about what is at stake in this game, and those who could inform us, journalists, work for enterprises now owned by the dinosaurs.

The rights of citizens to consume a large variety of information as well as to disseminate their own information widely are held to be fundamental public goods in the United States. Yale professor Yochai Benkler wrote in 2000 about the importance of diverse media to First Amendment rights:

> In a series of cases in which the Supreme Court reviewed various media regulations, the Court has steadily developed an understanding that decentralization of information production is a policy that serves values central to the First Amendment. Most pithily captured in Justice Black's statement in *United States v. Associated Press*, since adopted in other cases in this line— *Red Lion* and the two *Turner* cases—it is central to the values served by the First Amendment that we secure "the widest possible dissemination of information from diverse and antagonistic sources.[64]

Two centuries before Benkler, James Madison wrote the words that are carved in marble at the Library of Congress: "A popular Government, without popular information, or the means of acquiring it, is but a prologue to a farce or a tragedy; or, perhaps, both. Knowledge will forever govern ignorance; and a people who mean to be their own governors must arm themselves with the power which knowledge gives."[65]

If political decisions do leave people free to invent new varieties of smart mobs, the most important knowledge for designers and users of smart mob technologies could come from a comprehensive investigation of the dynamics of cooperation. Although the interdisciplinary studies discussed in Chapter 2 and Chapter 5 indicate a broad basis for such a body of knowledge, the gaps in what we know now are large enough to make the difference between higher levels of cooperation and a world in which nothing really works the way it's supposed to, and nobody understands why. Before attempting to build social accounting systems, we have to understand that we've only begun to understand how they work and how they can be cheated.

The hubris inherent in the idea of computerized reputation systems must be acknowledged, especially by those who design them. Although the first analyses of reputation systems in online markets indicates some hope for developing automated social accounting systems, common sense cautions that when it comes to characterizing the trustworthiness of human beings, errors can unfairly despoil the reputation of good citizens and loopholes can amplify the trust level of sophisticated cheaters. Such thus-far unquantified behaviors as redemption, maturation, and other forms of personal character change are not well represented by mathematical models of reputational data. As Ellul, Weizenbaum, and most religious systems contend, not every part of human nature can or should be digitized.

Considering the possible value of such knowledge to a humankind on the brink of six kinds of self-destruction, broad research into the precise dynamics of cooperation, management of common pool resources, and the powers and limits of social accounting systems could yield enormous benefits for the commons and for pioneering private enterprises.

The cognitive and social impacts of mobile and pervasive technologies are largely unknown, the potential for negative side effects is high, and the possibility of unexpected emergent behaviors is nearly certain. Before individuals, families, or communities can make decisions about how to adopt, use, constrain, or appropriate emerging technologies, we need better information about what mobile and pervasive media do to our minds and societies.

We need to know more about the ways mobile and pervasive media are changing the way people use cities, because the changes are well underway. Steven Johnson revealed in *Emergence* how "cities, like ant colonies, possess a kind of emergent intelligence: an ability to store and retrieve information, to recognize and respond to patterns in human behavior."[66] Swarming supported by texting and mobile telephony, untethered ubiquitous Internet access, location-aware services, and device-readable information associated with specific places are only the beginnings of significant changes in the way people use urban spaces.

"Even before wireless access, we saw people leaving their cubicles to work on park benches with their laptops and cell phones," said Anthony Townsend, the same research scientist at New York University's Taub Urban Research Center and NYCWireless cofounder we met in Chapter 6.[67] When I called Townsend to talk about community wireless networking, we also talked about the way changes in communication practices influence the way people use cities. I knew that he had written about the subject: "The modern city of office towers is as much an artifact of the invention of the telephone as the decentralization of manufacturing and residences to the suburbs."[68] Wireless Internet access points provided by

NYCWireless in Washington Square Park in 2001 and Bryant Square Park in 2002 are changing the way the people who work in those neighborhoods go about their business—in ways that Townsend believes can be more convivial than constant confinement in cubicles.

As an urban researcher, Townsend sees both opportunities and dangers. "The digital divide with location-based services," he told a reporter in 2001, "is going to be about who controls the information about your community. When I go to Harlem, do I get information that's created by the residents of Harlem, or by Yahoo! in Santa Clara, or by Verizon and the Yellow Pages?"[69] Townsend believes swarming is already accelerating urban metabolism and that wide diffusion of mobile devices and citywide information structures has created new feedback patterns he calls "the real-time city." He has warned urban planners that "the city will change far faster than the ability to understand it from a centralized perspective, let alone formulate plans and politics that will have the desired outcomes."[70]

William J. Mitchell, professor of architecture at MIT, foresaw in 1995 that mobile, pervasive, and wearable media would turn future cities into even more complex information systems than they already are. In *City of Bits,* Mitchell argued that designers and planners need to think about the kind of lives people want to live, not just the mechanics of digging up streets and installing fiber optic cables.[71] In 2001, Mitchell noted the use of mobile telephones to facilitate swarming by people who "rely on their electronics to deliver relevant information at the right moment, to guide them where they want to go, and to tell them what they will find when they get there. In SwarmCity.org, landmarks are physical places that (maybe temporarily) have lots of electronic pointers in their direction. And obscure backwaters are just places without pointers."[72]

Adding dynamic, location-specific information to cities is changing them, but without adequate knowledge of the dynamics of such changes and of how people would prefer their lives to change, there is no guarantee that new uses of communication technology will improve the urban experience. We need to understand the kinds of shifts in pedestrian experience enabled by swarming, observe the way people prefer to work when information and communication access is untethered from desktops, and balance technical and political issues in negotiating standards for informating places. If this understanding can be applied widely, smart mob technology could do more than spawn surveillance, cyborgs, flocking teenage-culture consumers, and swarming terrorists. If we know what we're doing, perhaps we could enable cooperation amplification through smart mob infrastructure, the way dedicated dreamers transformed computers from weapons into telescopes of the mind.

Cooperation Amplification

With all the dangers, threats, and pitfalls of smart mob technology, why bother with it?

The answer to this question is the same one that could have been given to the same question asked when language, writing, and printing were introduced: Creating knowledge technologies and applying them to larger and larger scales of cooperative enterprise is inextricable from what it is to be human. Cognitive scientist Andy Clark believes that humans have been cyborgs for some time, "not in the merely superficial sense of combining flesh and wires, but in the most profound sense of being human-technology symbionts: thinking and reasoning systems whose minds and selves are spread across biological brain and non-biological circuitry."[73] By "non-biological circuitry," Clark means the combination of external technologies and internal knowledge skills involved in encoding and exchanging knowledge through alphabets, numbers, and images. Clark calls these media and the literacies that make them broadly useful "mindware upgrades," which not only have extended human cognitive abilities but have transformed them.

Clark believes that future cognitive technologies will make it harder to draw the line between tool and user: "What are these technologies? They include potent, portable machinery linking the user to an increasingly responsive World Wide Web. But they include also, and perhaps ultimately more importantly, the gradual smartening up and interconnection of the many everyday objects which populate our homes and offices."[74] Clark's notions support the conjecture that smart mobs in computation-pervaded environments could enable some people to transform the way they think and the way civilization operates, the way some people used printing presses, literacy, the scientific method, and new social contracts to transform feudalism into modernism. Enlightenment rationality has its limits, but the reason it is called "the Enlightenment" is that the changes enabled by the systematic use of reason, aided by mathematics and literacy, represented a step toward a more democratic and humane world. Part of taking that step involved learning to think in new ways, aided by cognitive technologies—learning to become new kinds of humans.

It would be a mistake, Clark cautions, to try to nail "human nature" down to what humans used to be, because "ours are (by nature) unusually plastic brains whose biologically proper functioning has always involved the recruitment and exploitation of non-biological props and scaffolds. More so than any other creature on this planet, we humans emerge as natural-born cyborgs, factory tweaked and primed so as to be ready to grow into extended cognitive and computational architectures: ones whose systematic boundaries far exceed those of skin and skull."[75] Clark doesn't claim a final word on the subject, but he declares the opening of a new territory for cognitive science research—the dynamics of human-technology symbiosis. "Understanding what is distinctive about human reason thus involves understanding the complementary contributions of both biology and (broadly) speaking technology, as well as the dense, reciprocal patterns of causal and co-evolutionary influence that run between them."[76]

Coevolution seems to me a key word. If Heidegger, Ellul, and Weizenbaum represent the shadow aspects of technology as an extension of the brutally mechanical and exploitive part of human nature, perhaps Clark points to a complementary way of looking at the same trait. Perhaps the transaction between danger and opportunity necessitated by our tool-making nature is not a zero-sum game but a balancing act. Certainly, we wouldn't be using personal computers with graphic interfaces to explore a worldwide network if machines that entered the world as weapons had not been repurposed by determined people who saw them as "mindware upgrades." The first electronic digital computer was created by U.S. Department of Defense contractors to perform artillery and nuclear weapons calculations but was transformed into something else entirely by a few idealists who were convinced that computers could help people think more effectively.[77]

Vannevar Bush, who commanded the scientific war effort for the United States during World War II, saw that the collective scientific enterprise around the world was creating knowledge at such a growing rate that keeping track of what we know loomed as a future problem. In a visionary article in the *Atlantic Monthly* in July 1945, titled "As We May Think," Bush proposed a future technology that would help people navigate through knowledge more effectively.[78] Bush planted the seminal idea that we needed to build machines to manage the knowledge amassed by our knowledge technologies.

Early computer research, both government- and industry-sponsored, concentrated on turning the huge, computationally puny mainframe computers of the 1950s into "artificial intelligence." Computer scientists and the first commercial computer vendors saw the technology as a brute force instrument, a pile driver for calculations, an internal-combustion engine for data processing. Licklider and Engelbart looked at the primitive computers of the early 1960s and saw how one day they could become more like alphabets or telescopes than pile drivers or accounting engines—amplifiers of human minds, not substitutes for them.

Licklider, an MIT researcher studying bioacoustics, had the opportunity to work with the first computer that had been rigged so that the programmer could directly interact with it.[79] When I interviewed Licklider in 1983, I asked him about that experience and he said, "I had a kind of religious conversion. The PDP-1 opened me up to ideas about how people and machines like this might operate in the future, but I never dreamed at first that it would ever become economically feasible to give everybody their own computer."[80] It did occur to him that these new computers were excellent candidates for the super-mechanized libraries that Vannevar Bush had prophesied. In 1960, Licklider's article, "Man-Machine Symbiosis" envisioned computers as neither substitute nor slave but partner for human thought: "The hope is that, in not too many years, human brains and computers will be coupled together very tightly, and that the resulting partnership will think as no human being has ever thought and process data in a way not approached by the information-handling machines we know today."[81]

Licklider's vision might have remained obscure if Sputnik had not frightened the U.S. Department of Defense into creating ARPA, the Advanced Research Projects Agency, to fund wild ideas that could leapfrog conventional research. Licklider was put in charge of ARPA's Information Processing Technology Office in the early 1960s, where he sponsored the creation of blue sky technologies that conventional computer manufacturers weren't interested in—the graphical interface, the personal computer, and computer networks.[82] The problems to be overcome in achieving such a partnership between computers and humans were only partially a matter of building better computers and only partially a matter of learning how minds interact with information. The most important questions were not about either the brain or the technology, but about the organizational restructuring that would inevitably occur when a new way to think was introduced. As it turned out, another maverick thinker in California, Douglas Engelbart, had been pursuing exactly this problem for years.

Engelbart, a twenty-five-year-old veteran, had been a radar operator in World War II. When he read "As We May Think," while awaiting a ship home from the Pacific, he realized that the postwar world would be dominated by problems of unprecedented complexity. He returned from the war and started working as an engineer in what was to become Silicon Valley but at that time was the world's largest fruit orchard. One day in 1950, while driving to work, he realized that computers might be able to display information on cathode screens the way radar did and that people could use these specially designed symbol manipulating devices to solve complex problems together. From the beginning, he saw a combination of languages, methodologies, and machines supporting new ways to think, communicate, collaborate, and learn. Much of the apparatus was social, and therefore nonmechanical. After failing to recruit support from computer science or computer manufacturers, Engelbart wrote his seminal paper, "A Conceptual Framework for the Augmentation of a Man's Intellect," in order to explain what he was talking about.[83] Engelbart came to the attention of Licklider. ARPA sponsored a laboratory at the Stanford Research Institute (SRI), the "Augmentation Research Center," where Engelbart and a group of hardware engineers, programmers, and psychologists who shared Engelbart's dream started building the computer as we know it today.

I had stayed in touch with Engelbart since I had first interviewed him in 1983. He has always been frustrated by the attention paid to the easy part of his vision, creating computers that could amplify intellectual activities, and by the lack of attention devoted to the hard part, learning how groups can "raise the IQ of organizations." Changing old habits of thought and communication turned out to be a great deal harder than creating multimedia supercomputers and the foundations of the Internet. Engelbart was one of the first to learn how new ways to cooperate involve knowledge different from that required to design chips or write programs.

While the computer and telecommunication industries fight trillion-dollar battles, the spirit of cooperation for the fun of it finds its own channels. After the dotcom and telecom bubbles burst, the emergence of new voluntary community resources, from SETI@home to blogging, made it clear again that the big IPO is not the only reason people decide to work together.

Is the kind of return on contributed investment that Moore's, Metcalfe's, and Reed's laws describe applicable to cooperation beyond the world of software and e-commerce? What theory or metatechnology could provide a general framework for human-technology coevolution that is not hopelessly deterministic, naively utopian, cynically selfish, or dependent on altruism beyond self-interest?

If Ostrom, Axelrod, Foucault, Licklider, and Engelbart provide essential parts of a foundation for a new theory of cooperation amplification, Robert Wright provides a framework to fit them together. In his book, *Nonzero: The Logic of Human Destiny,* Wright applied to the history of civilization the same game theory that Axelrod had used to explain biological and social phenomena.[84] Wright's controversial conclusion is that humans throughout history have learned to play progressively more complex non-zero-sum games with the help of technologies like steam engines and algorithms and metatechnologies like money and constitutions. Wright avoided using the word "cooperation," because the research he cites covers instances in which participation in non-zero-sum games is not consciously cooperative. I have used the term "smart mobs" because I believe the time is right to combine conscious cooperation, the fun kind, with the unconscious reciprocal altruism that is rooted in our genes. The technologies of mobile communication and pervasive computation could elevate to a new level the non-zero-sum game-playing Wright chronicles.

Recall from Chapter 2 that a zero-sum game is winner-take-all. For every winner, there has to be a loser. Games like the Prisoner's Dilemma have more subtle gradations of reward and punishment. In some non-zero-sum games, all players benefit if they cooperate. More people playing more complex non-zero-sum games create emergent effects like vibrant cities, bodies of knowledge, architectural masterpieces, marketplaces, and public health systems. Wright wrote that "cultural evolution has pushed society through several thresholds over the past 20,000 years. And now it is pushing society through another one."[85]

The world has not and is not likely to become a happy-all-the-time, win-win enterprise. Starkly competitive zero-sum games coexist with increasingly sophisticated non-zero-sum games. We band together to bring down the big game and then fight over how to divide it. Humans did not stop committing atrocities when print literacy made science and democratic nation-states possible. Enormous suffering and huge disparities in wealth and opportunity exist, and at the same time, more people are more prosperous, healthy, and politically free than ever before. Wright's cultural evolution is not a utopian concept, although it does offer hope that the trajectory of cultural evolution points in a generally positive direction—the more people find that they can harvest personal benefits by investing trust and practicing cooperation, the more they will invest in cooperative enterprise and help others join the venture. With the right knowledge, I believe we can catalyze this process, cultivate it, and nurture its growth. We can make a conscious effort to manage what Wright claims to be an unconscious human predilection that has driven cultural evolution.

Certain technologies, Wright argued, can trigger human societies to reorganize at a higher level of cooperation. As an example, Wright offered the Shoshone, a Native American tribe that lived in a territory with no big game to hunt but an abundance of jackrabbits at certain times of year. Because of their stark environment, the Shoshone normally existed at a simple level of social organization, with every extended family foraging for itself. When the rabbits were running, however, the families banded together into a larger, closely coordinated group, to wield a tool too large for any one family to handle or maintain—a huge net. Working together with the net, the entire Shoshone hunting group could capture more protein per person than they could working apart. Wright declared that "the invention of such technologies—technologies that facilitate or encourage non-zero-sum interaction—is a reliable feature of cultural evolution everywhere. New technologies create new chances for positive sums. And people maneuver to seize those sums, and social structure changes as a result."[86]

Wright noted that people who interact with each other in mutually profitable ways are not always aware that they are cooperating; he cited evolutionary psychologists in asserting that unconscious underpinnings of cooperation—like affection and indignation—are rooted in genetic traits:

> Natural selection, via the evolution of "reciprocal altruism" has built into us various impulses which, however warm and mushy they may feel, are designed for the cool, practical purpose of bringing beneficial exchange.
>
> Among these impulses: generosity (if selective and sometimes wary); gratitude, and an attendant sense of obligation; a growing empathy for, and trust of, those who prove reliable reciprocators (also known as "friends"). These feelings, and the behaviors they fruitfully sponsor, are found in all cultures. And the reason, it appears, is that natural selection "recognized" non-zero-sum logic before people recognized it. (Even chimpanzees and bonobos, our nearest relatives, are naturally disposed to reciprocal altruism, and

neither species has yet demonstrated a firm grasp of game theory). Some degree of social structure is thus built into our genes. . . .

In the intimate context of hunter-gatherer life, moral indignation works well as an anti-cheating technology. It leads you to withhold generosity from past nonreciprocators, thus insulating yourself from future exploitation; and all the grumbling you and others do about these cheaters leads people in general to give them the cold shoulder, so chronic cheating becomes a tough way to make a living. But as societies grow more complex, so that people exchange goods and services with people they don't see on a regular basis (if at all), this sort of mano-a-mano indignation won't suffice; new anti-cheating technologies are needed. And, as we'll see, they have materialized again and again—via cultural, not genetic, evolution.[87]

The cultural innovations that reorganize social interaction in light of new technologies are "social algorithms governing the uses of technology." Wright called these social methodologies "metatechnologies." Perhaps gossip and reputation were the metatechnologies that emerged from speech. In the Middle Ages, the metatechnologies of capitalism—currency, banking, finance, insurance—pushed the hierarchical machinery of feudal society to transform into a new way of organizing social activity: the market. "The metatechnology of capitalism then combined currency and writing to unleash unprecedented social power."[88] Wright claimed that the emerging merchant class pushed for democratic means of governance not out of pure altruism but in order to be free to buy and sell and make contracts. Throughout this process, powerful people always seek to protect and extend their power, but new technologies always create opportunities for power shifts, and at each stage from writing to the Internet, more and more power decentralizes: "I mean that new information technologies in general—not just money and writing—very often decentralize power, and this fact is not graciously conceded by the powers that be. Hence a certain amount of history's turbulence, including some in the current era."[89]

We're heading into more of that turbulence that Wright mentioned. The metatechnologies that could constrain the dangers of smart mob technologies and channel their power to beneficial ends are not fully formed yet. I believe we can do wonderful things together, if enough people learn how. How might a new literacy of cooperation look? Technologies and methodologies of cooperation are embryonic today, and the emergence of democratic, convivial, intelligent new social forms depends on how people appropriate, adopt, transform, and reshape the new media once they are out of the hands of engineers—as people always do.

Over the next few years, will nascent smart mobs be neutralized into passive, if mobile, consumers of another centrally controlled mass medium? Or will an innovation commons flourish, in which a large number of consumers also have the power to produce? The convergence of smart mob technologies is inevitable. The way we choose to use these technologies and the way governments will allow us to use them are very much in question. Technologies of cooperation, or the ultimate disinfotainment apparatus? The next several years are a crucial and unusually malleable interregnum. Especially in this interval before the new media sphere settles into its final shape, what we know and what we do matters.

NOTES

Introduction

1. The Shibuya Crossing in Tokyo, Japan, has the highest mobile phone density in the world. On weekdays an average of 190,000 people and on weekends an average of 250,000 people pass this crossing per day (Source: CCC, Tsutaya), around 1,500 people traverse at each light change, and 80 percent of them carry a mobile phone. <http://nooper.co.jp/showcase/gallery.php?s=4&l=en> (24 January 2002).

2. Karlin Lillington, "Mobile but Without Direction," *Wired News*, 21 September 2000, <http://www.wired.com/news/business/0,1367,38921,00.html> (28 January 2002).

3. Howard Rheingold, *Tools for Thought: The History and Future of Mind-Expanding Technology* (New York: Simon & Schuster, 1985).

4. Howard Rheingold, *The Virtual Community: Homesteading on the Electronic Frontier* (Reading, Mass.: Addison-Wesley, 1993).

5. Arturo Bariuad, "Text Messaging Becomes a Menace in the Philippines," *Straits Times*, 3 March 2001.

6. Lisa Takeuchi Cullen, "Dialing for Dollars," *Time Magazine* 157 (22), 4 June 2001, <http://www.timeinc.net/time/interactive/business/money_np.html> (4 February 2002). See also: Kevin Werbach, "Location-Based Computing: Wherever You Go, There You Are," *Release 1.0* 18 (6), June 2000, <http://release1.edventure.com/abstracts.cfm?Counter=8096700> (4 February 2002).

7. "Japan's Lonely Hearts Find Each Other with 'Lovegety,'" *CNN.com*, 7 June 1998, <http://www.cnn.com/WORLD/asiapcf/9806/07/fringe/japan.lovegety/> (26 January 2002).

8. Howard Rheingold, "You Got the Power," *Wired* 8.08, August 2000, <http://www.wired.com/wired/archive/8.08/comcomp.html> (29 March 2002).

9. See: eBay, <http://www.ebay.com>; Epinions, <http://www.epinions.com>; Slashdot, <http://www.slashdot.org>; and Plastic, <http://www.plastic.com>.

10. J. Carey, "Space, Time and Communications: A Tribute to Harold Innis," in *Communication as Culture* (New York: Routledge, 1989), 12.

Chapter 1

Epigraph: Tom Standage, "The Internet, Untethered," *Economist*, 11 October 2001, http://www.economist.com/surveys/displaystory.cfm?story_id=811934. October 2001.

1. Raritan River Akita Club Inc. (RRACI), "Hachiko," <http://www.nylana.org/RRACI/hachiko.htm> (28 January 2002).

2. Thomas Schelling, *The Strategy of Conflict* (Cambridge: Harvard University Press, 1960).

3. Guy Debord, *La Société du Spectacle* (Paris: Buchet-Chastel, 1967).

4. "Mad Wing Cyber Girl Gang Arrested," *Japan Today*, 8 August 2001, <http://www.japantoday.com/e/?content=news&id=51700> (22 January 2002).

5. Howard Rheingold, *Virtual Reality* (New York: Summit, 1991).

6. Mizuko Ito, "Mobile Phones, Japanese Youth, and the Re-placement of Social Contact," Society for the Social Studies of Science Meetings, Boston, 2001, <http://www.itofisher.com/PEOPLE/mito/Ito.4S2001.mobile.pdf> (14 November 2001).

7. Ibid.

8. Ibid.

9. Mizuko Ito et al., conversation with the author, October 2001, Tokyo.

10. Ibid.

11. Eija-Liisa Kasasniemi and Pirjo Rautianen, "Mobile Culture of Children and Teenagers in Finland," in *Perpetual Contact: Mobile Communication, Private Talk and Public Performance,* ed. Mark Aakhus and James Katz (Cambridge: Cambridge University Press, 2002).

12. Rich Ling and Birgitte Yttri, "Hyper-Coordination via Mobile Phones in Norway," in *Perpetual Contact: Mobile Communication, Private Talk and Public Performance,* ed. Mark Aakhus and James Katz (Cambridge: Cambridge University Press, 2002), 143.

13. Connie Garfalk, "Kids on the Move," *Telenor Xpress* 1, 2001, <http://www.telenor.com/xpress/2001/1/kids_move.shtml> (26 January 2002).

14. Ito et al., conversation with the author.

15. Ling and Yttri, "Hyper-Coordination via Mobile Phones in Norway," 153.

16. "Don't Leave Home Without It," *J@pan Inc.*, <http://www.japaninc.net/mag/comp/2001/04/apr01_blowfish.html> (4 February 2002).

17. Dmitri Ragano, "Growing Up in the Age of the Keitai," TheFeature.com, <http://www.thefeature.com/printable.jsp?pageid=14395>.

18. Michael M. Lewis, *Next: The Future Just Happened* (New York: Norton, 2001).

19. Rob Guth, "Japan's NTT Goes Global with New Company," *E-Business World*, 29 June 1999, <http://www.e-commerceworld.com/idgns/1999/06/29/JapansNTTGoesGlobalWithNew.shtml> (24 February 2002). See also: Forbes International 500, <http://www.forbes.com/international/> (24 February 2002).

20. Mari Matsunaga, *The Birth of i-mode* (Singapore: Chuang Yi Publishing Pte Lt, 2001).

21. Ibid., 64.

22. Ibid., 78.

23. Ibid., 119.

24. "Secrets of DoCoMo's Success," *Wireless World Forum*, 25 July 2001, <http://www.wirelessworldforum.com/printout2.php/10235/0> (4 February 2002).

25. Matsunaga, *The Birth of i-mode*, 151.

26. Takeshi Natsuno, interview by author, 17 October 2001, Tokyo.

27. Ibid.

28. Michele Yamada, "NTT DoCoMo to Launch Global Positioning Svc on Nov. 27," *Dow Jones*, 20 November 2001, <http://sg.biz.yahoo.com/011120/15/1uh7d.html> (28 January 2002).

29. Kenny Hirschhorn, interview by author, April 2001, London.

30. Steve Silberman, "Just Say Nokia," *Wired* 7.09, September 1999, <http://www.wired.com/wired/archive/7.09/nokia.html> (28 January 2002).

31. Kenneth Klee and Jennifer Bensko, "The Future Is Finnish," *Newsweek International*, 24 May 1999, <http://discuss.washingtonpost.com/nwsrv/Issue/21_ppa/printed/int/eur/ov3121_1.htm> (28 July 2001).

32. Risto Linturi, interview by author, May 2001, Helsinki.

33. Ibid.

34. Klee and Bensko, "The Future Is Finnish."

35. Linturi, interview by author.

36. Helsinki Arena 2000 Project, <http://www.arenanet.fi/english/index.html> (28 January 2002).

37. Geographic Information Systems, <http://www.usgs.gov/research/gis/title.html> (29 March 2002).

38. David Gelernter, *Mirror Worlds, or: The Day Software Puts the Universe in a Shoebox . . . How It Will Happen and What It Will Mean* (Oxford: Oxford University Press, 1992).

39. William Shaw, "In Helsinki Virtual Village . . . ," *Wired* 9.03, March 2001, 157–163, <http://www.wired.com/wired/archive/9.03/helsinki.html> (29 March 2002).

40. Ilkka Innamaa, interview by author, May 2000, Helsinki.

41. C. Alexander et al., *A Pattern Language* (New York: Oxford University Press, 1977).

42. Silberman, "Just Say Nokia."

43. Richard Quest, "Nokia Keeps Finland Mobile," *Time*, 157, 4 June 2001, <http://www.time.com/time/interactive/business/nokia_np.html> (12 October 2001).

44. Klee and Bensko, "The Future Is Finnish."

45. Ibid.

46. Puneet Gupta, "Short Message Service: What, How and Where?," *Wireless Developer Network*, <http://www.wirelessdevnet.com/channels/sms/features/sms.html> (4 February 2002).

47. Michael Pastore, "SMS Continues to Take Messaging World by Storm," *Cyberatlas*, 4 April 2001, <http://cyberatlas.internet.com/markets/wireless/article/0,10094_733811,00.html> (28 January 2002).

48. Logica, "SMS to Drive Wireless Internet Forward," 26 June 2000, <http://www.nua.ie/surveys/index.cgi?f=VS&art_id=905355866&rel=true> (28 December 2001).

49. Howard Rheingold, *The Virtual Community: Homesteading on the Electronic Frontier* (Reading, Mass.: Addison-Wesley, 1993).

50. Kasasniemi and Rautianen, "Mobile Culture of Children and Teenagers in Finland."

51. Ibid.

52. Ibid., 171–183.

53. Pasi Mäenpää, "Mobile Communication as a Way of Urban Life," in *Ordinary Consumption*, ed. Jukka Gronow and Allen Warde (London: Routledge, 2001), 107–124.

54. Tuomas Toivonen, unpublished thesis, Helsinki University of Technology, 2001, <http://www.aula.cc/hakuhodo/aula_thesis/> (22 January 2002).

55. Ibid.

56. Ibid.

57. Alan Goldstein, "Information-Savvy Sweden Offers a Glimpse into the Future of the Mobile Internet," *Dallas Morning News*, 29 March 2001, <http://www.mformobile.com/main.asp?pk=13755&pollid=x> (1 August 2001).

58. Maija Pesola, "Simplicity Seems the Key for Location-Based Mobile Phone Games," *Wireless Word*, 20 July 2001.

59. LunarMobil, <http://www.lunarmobil.se> (5 February 2002).

60. Anne Torres, "4 Sme, Txtng is Lyf," *TheFeature*, 18 April 2001, <http://www.thefeature.com/index.jsp?url=article.jsp?pageid=10667> (11 January 2002).

61. Benjamin Pimentel, "Cell Phone Craze May Be Key to Philippines' Future," *San Francisco Chronicle*, 11 February 2001, <http://www.sfgate.com/cgi-bin/article.cgi?file=/chronicle/archive/2001/02/11/BU166485.DTL> (24 May 2001).

62. Ibid.

63. Torres, "4 Sme, Txtng is Lyf."

64. Xinhua News Agency, "Thailand: Mobile Phone Network Paralyzed by Flood of Love Messages," 15 February 2001, <http://www.ayg.com/sms/Article.po?id=339231> (20 January 2002).

65. Orange.com, "The Survey Said: Text Messaging the Ultimate Flirting Tool," 26 March 2001, <http://www.orange.com/english/press_releases.html> (15 July 2001).

66. Leopoldina Fortunati, "The Ambiguous Image of the Mobile Phone," in *Communications on the Move: The Experience of Mobile Telephony in the 1990s,* ed. L. Haddon, a report to the COST248 work group, sponsored and published by Telia, AB. <http://members.aol.com/leshaddon/OINTRO.html>

67. Mark Ashurst, "Africa: Now, a 'Quiet Revolution': Mobile Phones Leapfrog an Obstacle to Development," *Newsweek International*, 27 August 2001.

68. Sadie Plant, "On the Mobile: The Effects of Mobile Telephones on Social and Individual Life," <http://www.motorola.com/mot/documents/0,1028,297,00.doc> (11 November 2001).

69. David Bennahum, interview with author, 10 November 2001, New York.

70. Ibid.

71. Douglas Century, "Motorola Versus Blackberry: Texting Cultures, A World Divided into Two-Way-Pager Camps," 14 January 2001, <http://www.xent.com/dec00/0761.html> (28 January 2002).

72. Fushi Tarazu, "DoCoMo's i-Mode Abroad?," *The Motley Fool,* 11 December 2000, <http://www.fool.com/community/views/2000/view001211.htm?ref=yhoolnk> (23 February 2001).

73. Tony Emerson, "The Next Big Thing," *Newsweek,* 6 August 2001, <http://www.msnbc.com/news/606561.asp#BODY> (12 January 2002).

74. Mizuko Ito, email correspondence with author, 14 January 2002.

75. Julian E. Barnes, "For Cellphone Holdouts, Worry Closes the Sale," *New York Times,* 19 September 2001, C6.

76. Simon Romero, "The Simple BlackBerry Allowed Contact When Phones Failed," *New York Times,* 20 September 2001, <http://www.nytimes.com/2001/09/20/technology/circuits/20BERR.html> (28 January 2002).

77. Stewart Brand, "Founding Father: Interview with Paul Baran," *Wired* 9.03, March 2001, <http://www.wired.com/wired/archive/9.03/baran.html> (13 May 2001).

78. Ling and Yttri, "Hyper-Coordination via Mobile Phones in Norway."

79. Mark Aakhus and James Katz, eds., *Perpetual Contact: Mobile Communication, Private Talk and Public Performance* (Cambridge: Cambridge University Press, 2002).

80. Erving Goffman, *The Presentation of Self in Everyday Life* (Garden City, N.Y.: Doubleday, 1959).

81. Ling and Yttri, "Hyper-Coordination via Mobile Phones in Norway," 159.

82. Ibid., 158.

83. Garfalk, "Kids on the Move."

84. Alex S. Taylor and Richard Harper, "Talking 'Activity': Young People and Mobile Phones," paper presented at the CHI 2001 Conference on Human Factors

in Computing Systems, Seattle, 31 March–5 April 2001, <http://www.cs.colorado.edu/~palen/chi_workshop/papers/TaylorHarper.pdf> (24 February 2002).

85. Ling and Yttri, "Hyper-Coordination via Mobile Phones in Norway."

86. Alexandra Weilenmann and Catrine Larsson, "Local Use and Sharing of Mobile Phones," in *Wireless World: Social and Interactional Aspects of the Mobile Age,* ed. B. Brown et al. (London: Springer-Verlag, 2001), 95.

87. Marko Ahtisaari, "Social Mobility," *Out of the Blue—The J. Walter Thompson Magazine for Europe,* Winter 2000/2001, 26.

88. Leslie Haddon, "The Social Consequences of Mobile Telephony: Framing Questions," in *The Social Consequences of Mobile Telephony: The Proceedings from a Seminar About Society, Mobile Telephony and Children,* Telenor R&D N 38/2000, eds. Rich Ling and Kristin Trane, 26 June 2000, 2–6, <http://www.telenor.no/fou/prosjekter/Fremtidens_Brukere/seminarer/mobilpresentasjoner/Proceedings%20_FoU%20notat_.pdf> (31 January 2002).

89. Erving Goffman, "Alienation from Interaction," in *Communication and Culture,* ed. Alfred G. Smith (New York: Holt, Rinehart and Winston, 1966).

90. Plant, "On the Mobile."

91. Leysia Palen, Marilyn Salzman, and Ed Youngs, "Discovery and Integration of Mobile Communications in Everyday Life," *Personal and Ubiquitous Computing Journal,* vol. 5 (2001): 109–122, <http://www.cs.colorado.edu/%7Epalen/Papers/cscwPalen.pdf> (5 February 2002).

92. Mizuko Ito, email correspondence with author, 14 January 2002.

Chapter 2

Epigraph: David Hume, *A Treatise of Human Nature,* ed. Ernest C. Mossner (New York: Viking, 1986).

1. Netscan, <http://netscan.research.microsoft.com> (5 February 2002).

2. Howard Rheingold, *The Virtual Community: Homesteading on the Electronic Frontier* (Reading, Mass.: Addison-Wesley, 1993).

3. Erving Goffman, *The Presentation of Self in Everyday Life* (Garden City, N.Y.: Doubleday, 1959).

4. Matt Ridley, *The Origins of Virtue: Human Instincts and the Evolution of Cooperation* (London: Penguin, 1996).

5. Ibid.

6. Garrett Hardin, "The Tragedy of the Commons," *Science* 162 (13 December 1968): 1243–1248.

7. Thomas Hobbes, *Leviathan,* ed. Richard E. Flathman and David Johnston (New York: W. W. Norton, 1997).

8. John Locke, *Two Treatises of Government* (New York: Prentice-Hall, 1952).

9. Mancur Olson Jr., *The Logic of Collective Action: Public Goods and the Theory of Group* (Cambridge: Harvard University Press, 1965).

10. Mancur Olson Jr., "The Logic of Collective Action," in *Rational Man and Irrational Society*, ed. Brian Barry and Russell Hardin (Beverly Hills, Calif.: Sage, 1982), 44.

11. Elinor Ostrom, *Governing the Commons: The Evolution of Institutions for Collective Action* (Cambridge: Cambridge University Press, 1990).

12. Ibid., 96.

13. Ibid., 90.

14. Ridley, *The Origins of Virtue*.

15. Ostrom, *Governing the Commons*, 27.

16. H. Scott Gordon, "The Economic Theory of a Common-Property Resource: The Fishery," *Journal of Political Economy* 62 (1954): 124–142; Anthony D. Scott, "The Fishery: The Objectives of Sole Ownership," *Journal of Political Economy* 65 (1955): 116–124.

17. Charlotte Hess, "Is There Anything New Under the Sun? A Discussion and Survey of Studies on New Commons and the Internet," presented at Constituting the Commons: Crafting Sustainable Commons in the New Millennium, the Eighth Conference of the International Association for the Study of Common Property, Bloomington, Indiana, 31 May–4 June 2000.

18. Ostrom, *Governing the Commons*, 25.

19. Marc A. Smith, "Mapping Social Cyberspaces: Measures and Maps of Usenet, a Computer Mediated Social Space" (Ph.D. diss., UCLA, 2001), 18.

20. Thomas Henry Huxley, "The Struggle for Existence in Human Society," in *Evolution and Ethics, and Other Essays* (London, 1894), 202–218.

21. Peter Kropotkin, *Mutual Aid. A Factor of Evolution* (Montreal: Black Rose Books, 1989), 78.

22. Stephen J. Gould, *Bully for Brontosaurus: Reflections on Natural History* (New York: W. W. Norton, 1991).

23. Kropotkin, *Mutual Aid*, 171.

24. J. Paradis and G. C. Williams, *Evolution and Ethics: T. H. Huxley's Evolution and Ethics with New Essays on Its Victorian and Sociobiological Context* (Princeton: Princeton University Press, 1989).

25. W. D. Hamilton, "The Genetical Evolution of Social Behavior," *Journal of Theoretical Biology* 7 (1964): 1–52.

26. Richard Dawkins, *The Selfish Gene* (Oxford: Oxford University Press, 1976).

27. Hobbes, *Leviathan*, 95.

28. John von Neumann and Oskar Morgenstern, *Theory of Games and Economic Behavior* (Princeton: Princeton University Press, 1944).

29. William Poundstone, *Prisoner's Dilemma: John von Neumann, Game Theory, and the Puzzle of the Bomb* (New York: Doubleday, 1992).

30. J. Bronowski, *The Ascent of Man* (Toronto: Little, Brown, 1973).

31. Herman Kahn, *On Thermonuclear War* (Princeton: Princeton University Press, 1960).

32. Jean-Jacques Rousseau, *A Discourse on Inequality* (London: Penguin, 1984).

33. Merrill M. Flood, "Some Experimental Games," Research Memorandum RM–789 (Santa Monica, Calif.: RAND Corporation, 1952).

34. A. W. Tucker, "On Jargon: The Prisoner's Dilemma," *UMAP Journal* 1 (1950): 101.

35. Robert Axelrod, *The Evolution of Cooperation* (New York: Basic Books, 1985).

36. Ibid., 12.

37. Ibid., 31.

38. Ibid., viii–ix.

39. Ibid., 21.

40. R. L. Trivers, "The Evolution of Reciprocal Altruism," *Quarterly Review of Biology* 46 (1971): 35–37.

41. Axelrod, *The Evolution of Cooperation.*

42. G. S. Wilkinson, "Reciprocal Food Sharing in the Vampire Bat," *Nature* 308 (March 8, 1984): 181–184.

43. Manfred Milinski, "TIT FOR TAT in Sticklebacks and the Evolution of Co-operation," *Nature* 325 (29 January 1987): 433–435.

44. P. Farb, *Man's Rise to Civilization as Shown by the Indians of North America from Primeval Times to the Coming of the Industrial State* (New York: Dutton, 1968).

45. Steven Levy, *Hackers: Heroes of the Computer Revolution* (New York: Doubleday, 1984).

46. J. H. Saltzer, D. P. Reed, and D. D. Clark, "End-to-End Arguments in System Design," *ACM Transactions on Computer Systems* 2 (November 1984): 277–288.

47. Howard Rheingold, *Tools for Thought* (Cambridge: MIT Press, 2000).

48. Katie Hafner and Matthew Lyon, *Where Wizards Stay Up Late: The Origins of the Internet* (New York: Touchstone, 1998).

49. Levy, *Hackers.*

50. Hafner and Lyon, *Where Wizards Stay Up Late.*

51. J.C.R. Licklider and R. W. Taylor, "The Computer as a Communication Device," *Science and Technology* (April 1968): 21–31.

52. William Henry Gates III, "An Open Letter to Hobbyists," *Altair Users' Newsletter,* 3 February 1976.

53. Dennis M. Ritchie, "The Evolution of the Unix Time-Sharing System," *AT&T Bell Laboratories Technical Journal* 63 (October 1984): 1577–1593.

54. Nick Moffit, "Nick Moffit's $7 History of Unix," <http://crackmonkey.org/unix.html> (29 January 2002).

55. Ritchie, "The Evolution of the Unix Time-Sharing System."

56. Moffit, "Nick Moffit's $7 History of Unix."

57. Richard Stallman, "The Free Software Definition," The GNU Project, Free Software Foundation, 2000, <http://www.gnu.org/philosophy/free-sw.html> (17 June 2001).

58. Ibid. See also: Michael Stutz, "Freed Software Winning Support, Making Waves," *Wired News*, 30 January 1998, <http://www.wired.com/news/technology/0,1282,9966,00.html> (5 February 2002).

59. Eric Raymond, *The Cathedral and the Bazaar: Musings on Linux and Open Source by an Accidental Revolutionary* (Sebastopol, Calif.: O'Reilly and Associates, 1997). See also: <http://www.tuxedo.org/~esr/writings/homesteading/> (29 January 2002).

60. BIND (Berkeley Internet Name Domain), <http://www.isc.org/products/BIND/> (16 January 2002).

61. Network Working Group, ed. B. Carpenter, "Architectural Principles of the Internet," June 1996, <http://www.ietf.org/rfc/rfc1958.txt> (26 November 2001).

62. Ibid.

63. Tim Berners-Lee, "Information Management: A Proposal," 1989, <http://www.w3.org/History/1989/proposal.html> (29 January 2002).

64. Andy Server, "It Was My Party—and I Can Cry If I Want To," *Business 2.0*, March 2001, <http://www.business2.com/articles/mag/0,1640,9662,FF.html> (12 August 2001).

65. Daniel Dern, "A Real Brief History of Usenet," *BYTE Magazine*, 4 September 1999.

66. Smith, "Mapping Social Cyberspaces," 12.

67. Ibid., 11.

68. Lawrence Lessig, *The Future of Ideas* (New York: Random House, 2001).

69. "FCC Launches Proceeding to Promote Widespread Deployment of High-speed Broadband Internet Access Services," 14 February 2002, <http://www.fcc.gov/Bureaus/Common_Carrier/News_Releases/2002/nrcc0202.html> (24 February 2002).

70. "Cable TV Lobby, Including Comcast, Tells FCC: Give Us a "Closed" Broadband Net," *Center for Digital Democracy*, 15 February 2002, <http://www.democraticmedia.org/news/washingtonwatch/cableletter.html> (25 February 2002). See also: Cable Industry FCC Lobbying Document, *Center for Digital Democracy*, 8 February 2002, <http://www.democraticmedia.org/resources/filings/cableFCCLobbyingDocument.pdf> (25 February 2002).

71. "FCC Sides with Cable Net Firms," *Associated Press*, 14 March 2002, <http://www.wired.com/news/politics/0,1283,51061,00.html> (29 March 2002).

72. L. Garton, C. Haythornthwaite, and B. Wellman, "Studying Online Social Networks," *Journal of Computer-Mediated Communication* 3, 1 (1997): 1.

73. Barry Wellman, "Physical Place and CyberPlace: The Rise of Personalized Networking," *International Journal of Urban and Regional Research* 25, 2 (2001):

227–252, <http://www.chass.utoronto.ca/~wellman/publications/individualism/ijurr3a1.htm> (29 March 2002).

74. Ibid., 227.

75. Ibid., 228.

76. Ibid., 233, 238.

77. Alun Anderson, "The Mathematics of Mayhem," in *The World in 2001*, <http://www.theworldin.com/arts/sci/fs1.html> (5 May 2001).

78. Gordon E. Moore, "Cramming More Components onto Integrated Circuits," *Electronics* 38, 8 (19 April 1965):114–117.

79. "Moore's Law," Intel Corporation, <http://www.intel.com/research/silicon/mooreslaw.htm> (21 December 2001).

80. Scott Kirsner, "The Legend of Bob Metcalfe," *Wired* 6.11, November 1998, <http://www.wired.com/wired/archive//6.11/metcalfe.html?person=bob_metcalfe&topic_set=wiredpeople> (27 January 2002).

81. David P. Reed, "That Sneaky Exponential: Beyond Metcalfe's Law to the Power of Community Building," originally appeared in *Context Magazine*, Spring 1999 (by permission of DiamondCluster International, Inc. © 1999) <http://www.contextmag.com/archives/199903/digitalstrategyreedslaw.asp> (25 January 2002).

82. David P. Reed, interview by author, Cambridge, Mass., November 2001.

83. Francis Fukuyama, *Trust: The Social Virtues and the Creation of Prosperity* (New York: Free Press, 1995).

84. Reed, interview by author, 2001.

85. Reed, "That Sneaky Exponential," 1999.

Chapter 3

Epigraph: Cory Doctorow, "My Date with the Gnomes of San Jose," *Mindjack*, 15 October 2000.http://www.mindjack.com/feature/p2p.html. (25 January 2002).

1. Charlene Anderson, "SETI@home and the Planetary Society: A Reminiscence and a Hope for the Future," May 2000, <http://www.planetary.org/UPDATES/seti/seti@home_and_planetary_society.html> (20 January 2002). See also: Roving Mouse, "SETI@home Stats," <http://www.roving-mouse.com/setiathome/> (25 January 2002).

2. Robert Wright, *Nonzero: The Logic of Human Destiny* (New York: Vintage, 2000).

3. David P. Reed, "That Sneaky Exponential: Beyond Metcalfe's Law to the Power of Community Building," *Context Magazine*, Spring 1999 (by permission of DiamondCluster International, Inc. © 1999) <http://www.contextmag.com/archives/199903/digitalstrategyreedslaw.asp> (1 February, 2002).

4. David Anderson, interview by author, summer 2000.

5. John F. Shoch and Jon A. Hupp, "Notes on the 'Worm' Programs—Some Early Experience with a Distributed Computation," Xerox PARC, September 1980.

6. Ibid., 1. See also: John Brunner, *Shockwave Rider* (New York: Del Rey, 1975), 249–252.

7. Miron Livny and Udi Manber, "Distributed Computation Via Active Messages," *IEEE Transactions on Computers* 34, 12 (1985): 1185–1190.

8. Richard Crandall, telephone interview by author, June 2000.

9. "Deepest Computation in History for a Yes/No Answer," *Technical News Release*, 29 September 1999, <http://www.perfsci.com/F24release.html> (1 February 2002).

10. "GIMPS Finds First Million-Digit Prime, Stakes Claim to $50,000 EFF Award," 30 June 1999, <http://www.mersenne.org/6972593.htm> (30 January 2002).

11. "Distributed Computing for Global Climate Research at Rutherford Appleton Laboratory," <http://www.climate-dynamics.rl.ac.uk/index.html> (25 January 2002).

12. Ibid.

13. United Devices, <http://www.ud.com/> (1 February 2002).

14. "The United Devices Cancer Research Program," <http://www.intel.com/cure/united.htm> (23 December 2001).

15. Henry Norr, "Idle Computer Time Can Fight Cancer," *San Francisco Chronicle*, 4 April 2001, B1.

16. Paul Marks, "Anthrax Screensaver Finds Promising New Drugs," *NewScientist.com*, 19 February 2002, <http://www.newscientist.com/news/news.jsp?id=ns99991953> (19 February 2002).

17. Google Compute, <http://toolbar.google.com/dc/faq_dc.html> (6 March 2002).

18. Harry McCracken, "The Digital Century," *PC World*, December 1999, <http://www.pcworld.com/resource/article.asp?aid=13531> (5 February 2002).

19. Matt Richtel, "With Napster Down, Its Audience Fans Out," *New York Times*, 20 July 2001, <http://www.nytimes.com/2001/07/20/college/coll20MUSI.html> (2 February 2002); Ron Harris, "Technology: Copyright Laws at Stake in Napster Case," *Nando Times*, 2 March 2001, <http://archive.nandotimes.com/technology/story/0,1643,500458967–500698582–503788773–0,00.html> (5 February 2002).

20. Dan Bricklin, "The Cornucopia of the Commons," in *Peer-to-Peer: Harnessing the Power of Disruptive Technologies,* ed. Andy Oram (Sebastopol, Calif.: O'Reilly and Associates, 2001).

21. Ashlee Vance, "Napster Serenades Songwriters, Ready to End Lawsuit," *Unlimited Net,* 26 September 2001, <http://www.unlimited.net.nz/unlimited/unlimited.nsf/ArchiveByAuthor/3CC3423C3EA87267CC256AD2006D2BA9?OpenDocument> (5 February 2002).

22. "Napster Offers $1 Billion to Settle Suit," *CNN.com*, 21 February 2001, <http://www.cnn.com/2001/LAW/02/20/napster.settlement.03/> (5 February 2002).

23. Gene Kan, "Gnutella," in *Peer-to-Peer: Harnessing the Power of Disruptive Technologies,* ed. Andy Oram (Sebastopol, Calif.: O'Reilly and Associates, 2001);

"What Is Gnutella?" *Gnutella News,* <http://www.gnutellanews.com/information/what_is_gnutella.shtml> (2 February 2002).

24. Nullsoft, Inc., <http://www.nullsoft.com/> (29 January 2002).

25. David E. Weekly, "Client as Server: The New Model," *Freshmeat.net,* 16 April 2000, <http://freshmeat.net/articles/view/155/ > (2 February 2002).

26. Ibid.

27. *Gnutella News.*

28. Ibid.

29. Kelly Truelove, "Gnutella and the Transient Web," *OpenP2P.com,* 22 March 2001, <http://www.openp2p.com/pub/a/p2p/2001/03/22/truelove.html> (17 January 2002).

30. Eytan Adar and Bernardo A. Huberman, "Free Riding on Gnutella," *First Monday* 5, 10 (2000), <http://www.firstmonday.dk/issues/issue5_10/adar/index.html> (2 February 2002).

31. Mojo Nation, <http://www.mojonation.net/> (23 January 2002).

32. Cory Doctorow, email correspondence with author, 19 February 2002.

33. Steven Johnson, "The Taste Test," *Feed,* 8 May 2001, <http://www.feedmag.com/templates/default.php3?a_id=1703> (23 December 2001).

34. Lou Gerstner, addressing the eBusiness Conference Expo in New York City, 12 December 2000, <http://www.ibm.com/lvg/1212.phtml> (2 February 2002).

35. Michelle Delio, "The Grid Draws Its Battle Lines," *Wired News*, 20 February 2002, <http://www.wired.com/news/technology/0,1282,50538,00.html> (29 March 2002).

36. Ian Foster, "Internet Computing and the Emerging Grid," *Nature,* 7 December 2000, <http://www.nature.com/nature/webmatters/grid/grid.html> (23 November 2001).

37. Ibid.

38. John Markoff, "The Soul of the Ultimate Machine," *New York Times*, 12 December 2000, <http://www.nytimes.com/2000/12/10/technology/10SMAR.html> (24 January 2002).

39. Ibid.

40. Ibid.

41. Steve Lohr, "IBM Making a Commitment to Next Phase of the Internet," *New York Times*, 2 August 2001, <http://www.nytimes.com/2001/08/02/technology/02BLUE.html>

42. Ann Harrison, "The Crime of Distributed Computing," *Register,* 12 December 2001, <http://www.theregister.co.uk/content/6/23477.html> (1 February 2002).

43. Steven Bonisteel, "Criminal Charges Settled in Distributed-Computing Case," *Newsbytes,* 17 January 2002, <http://www.newsbytes.com/news/02/173751.html>.

44. Lawrence Lessig, *The Future of Ideas* (New York: Random House, 2001).

Chapter 4

Epigraph: Mark Weiser, "The Computer for the 21st Century," *Scientific American*, September 1991, p. 94—104. http://www.ubiq.com/hypertext/weiser/Sci-AmDraft3.html. 2 February 2002.

1. Howard Rheingold, *Tools for Thought* (New York: Simon & Schuster, 1985).

2. Joel Garreau, "You Are So Here," *Washington Post*, 19 August 2001: C01, <http://www.washingtonpost.com/wp-dyn/articles/A33379–2001Aug19.html> (22 January 2002).

3. "Sensor Networks for Healthcare, the Environment, and Homeland Defense," <http://www.soe.ucsd.edu/Research_Review/agenda.html> (1 January 2002).

4. Saikat Chatterjee, "Netravali Sees a Networked Sphere in Ten Years," *Business Times, The Times of India*, New Delhi, 9 June 2000.

5. Patrick Gelsinger, Keynote Speech at Intel Developer Forum, Spring 2002, 28 February 2002, <http://www.intel.com/pressroom/archive/speeches/gelsinger20020228.htm> (6 March 2002), See also: "Intel Expands Moore's Law Into New Technologies and Applications,"<http://www.intel.com/pressroom/archive/releases/20020228corp.htm> (6 March 2002).

6. M. Weiser, R. Gold, and J. S. Brown, "The Origins of Ubiquitous Computing Research at PARC in the Late 1980s," *IBM Systems Journal* 38, 4 (1999): 693–696, <http://www.research.ibm.com/journal/sj/384/weiser.html> (2 February 2002).

7. Mark Weiser, "Ubiquitous Computing," <http://www.ubiq.com/hypertext/weiser/UbiHome.html> (29 January 2002).

8. Weiser, "The Computer for the 21st Century."

9. Ibid.

10. "The Trojan Room Coffee Machine," <http://www.cl.cam.ac.uk/coffee/coffee.html> (22 January 2002).

11. Weiser, "The Computer for the 21st Century."

12. Howard Rheingold, *Virtual Reality* (New York: Summit, 1991).

13. Myron Krueger, *Artificial Reality* (Reading, Mass.: Addison-Wesley, 1983).

14. Myron Krueger, "Responsive Environments," *NCC Proceedings*, 1977, 422–433.

15. Warren Robinett, "Electronic Expansion of Human Perception," *Whole Earth Review*, Fall 1991, 16–21.

16. Alex Pentland, "The Dance of Bits and Atoms," <http://www.white.media.mit.edu/people/sandy/profile.html> (2 February 2002).

17. Ivan E. Sutherland, "The Ultimate Display," *Proceedings of IFIPS Congress* 2 May 1965, 506–508.

18. Alex P. Pentland, "Smart Rooms," *Scientific American* 274 (April 1996): 68–76, <http://www.sciam.com/0496issue/0496pentland.html> (11 December 2001).

19. Elisa Batista, "Big Blue's Big Brother Lab," *Wired News*, 24 April 2001, <http://www.wired.com/news/technology/0,1282,43186,00.html> (24 February 2002).

20. Jim Spohrer, interview by author, November 2001.

21. J. C. Spohrer, "Information in Places," *IBM Systems Journal* 38, 4 (1996), <http://www.research.ibm.com/journal/sj/384/spohrer.html> (24 November 2001).

22. Ivan E. Sutherland, "Sketchpad: A Man-Machine Graphical Communication System," *Proceedings of the Spring Joint Computer Conference*, Detroit, Michigan, May 1963, and MIT Lincoln Laboratory Technical Report #296, January 1963.

23. Ivan E. Sutherland, "A Head-Mounted Three-Dimensional Display," *AFIPS Conference Proceedings* 33, Part I, 1968, 757–764.

24. S. Feiner, B. MacIntyre, and D. Seligmann, "Knowledge-Based Augmented Reality," *Communications of the ACM* 36 (July 1993): 52–62.

25. Spohrer, "Information in Places."

26. Ibid.

27. Per Persson and Fredrik Espinoza, "GeoNotes: Social Enhancement of Physical Space," *ERCIM News* 47, October 2001, <http://www.ercim.org/publication/Ercim_News/enw47/persson.html> (2 February 2002).

28. Jun Rekimoto, Yuji Ayatsuka, and Kazuteru Hayashi, "Augment-able Reality: Situated Communication through Physical and Digital Spaces," *Proceedings of the International Symposium on Wearable Computing*, 1998, <http://www.csl.sony.co.jp/person/rekimoto/papers/iswc98.pdf> (22 December 2001).

29. Ismail Haritaoglu, "InfoScope: Link from Real World to Digital Information Space," in *Ubicomp 2001: Ubiquitous Computing. Third International Conference, Atlanta, Georgia, September 30–October 2, 2001: Proceedings*, ed. Gregory C. Abowd, Barry Bromitt, and Steven A. Shafer, 247–255. Lecture Notes in Computer Science, 2201, Springer 2001, <http://link.springer.de/link/service/series/0558/papers/2201/22010247.pdf>

30. Salil Pradhan et al., "Websigns: Hyperlinking Physical Locations to the Web," *IEEE Computer* 34 (August 2001): 42–46.

31. Steven Feiner et al., "A Touring Machine: Prototyping 3D Mobile Augmented Reality Systems for Exploring the Urban Environment," *Proceedings of the First International Symposium on Wearable Computers* (1997): 74–81, <http://www.computer.org/conferen/proceed/8192/pdf/81920074.pdf> (5 February 2002).

32. Scott Fisher, "Environmental Media: Linking Virtual Environments to the Physical World," *Proceedings of the Second International Symposium on Mixed Reality*, Yokohama, Japan, March 2001, <http://www.wem.sfc.keio.ac.jp/wem/RawMedia/Fisher.pdf> (3 February 2002).

33. David S. Bennahum, "Be Here Now," *Wired* 9.11, November 2001, <http://www.wired.com/wired/archive/9.11/location.html> (3 February 2002).

34. Garreau, "You Are So Here."

35. "Direction Finding CDMA Handset from KDDI," 27 February 2002, <http://www.cellular-news.com/story/5932.shtml> (6 March 2002).

36. Universal Design of Digital City Project Overview, <http://www.digitalcity.jst.go.jp/about-e.html> (3 February 2002).

37. Risto Linturi, Marja-Riitta Koivunen, and Jari Sulkanen, "Helsinki Arena 2000—Augmenting a Real City to a Virtual One," *Digital Cities 2000*, 83–96, <http://www.linturi.fi/HelsinkiArena2000/> (11 January 2001).

38. The Center for Information Technology Research in the Interest of Society (CITRIS), <http://www.citris.berkeley.edu/about_citris.html> (3 February 2002).

39. Wade Roush, "Networking the Infrastructure," *Technology Review*, December 2001, <http://www.technologyreview.com/articles/roush1201.asp> (11 December 2001).

40. Russ Adams, "Bar Code History Page," *BarCode* 1, 16 (March 2001), <http://www.adams1.com/pub/russadam/history.html> (3 February 2002); see also: "The Origins of a Bar Code," *Uniform Code Council*, 2002, <http://www.uc-council.org/about_ucc/uc_bar_code_origin.html> (11 January 2002).

41. Charlie Schmidt, "Beyond the Bar Code," *Technology Review*, March 2001, <http://www.technologyreview.com/articles/schmidt0301.asp> (6 January 2002).

42. Barpoint, <http://www.barpoint.com> (3 February 2002).

43. "Organic Transistors and the Death of the Bar Code," *Berkeley Engineering Lab Notes* 2 (February–March 2002), <http://www.coe.berkeley.edu/labnotes/0202/barcode.html> (29 March 2002).

44. Auto-ID Center, <http://www.autoidcenter.org/main.asp> (29 March 2002).

45. Junko Yoshida, "Euro Bank Notes to Embed RFID Chips by 2005," *EE Times*, 19 December 2001, <http://www.eet.com/story/OEG20011219S0016> (29 January 2002).

46. Wes Vernon, "Latest Privacy Nightmare: Money That Tracks You," *NewsMax.com*, 28 July 2001, < http://www.newsmax.com/archives/articles/2001/7/27/212324.shtml> (3 February 2002).

47. Will Knight, "Tiny Radio Chip Gives Paper an ID," *New Scientist*, 4 July 2001, <http://www.newscientist.com/news/news.jsp?id=ns9999967> (3 February 2002); "Hitachi Announces World's Smallest RFID IC, the *mu-chip*," 5 July 2001, <http://www.hitachi.com/products/electronic/semiconductorcomponent/elecrfid/> (5 February 2002).

48. Kris Pister, Joe Kahn, and Bernhard Boser, "Smart Dust: Autonomous Sensing and Communication in a Cubic Millimeter," *Berkeley Sensor and Actuator Center*, <http://www-bsac.EECS.Berkeley.EDU/~pister/SmartDust/> (2 February 2002).

49. Duncan Graham-Rowe, "Dust Bugs," *New Scientist*, 28 August 1999, <http://www-bsac.eecs.berkeley.edu/~warneke/research/press/newscientist.html> (30 January 2002).

50. Jack Smith, "Computer in a Speck of Dust," *ABCNEWS.com*, 22 November 1999, <http://www.rense.com/politics5/minitech_p.htm> (3 February 2002).

51. Jun Rekimoto, "NaviCam: A Magnifying Glass Approach to Augmented Reality Systems," *Presence: Teleoperators and Virtual Environments* 6, 4 (1997): 339–412.

52. Jun Rekimoto, <http://www.csl.sony.co.jp/person/rekimoto.html> (3 February 2002).

53. Neil Gershenfeld, *When Things Start to Think* (New York: Henry Holt, 1999).

54. William Butera, "Programming a Paintable Computer," (Ph.D. diss., MIT, 2002), <http://web.media.mit.edu/~vmb/papers/buteraphd.pdf> (June 2002).

55. Gershenfeld, *When Things Start to Think,* 10.

56. Steve Mann and Hal Niedzviecki, *Cyborg: Digital Destiny and Human Possibility in the Age of the Wearable Computer* (Mississauga: Doubleday Canada, 2001), 30.

57. "A Brief History of Wearable Computing," <http://wearables.www.media.mit.edu/projects/wearables/lizzy/timeline.html#1989> (3 February 2002).

58. J. Peter Bade, G. Q. Maguire Jr., and David F. Bantz, *The IBM/Columbia Student Electronic Notebook Project,* 29 June 1990.

59. "A Brief History of Wearable Computing."

60. The Wearable Group at Carnegie Mellon, <http://www.wearablegroup.org/> (6 March 2002). See also: VuMan, <http://www-2.cs.cmu.edu/~wearable/vuman.html> (6 March 2002).

61. Mann and Niedzviecki, *Cyborg,* 42.

62. Ibid., 48–49.

63. *Cyberman,* directed by Peter Lynch, <http://cbc.ca/cyberman/> (29 March 2002).

64. Thad Starner's Home Page, <http://www.cc.gatech.edu/fac/Thad.Starner/> (25 January 2002).

65. Thad Starner, "Wearable Computing and Context Awareness" (Ph.D. diss., MIT, 1999), 64.

66. Mann and Niedzviecki, *Cyborg,* 71.

67. Steve Mann, "Smart Clothing: The Shift to Wearable Computing," *Proceedings of CACM* 39 (August 1996): 23–24.

68. "The MIThril Vision," <http://www.media.mit.edu/wearables/mithril/vision.html> (21 January 2002).

69. Scott Stemberger, "New Body Art: Wearable Wireless Devices," *IBM DeveloperWorks,* January 2002, <http://www-106.ibm.com/developerworks/wireless/library/wi-wear.html?t=gr,p=Wearem-Wireless> (3 February 2002).

70. Ibid.

71. Ibid.

72. Wearable Internet Appliance, <http://www.hitachi.co.jp/Prod/vims/wia/eng/main.html> (3 February 2002).

73. "Timex Watch to Incorporate Speedpass Technology," *Associated Press,* 28 February 2002, <http://www.usatoday.com/life/cyber/tech/review/2002/2/28/timex-speedpass.htm> (6 March 2002).

Chapter 5

Epigraph: Bruce Sterling, *Distraction, A Novel* (New York: Bantam, 1998).

1. Upendra Shardanand and Pattie Maes, "Social Information Filtering: Algorithms for Automating Word of Mouth," *Proceedings of ACM CHI'95 Conference on Human Factors in Computing Systems,* 1995, <http://www.acm.org/sigchi/chi95/Electronic/documnts/papers/us_bdy.htm> (9 February 2002).

2. Cameron Barrett, "Online Community Technologies and Concepts," *Camworld.com,* December 2001, <http://www.camworld.com/essays/communities.html> (9 February 2002).

3. Howard Rheingold, *The Virtual Community: Homesteading on the Electronic Frontier* (Reading, Mass.: Addison-Wesley, 1993).

4. Howard Rheingold, "Virtual Communities," *Whole Earth Review* 61 (Winter 1988): 14.

5. David Goldberg et al., "Using Collaborative Filtering to Weave an Information Tapestry," *Communications of the ACM* 35 (December 1992): 61–70.

6. Usenet FAQ Archive, <ftp://rtfm.mit.edu/pub/usenet-by-hierarchy/> (9 February 2002).

7. Paul Resnick et al., "GroupLens: An Open Architecture for Collaborative Filtering of Netnews," *Proceedings of ACM 1994 Conference on Computer Supported Cooperative Work,* 1994, 175–186, <http://www.si.umich.edu/~presnick/papers/cscw94/> (9 February 2002).

8. The Reputations Research Network, <http://databases.si.umich.edu/reputations/> (14 January 2002).

9. MovieLens, <http://movielens.umn.edu/> (9 February 2002).

10. Hui Guo, Thomas Kreifelts, and Angi Voss, "SOaP: Social Filtering through Social Agents," in *ECRIM Workshop Proceedings, No. 98/W001 of the 5th DELOS Workshop on Filtering and Collaborative Filtering,* 291–298, <http://www.ercim.org/publication/ws-proceedings/DELOS5/guo.pdf> (10 February 2002).

11. Ibid.

12. Steven Johnson, *Emergence: The Connected Lives of Ants, Brains, Cities, and Software* (New York: Scribner, 2001).

13. Epinions, <http://www.epinions.com> (9 February 2002).

14. Mark Frauenfelder, "Revenge of the Know-It-Alls," *Wired* 8.07, July 2000, <http://www.wired.com/wired/archive/8.07/egoboo.html> (31 January 2002).

15. Ibid.

16. Ibid.

17. Katie Hafner, "Web Sites Begin to Self Organize," *New York Times,* 18 January 2001, <http://www.nytimes.com/2001/01/18/technology/18SELF.html> (24 January 2002).

18. Everything2, <http://www.everything2.com/> (9 February 2002).

19. Blogger, <http://www.blogger.com> (5 February 2002).

20. Farhad Manjoo, "Blah, Blah, Blah, and Blog," *Wired News,* 18 February 2002, <http://www.wired.com/news/print/0,1294,50443,00.html> (24 February 2002).

21. Henry Jenkins, "Digital Renaissance," *Technology Review,* March 2002, <http://www.technologyreview.com/articles/jenkins0302.asp> (24 February 2002).

22. Slashdot FAQ, <http://slashdot.org/faq/> (9 February 2002).

23. Ibid.

24. eBay, <http://pages.ebay.com/community/aboutebay/overview/index.html> (5 February 2002).

25. Peter Kollock, "The Production of Trust in Online Markets," in *Advances in Group Processes* 16, ed. E. J. Lawler et al. (Greenwich, Conn.: JAI Press, 1999), <http://www.sscnet.ucla.edu/soc/faculty/kollock/papers/online_trust.htm> (9 February 2002).

26. "Crime Low on eBay Site," *Marin Independent Journal,* 29 December 2000, B4, B6.

27. Judith H. Dobryzynski, "In Online Auctions, Rings of Bidders," *New York Times,* 2 June 2000, <http://www.nytimes.com/library/tech/00/06/biztech/articles/02ebay.html> (11 January 2002).

28. Peter Kollock, "The Production of Trust in Online Markets," 99.

29. Paul Resnick and Richard Zeckhauser, "Trust Among Strangers in Internet Transactions: Empirical Analysis of eBay's Reputation System," Working Paper for the NBER Workshop on Empirical Studies of Electronic Commerce, 5 February 2001, <http://www.si.umich.edu/~presnick/papers/ebayNBER/index.html> (10 February 2002).

30. Paul Resnick et al., "Reputation Systems," *Communications of the ACM,* 43 (December 2000), <http://www.si.umich.edu/~presnick/papers/cacm00/reputations.pdf> (9 February 2002).

31. "Reputation Bibliography," The Reputations Research Network, <http://databases.si.umich.edu/reputations/bib/bib.html> (23 October 2001).

32. Richard Lethin, "Reputation," in *Peer-to-Peer: Harnessing the Power of Disruptive Technologies,* ed. Andy Oram (Sebastopol, Calif.: O'Reilly and Associates, 2001).

33. William Stallings, "How to Certify Public Keys Without a Central Authority," *Byte,* February 1995, <http://www.byte.com/art/9502/sec13/art4.htm> (9 February 2002).

34. Chrysanthos Dellarocas, interview by author, November 2001, New York.

35. Chrysanthos Dellarocas, "Building Trust On-Line: The Design of Reliable Reputation Reporting Mechanisms for Online Trading Communities," *eBusiness@MIT,* July 2001, <http://ebusiness.mit.edu/research/papers/101%20Dellarocas,%20Trust%20Management.pdf> (19 September 2001).

36. Kirsten Hawkes, "Why Hunter-Gatherers Work: An Ancient Version of the Problem of Public Goods," *Current Anthropology* 34, 4 (1993): 341–361.

37. Josh Whitfield, "Men Fish for Compliments," *Nature* 9 (April 2001), <http://www.nature.com/nsu/010412/010412–1.html> (9 February 2002).

38. G. Pollock and L. A. Dugatkin, "Reciprocity and the Evolution of Reputation," *Journal of Theoretical Biology* 159 (1992): 25–37.

39. Robin Dunbar, "Why Gossip Is Good for You," *New Scientist,* 21 November 1992.

40. Karl Sigmund, Ernst Fehr, and Martin A. Nowak, "The Economics of Fair Play," *Scientific American,* January 2002, 83–87.

41. Ernst Fehr and Simon Gachter, "Altruistic Punishment in Humans," *Nature* 115 (2002). 137–140.

42. Karl Sigmund, Christoph Hauert, and Martin A. Nowak, "Reward and Punishment in Minigames," paper presented at conference in Steyr, Austria, July 6–7, 2001, <http://www.umass.edu/preferen/mpapers/Sigmund.pdf> (9 February 2002).

43. Natalie Angier, "The Urge to Punish Cheats: Not Just Human, but Selfless," *New York Times,* 22 January 2002, <http://www.nytimes.com/2002/01/022/science/social/22CHEA.html> (23 January 2002).

44. Ibid.

45. Marc A. Smith, "Mapping Social Cyberspaces: Measures and Maps of Usenet, a Computer Mediated Social Space" (Ph.D. diss., UCLA, 2001), 157–158.

Chapter 6

Epigraph: Lawrence Lessig, interviewed by author, November 2001.

1. Elektrosmog Timeline, <http://elektrosmog.nu/timeline.html> (22 February 2002).

2. "Starbucks and Microsoft Blend Coffee Retailer's Expertise with Technology Leader's Software and Services to Deliver Wireless Coffeehouse Experience," <http://www.mobilestar.com/news_pressreleases_starbux.asp> (20 February 2002).

3. Surf and Sip, Inc., <http://www.surfandsip.com/> (21 February 2002).

4. Bob Liu, "VoiceStream to Acquire MobileStar Assets," *80211Planet.com,* 12 November 2001, <http://www.80211-planet.com/news/article/0,4000,1481_922241,00.html> (21 February 2002). See also: Ben Charny, "MobileStar Lays Off

Staff, Seeks Sale," *CNET News.com,* 10 October 2001, <http://news.com.com/2100–1033–274214.html?legacy=cnet> (21 February 2002).

5. Mark Ashurst, "Africa: Now, a 'Quiet Revolution': Mobile Phones Leapfrog an Obstacle to Development," *Newsweek International,* 27 August 2001. See also: Stefan Lehmann, "Wireless Brings the World to Africa," *Connect-World Africa 2001,* October 2001, <http://www.connect-world.com/docs/articles/cwafrica01/lehmann_radio_cwafrica01.asp> (22 February 2002).

6. Rob Flickenger, "802.11b Tips, Tricks, and Facts," *O'Reilly Network,* 2 March 2001, <http://www.oreillynet.com/pub/a/wireless/2001/03/02/802.11b_facts.html> (21 February 2002).

7. Ibid.

8. "Communications Law: An Overview," *Legal Information Institute* (Cornell Law School), <http://www.law.cornell.edu/topics/communications.html> (21 February 2002). See also: "Communications Act Of 1934," *Federal Communications Commission,* <http://www.fcc.gov/Reports/1934new.pdf> (21 February 2002).

9. "Three Telecommunications Laws: Their Impact and Significance," Center for Educational Priorities, <http://www.cep.org/laws.html> (21 February 2002).

10. Jessica Litman, *Digital Copyright* (New York: Prometheus Books, 2001).

11. R. H. Coase, "The Federal Communications Commission," *Journal of Law and Economics* 2 (1959): 10.

12. Lawrence Lessig, "The Internet Under Siege," *Foreign Policy,* November-December 2001, <http://www.foreignpolicy.com/issue_novdec_2001/lessig.html> (21 February 2002).

13. Kevin Maney, "Wireless Technology Could Sting Cellular Networks," *USA Today,* 1 August 2001, <http://www.usatoday.com/life/cyber/ccarch/2001–08–01-maney.htm> (23 February 2002).

14. See Chapter 2 for an explanation of Moore's, Metcalfe's, and Reed's Laws.

15. Leander Kahney, "Free the Wireless Net!" *Wired News,* 20 September 2000, <http://www.wired.com/news/print/0,1294,38803,00.html> (21 February 2002).

16. Consume the Net, <http://www.consume.net> (22 February 2002).

17. Elektrosmog Timeline.

18. Kahney, "Free the Wireless Net!"

19. WirelessAnarchy, <http://www.wirelessanarchy.com> (21 February 2002).

20. Anthony Townsend, telephone interview by author, 12 February 2002.

21. Peter Meyers, "Motley Crew Beams No-Cost Broadband to New York: High Speed, Freed," *Village Voice,* 15–21 August 2001, <http://www.villagevoice.com/issues/0133/meyers.php> (22 February 2002).

22. NYCWireless, <http://www.nycwireless.net> (16 January 2002).

23. Erika Jonietz, "Unwiring the Web," *Technology Review,* December 2001, <http://www.technologyreview.com/articles/innovation11201.asp> (22 February 2002).

24. Townsend, telephone interview by author.

25. Dana Spiegel, email correspondence, 29 January 2002.

26. Jonietz, "Unwiring the Web."

27. Peter Meyers, "In a Pinch, Wi-Fi Fills the Gap," *New York Times,* 4 October 2001, <http://www.nytimes.com/2001/10/04/technology/circuits/04ACCE. html?ex=100> (23 February 2002).

28. PlayaNet, <http://www.playanet.org> (23 February 2002).

29. Burning Man, <http://www.burningman.com> (23 February 2002).

30. Cory Doctorow, email correspondence, 25 February 2001.

31. "SFLan Manifesto," <http://www.sflan.com/index.html> (23 February 2002).

32. John Markoff, "The Corner Internet Network vs. the Cellular Giants," *New York Times*, 4 March 2002, <http://www.nytimes.com/2002/03/04/technology/ 04MESH.html> (6 March 2002).

33. Michael Behar, "The Broadband Militia," *Washington Monthly*, March 2002, <http://www.washingtonmonthly.com/features/2001/0203.behar.html> (6 March 2002).

34. Rob Flickenger, *Building Wireless Community Networks: Implementing the Wireless Web* (Sebastopol, Calif.: O'Reilly Associates, 2001), <http://www.oreillynet.com/pub/a/wireless/2001/03/06/recipe.html> (21 February 2002).

35. Personal Telco Project, <http://www.personaltelco.net> (28 July 2001).

36. Ben Charny, "EarthLink Founder Takes to the Air," *CNET News.com*, 19 December 2001, <http://news.cnet.com/news/0–1004 200–8237110.html> (21 February 2002.)

37. "Asia at the Forefront of Wireless LAN Industry," *Wireless World Forum*, 1 February 2002, <http://www.wirelessworldforum.com/w2fnews11530.html> (21 February 2002).

38. Ephraim Schwartz, "IBM Hints at Taking Wi-Fi Access National," *Infoworld*, 10 June 2002, <http://www.idg.net/go.cgi?id=697400>

39. John Edwards, "LANs Without Lines, *CIO Magazine*, 1 April 2001, <http://www.cio.com/archive/040101/et_content.html> (11 February 2002). See also: "Wireless Bares its Bluetooth at Comdex," *USA Today*, 15 November 2001, <http://www.usatoday.com/life/cyber/wireless/2001/11/15/comdex-bluetooth.htm> (24 February 2002).

40. Bob Brewin, "UPS to Deploy Bluetooth, Wireless LAN Network," *CNN.com*, 24 July 2001, <http://www.cnn.com/2001/TECH/industry/07/24/ ups.bluetooth.idg/> (23 February 2002).

41. Ephraim Schwartz, "Fearless Forecasts," *Infoworld.com*, 21 December 2001, <http://www.infoworld.com/articles/op/xml/01/12/24/011224opwireless.xml> (23 February 2002).

42. Microsoft chairman Bill Gates at the Microsoft Professional Developers Conference, 23 October 2001, reported by David Isenberg in *Smart Letter* #68, 17 March 2002, <http://isen.com/archives/020317.html> (29 March 2002).

43. Kevin Poulsen, "War Driving by the Bay," *The Register,* 13 April 2001, <http://www.theregister.co.uk/content/8/18285.html> (21 February 2002).

44. Ibid.

45. Meyers, "Motley Crew Beams No-Cost Broadband."

46. Michelle Delio, "Wireless Networks in Big Trouble," *Wired News,* 20 August 2001. <http://www.wired.com/news/wireless/0,1382,46187,00.html> (27 December 2001).

47. Paul Festa, "Free Wireless Net Access for the Masses," *CNET News.com,* 26 September 2001, <http://news.cnet.com/news/0–1004–200–7301549.html?tag=tp_pr> (11 October 2001).

48. RF Radiation and Electromagnetic Field Safety, <http://www.arrl.org/news/rfsafety/hbkrf.html> (29 March 2002).

49. Howard Rheingold, *Tools for Thought* (New York: Simon and Schuster, 1985), <http://www.rheingold.com/texts/tft/index.html> (23 February 2002).

50. Howard Rheingold, *The Virtual Community: Homesteading on the Electronic Frontier* (Reading, Mass.: Addison-Wesley, 1993).

51. Dave Hughes, telephone interview by author, January 2002.

52. Lawrence Lessig, *The Future of Ideas* (New York: Random House, 2001), 80.

53. Anna Couey, "The Birth of Spread Spectrum: How 'The Bad Boy of Music' and 'The Most Beautiful Girl in the World' Catalyzed a Wireless Revolution—In 1941," *MicroTimes* 166, 23 June 1997, <http://www.sirius.be/lamarr.htm> (23 February 2002). See also: Ashley Craddock, "Privacy Implications of Hedy Lamarr's Idea," *Wired News,* 11 March 1997, <http://www.wired.com/news/politics/0,1283,2507,00.html> (14 October 2001).

54. Chris Beaumont, "Hedy Lamarr, George Antheil, and the Secret Communications System Patent," <http://www.ncafe.com/chris/pat2/index.html> (23 February 2002).

55. Peter H. Dana, "Global Positioning System Overview," 1 May 2000, <http://www.colorado.edu/geography/gcraft/notes/gps/gps_f.html> (23 February 2002).

56. Dewayne Hendricks, email correspondence, 10 March 2002, See also: Tucson Amateur Packet Radio, <http://www.tapr.org> (29 March 2002).

57. Brent Hurtig, "Broadband Cowboy," *Wired* 10.01, January 2002, <http://www.wired.com/wired/archive/10.01/hendricks_pr.html> (23 February 2002).

58. Hughes, telephone interview by author.

59. "Wales' Digital Opportunity—Dave Hughes, Colorado." Produced by John Wilson. 20 min., videocassette, <http://www.digitalmatrixcymru.org.uk/webcast/index.htm> (23 February 2002).

60. Nobuo Ikeda, "The Spectrum as Commons: Digital Wireless Technologies and the Radio Policy," RIETI Discussion Paper Series 02-E–002, March 2002 <http://www.rieti.go.jp/jp/publications/dp/02e002.pdf> (29 March 2002).

61. "AN-MSI Tribal College Wireless Project Overview," <http://www.anmsi.org/committees/internet_conn/wireless_net.asp> (18 July 2001).

62. "HPWREN Collaborates with Palomar College and SCTCA's Tribal Digital Village: Computer Science Class Includes Multicast Technology Experiments," *High Performance Wireless Research and Education Network (HPWREN)*, 4 January 2002, <http://hpwren.ucsd.edu/news/020104.html> (20 February 2002).

63. Kade L. Twist, "Native Networking Trends: Wireless Broadband Networks," *Digital Beat*, 20 September 2001, <http://www.benton.org/DigitalBeat/db092001.html> (23 February 2002).

64. Robert X. Cringely, "The 100 Mile-Per-Gallon Carburetor: How Ultra Wide Band May (or May Not) Change the World," *The Pulpit*, 24 January 2002, <http://www.pbs.org/cringely/pulpit/pulpit20020124.html> (29 January 2002).

65. Tim Shepard, "Decentralized Channel Management in Scalable Multihop Spread-Spectrum Packet Radio Networks" (Ph.D. diss., MIT, 1995), <ftp://ftp.lcs.mit.edu/pub/lcs-pubs/tr.outbox/MIT-LCS-TR–670.ps.qz> (23 February 2002).

66. W. Brian Arthur, *Increasing Returns and Path Dependence in the Economy* (Ann Arbor: University of Michigan Press, 1994).

67. "A Radio on Every Chip in 10 Years," *The Register*, 4 March 2002, <http://www.theregister.co.uk/content/3/24267.html> (6 March 2002).

68. Steve Gillmor, "Man in the White Suit," *InfoWorld.com*, 4 January 2002, <http://www.infoworld.com/articles/op/xml/02/01/07/020107opcurve.xml> (24 January 2002).

69. "MeshNetworks Receives Experimental License from FCC Enabling Demonstration of its Mobile Broadband Network Technology," <http://www.meshnetworks.com/pages/newsroom/press_releases/release_01_09_02.htm> (23 February 2002).

70. "Nokia Introduces First-of-Its-Kind Wireless Broadband Solution at SUPERCOMM 2000," 7 June 2000, <http://press.nokia.com/PR/200006/782980_5.html> (29 January 2002).

71. Sam Joseph, "When Population Density is a Plus," *J@pan, Inc*, June 2001, <http://www.japaninc.com/mag/comp/2001/06/jun01_filter_pop.html> (23 February 2002).

72. Cybiko, Inc., <http://www.cybiko.com/> (23 January 2002). See also: Cybla.com, <http://www.cybla.com/main.shtml> (23 February 2002).

73. Sam Joseph, "P2P: The Japanese Angle," *J@pan Inc*, April 2001, <http://www.japaninc.net/print.php?articleID=112> (21 December 2001).

74. Jaap Haartsen, "Bluetooth: The Universal Radio Interface for Ad Hoc, Wireless Connectivity," *Ericsson Review* 3, 1998, <http://www.ericsson.com/about/publications/review/1998_03/article14.shtml> (14 December 2001).

75. The Bluetooth Special Interest Group (SIG), <http://www.bluetooth.com/sig/about.asp> (23 February 2002).

76. Brewin, "UPS to Deploy Bluetooth."

77. Guy Kewney, "Bluetooth Will Coexist with WLANs, Says Forrester," *ZDNET UK News,* 22 October 2001, <http://news.zdnet.co.uk/story/0,,t269-s2097796,00.html> (10 November 2001).

78. Hurtig, "Broadband Cowboy."

79. David S. Isenberg, "The Dawn of the Stupid Network," *ACM Networker* 2.1, February/March 1998, 24–31, <http://www.isen.com/papers/Dawnstupid.html> (29 March 2002).

80. Hughes, telephone interview by author.

81. GNU Radio, <http://www.gnu.org/software/gnuradio/gnuradio.html> (29 March 2002).

82. Lessig, interview by the author.

83. Yochai Benkler, "Overcoming Agoraphobia: Building the Commons of the Digitally Networked Environment," *Harvard Journal of Law and Technology* 287, 1998, <http://www.law.nyu.edu/benklery/agoraphobia.pdf> (18 November 2001).

84. Kevin Werbach, "Open Spectrum: The Paradise of the Commons," *Release 1.0,* 19, 10 (November 2001), <http://release1.edventure.com/abstracts.cfm?Counter=5423494> (23 February 2002).

85. Quentin Hardy, "The Great Wi-Fi Hope," *Forbes,* 18 March 2002, <http://www.forbes.com/forbes/2002/0318/056.html> (29 March 2002).

86. Lessig, interview by author.

87. Ibid.

88. David Reed, interview by author, November 2001 (described in Chapter 2).

89. Werbach, "Open Spectrum."

90. Joseph A. Schumpeter, *Capitalism, Socialism, and Democracy* (1942; reprint, New York: Harper, 1975), 82–85.

91. Niccolo Machiavelli, *The Prince,* 2nd ed. (London and New York: W. W. Norton, 1992), 17.

92. Lessig, *The Future of Ideas,* 230.

Chapter 7

Epigraph: Vincente Rafael, "The Cell Phone and the Crowd: Messianic Politics in Recent Phillipine History," 13 June 2001. http://communication.ucsd.edu/people/f_rafael.cellphone.html.

1. Michael Bociurkiw, "Revolution by Cell Phone," *Forbes,* 10 September 2001, <http://www.forbes.com/asap/2001/0910/028.html> (1 March 2002).

2. Ibid.

3. Paul de Armond, "Black Flag Over Seattle," *Albion Monitor* 72, March 2000, <http://www.monitor.net/monitor/seattlewto/index.html> (1 March 2002).

4. Alexander MacLeod, "Call to Picket Finds New Ring in Britain's Fuel Crisis," *Christian Science Monitor,* 19 September 2000. See also: Chris Marsden, "Britain's Labour Government and Trade Union Leaders Unite to Crush Fuel Tax Protest," *World Socialist Web Site,* 15 September 2000, <http://www.wsws.org/articles/2000/sep2000/fuel-s15.shtml> (1 March 2002).

5. Steve Mann and Hal Niedzviecki, *Cyborg: Digital Destiny and Human Possibility in the Age of the Wearable Computer* (Mississauga: Doubleday Canada, 2001), 177–178.

6. Critical Mass, <http://www.critical-mass.org/> (6 March 2002).

7. Anne Torres, "4 SME, Txtng is Lyf," *TheFeature.com,* 18 April 2001, <http://www.thefeature.com> (1 March 2002).

8. Bociurkiw, "Revolution by Cell Phone."

9. Rafael, "The Cell Phone and the Crowd."

10. Ibid.

11. Arturo Bariuad, "Text Messaging Becomes a Menace in the Philippines," *Straits Times,* 3 March 2001.

12. Wayne Arnold, "Manila's Talk of the Town Is Text Messaging," *New York Times,* 5 July 2000, C1.

13. Bariuad, "Text Messaging Becomes a Menace."

14. Rafael, "The Cell Phone and the Crowd."

15. Ibid.

16. Richard Lloyd Parry, "The TXT MSG Revolution," *Independent Digital,* 23 January 2001, <http://www.independent.co.uk/story.jsp?story=51748> (1 March 2002).

17. Rafael, "The Cell Phone and the Crowd."

18. de Armond, "Black Flag Over Seattle."

19. David Ronfeldt and John Arquilla, "Networks, Netwars, and the Fight for the Future," *First Monday* 6, 10 (October 2001), <http://firstmonday.org/issues/issue6_10/ronfeldt/index.html> (1 March 2002).

20. John Arquilla and David Ronfeldt, eds., *Networks and Netwars: The Future of Terror, Crime, and Militancy* (Santa Monica, Calif.: RAND, 2001).

21. Jim Lai, "The Future of Infantry," *Mindjack* 28, January 2002, <http://www.mindjack.com/feature/landwarrior.html> (1 March 2002).

22. Ian Sample, "Military Palmtop to Cut Collateral Damage," *New Scientist,* 9 March 2002, <http://www.newscientist.com/news/news.jsp?id=ns99992005> (29 March 2002).

23. Arquilla and Ronfeldt, eds., *Networks and Netwars,* 310–313.

24. Alexis de Tocqueville, *Democracy in America,* ed. J. P. Mayer and Max Lerner, trans. George Lawrence (New York: Harper and Row, 1966), 483–484.

25. Elinor Ostrom, *Governing the Commons: The Evolution of Institutions for Collective Action* (Cambridge: Cambridge University Press, 1990).

26. Nick Montfort, "My Pager, My Matchmaker," *Ziff Davis Smart Business*, 7 July 2000, <http://techupdate.zdnet.com/techupdate/stories/main/0,14179,2577889,00.html> (1 March 2002).

27. "Bleep at First Sight," *Reuters*, 15 May 1998, <http://www.wired.com/news/news/culture/story/12342.html> (1 March 2002).

28. Craig Wilson, "'Gaydar' Device Clears Up Mixed Signals," *USA Today*, 25 February 2000, <http://www.usatoday.com/life/cyber/tech/review/crg942.htm> (1 March 2002).

29. Montfort, "My Pager, My Matchmaker."

30. ImaHima, <http://www.imahima.com/index.jsp> (1 March 2002).

31. Diego Ibarguen, "Tracking Celebrities Via Cell Phones, Web Sites," *San Francisco Chronicle*, 21 January 2001.

32. Justin Hall, "Mobile Reporting: Peer-to-Peer News," *TheFeature.com*, 20 February 2002, <http://www.thefeature.com/printable.jsp?pageid=14274> (1 March 2002).

33. Mann and Niedzviecki, *Cyborg*.

34. Gerd Kortuem et al., "Close Encounters: Supporting Mobile Collaboration through Interchange of User Profiles," in *Proceedings of the First International Symposium on Handheld and Ubiquitous Computing (HUC99)*, 1999, Karlsruhe, Germany, <http://www.cs.uoregon.edu/research/wearables/Papers/HUC99-kortuem.pdf> (6 March 2002).

35. Neeraj Jhanji, interview by author, October 2001, Tokyo.

36. ImaHima Press Releases, <shttp://www.imahima.com/en/news3.html> (1 March 2002).

37. Deborah Mendez-Wilson, "Users Turned to Pagers When Phone Lines Went Down in Crisis," *Wireless Week*, 24 September 2001, <http://www.wirelessweek.com/index.asp?layout=story&articleId=CA160205> (1 March 2002).

38. John Geirland, "Mobile Community," *TheFeature.com*, 24 September 2001, <http://thefeature.com/article.jsp?pageid=12836> (1 March 2002).

39. Gordon Gould, Alex Levine, and Andrew Pimentel, interview by author, November 2001, New York.

40. ENGwear: Wearable Wireless Systems for Electronic News Gathering, <http://www.eyetap.org/hi/ENGwear/> (1 March 2002).

41. Mann and Niedzviecki, *Cyborg*, 175–176.

42. Ibid., 177–178.

43. Hall, "Mobile Reporting."

44. Henry Jenkins, "Digital Renaissance," *Technology Review*, March 2002, <http://www.technologyreview.com/articles/jenkins0302.asp> (24 February 2002).

45. Gerd Kortuem et al., "When Peer-to-Peer Comes Face-to-Face: Collaborative Peer-to-Peer Computing in Mobile Ad Hoc Networks," 2001 International Con-

ference on Peer-to-Peer Computing (P2P2001), 27–29 August 2001, Linköping, Sweden, <http://www.cs.uoregon.edu/research/wearables/Papers/p2p2001.pdf> (6 March 2002).

46. Gerd Kortuem, telephone interview by author, 27 February 2002.

47. T. G. Zimmerman, "Personal Area Networks: Near-Field Intrabody Communication," *IBM Systems Journal* 35, 3&4 (1996), <http://www.research.ibm.com/journal/sj/mit/sectione/zimmerman.html> (6 March 2002).

48. Kortuem et al., "When Peer-to-Peer Comes."

49. Paul Rankin, "Context-Aware Mobile Phones: The Difference Between Pull and Push, Restoring the Importance of Place," Philips Research Laboratories, Redhill, Surrey, U.K.

50. Jay Schneider et al., "Auranet: Trust and Face-to-Face Interactions in a Wearable Community," Technical Report WCL-TR15, July 2001, <http://www.cs.uoregon.edu/research/wearables/Papers/auranet.pdf> (6 March 2002).

51. Erving Goffman, *The Presentation of Self in Everyday Life* (Garden City, N.Y.: Doubleday, 1959).

52. Jay Schneider et al., "Disseminating Trust Information in Wearable Communities," 2nd International Symposium on Handheld and Ubiquitous Computing (HUC2K), 25–27 September 2000, Bristol, England, <http://www.cs.uoregon.edu/research/wearables/Papers/HUC2K.pdf > (6 March 2002).

53. Gerd Kortuem et al., "When Cyborgs Meet: Building Communities of Cooperating Wearable Agents," *Proceedings Third International Symposium on Wearable Computers*, 18–19 October 1999, San Francisco, California, <http://www.computer.org/proceedings/iswc/0428/04280124abs.htm> (6 March 2002).

54. Kortuem, telephone interview by author.

55. Natalie S. Glance and Bernardo A. Huberman, "The Dynamics of Social Dilemmas," *Scientific American*, March 1994, 76–81.

56. Mark Granovetter, "Threshold Models of Collective Behavior," *American Journal of Sociology* 83, 6 (1978): 1420–1443.

57. Michael Suk-Young Chwe, *Rational Ritual: Culture, Coordination, and Common Knowledge* (Princeton: Princeton University Press, 2001), <http://www.chwe.net/michael/r.pdf> (6 March 2002).

58. Kevin Kelly, *Out of Control* (Reading, Mass.: Addison-Wesley, 1994), <http://www.kk.org/outofcontrol/index.html> (6 March 2002).

59. Ibid.

60. William Benzon, *Beethoven's Anvil: Music in Mind and Culture* (New York: Basic Books, 2001).

61. William Benzon, email interview by author.

62. William Morton Wheeler, *Emergent Evolution and the Development of Societies* (New York: W. W. Norton, 1928).

63. Ibid.

64. Steven Johnson, *Emergence: The Connected Lives of Ants, Brains, Cities, and Software* (New York: Scribner, 2001).

65. Bernardo Huberman, interview by author, October 2001, Palo Alto, California.

66. Bernardo A. Huberman, "The Social Mind," in *Origins of the Human Brain,* ed. Jean-Pierre Changeux and Jean Chavaillon (Oxford: Clarendon Press, 1995), 250.

67. Kay-Yut Chen, Leslie R. Fine, and Bernardo Huberman, "Forecasting Uncertain Events with Small Groups," HP Laboratories, Palo Alto, California, 3 August 2001, <http://papers.ssrn.com/sol3/papers.cfm?abstract_id=278601> (6 March 2002).

68. Ibid.

69. Norman Johnson et al., "Symbiotic Intelligence: Self-Organizing Knowledge on Distributed Networks, Driven by Human Interaction," in *Artificial Life VI: Proceedings of the Sixth International Conference on Artificial Life (Complex Adaptive Systems,* No. 6), ed. C. Adami, R. Belew, H. Kitano, and C. Taylor (Cambridge: Bradford Books/MIT Press, 1998).

70. George Dyson, *Darwin Among the Machines: The Evolution of Global Intelligence* (Reading, Mass.: Addison-Wesley, 1997).

71. Johnson et al., "Symbiotic Intelligence."

Chapter 8

Epigraphs: Langdon Winner, "Whatever Happened to the Electronic Cottage?" *Tech Knowledge Review* 3.23, 27 July 2001. http://www.oreilly.com/people/staff/stevet/netfuture/2001/Jul2701_121.html#3. 17 March 2002.

Robert Wright, *Nonzero: The Logic of Human Destiny* (New York: Vintage, 2000).

1. Rich Ling and Per Helmersen, "It Must Be Necessary, It Has to Cover a Need: The Adoption of Mobile Telephony Among Pre-Adolescents and Adolescents," in *The Social Consequences of Mobile Telephony: The Proceedings from a Seminar About Society, Mobile Telephony, and Children,* Telenor R&D N 38/2000, ed. Rich Ling and Kristin Trane, 26 June 2000, 19–23, <http://www.telenor.no/fou/prosjekter/Fremtidens_Brukere/seminarer/mobilpresentasjoner/Proceedings%20_FoU%20notat_.pdf> (4 February 2002).

2. Nicola Green, "Outwardly Mobile: Young People and Mobile Technologies," in *Perpetual Contact: Mobile Communication, Private Talk, and Public Performance,* ed. by Mark Aakhus and James Katz (Cambridge: Cambridge University Press, 2002).

3. Howard Rheingold, "Look Who's Talking," *Wired* 7.01, January 1999, <http://www.wired.com/wired/archive/7.01/amish.html> (18 March 2002).

4. Jane Wakefield, "Watching Your Every Move," *BBC News Online,* 7 February 2002, <http://news.bbc.co.uk/hi/english/sci/tech/newsid_1789000/1789157.stm> (16 March 2002).

5. Stuart Millar and Paul Kelso, "Liberties Fear Over Mobile Phone Details," *The Guardian*, 27 October 2001, <http://politics.guardian.co.uk/attacks/story/0,1320,581861,00.html> (18 March 2002).

6. Declan McCullagh, "Call It Super Bowl Face Scan 1," *Wired News*, 2 February 2001, <http://www.wired.com/news/politics/0,1283,41571,00.html> (18 March 2002).

7. Ryan Naraine, "Face Recognition, Via Cell-Phones," *Symobile*, 27 March 2002, <http://www.symobile.com/comtex/content.cfm?transmit_id=2002086a9917> (29 March 2002).

8. George Orwell, *Nineteen Eighty-Four* (London: Martin Secker and Warburg, 1949).

9. David Lyon, *The Electronic Eye: The Rise of Surveillance Society* (Minneapolis: University of Minnesota Press, 1994).

10. Steve Mann, "Smart Clothing: The Wearable Computer and WearCam," *Personal Technologies* 1, 1 (March 1997), <http://wearcam.org/personaltechnologies/> (18 March 2002).

11. Steven K. Feiner, "The Importance of Being Mobile: Some Social Consequences of Wearable Augmented Reality Systems," *Proceedings of IWAR 99 (International Workshop on Augmented Reality)*, San Francisco, California, 20–21 October, 1999, 145–148, <http://www.cs.columbia.edu/graphics/publications/FEINERiwar99.pdf> (18 March 2002).

12. Ibid.

13. Graeme Wearden, "Can 3G Phones Capture Criminals?" *ZDNet News*, 22 March 2002, < http://zdnet.com.com/2100–1105–867005.html> (27 March 2002).

14. Gary T. Marx, "The Surveillance Society: The Threat of 1984-Style Techniques," *The Futurist*, June 1985, 21–26.

15. Gary T. Marx, *Undercover: Police Surveillance in America* (Berkeley: University of California Press, 1988).

16. Michel Foucault, *Power/Knowledge: Selected Interviews and Other Writings, 1972–1977*, ed. Colin Gordon (New York: Pantheon, 1980), 39.

17. Michel Foucault, *Discipline and Punish: The Birth of the Prison* (London: Tavistock, 1977), 27.

18. Michel Foucault, "Panopticism," in *Discipline and Punish: The Birth of the Prison*, trans. Alan Sheridan (New York: Vintage Books, 1995), 195–228.

19. Ibid.

20. Ibid.

21. Winner, "Whatever Happened to the Electronic Cottage?"

22. Jan English-Leuck et al., *The Silicon Valley Cultures Project*, <http://www.sjsu.edu/depts/anthropology/svcp/> (23 March 2002), quoted in Winner.

23. Byron Reeves and Clifford Nass, *The Media Equation: How People Treat Computers, Television, and New Media Like Real People and Places* (Cambridge, U.K.: Cambridge University Press, 1996).

24. D. C. Dryer, C. Eisbach, and W. S. Ark, "At What Cost Pervasive? A Social Computing View of Mobile Computing Systems," *IBM Systems Journal* 38, 4 (1999), <http://www.research.ibm.com/journal/sj/384/dryer.html> (29 March 2002).

25. Mark Pesce, *The Playful World: How Technology Is Transforming Our Imagination* (New York: Ballantine, 2000). See also: The Playful World, <http://www.playfulworld.com/> (23 March 2002).

26. Leslie Haddon, "The Social Consequences of Mobile Telephony: Framing Questions," in *The Social Consequences of Mobile Telephony: The Proceedings from a Seminar About Society, Mobile Telephony, and Children*, Telenor R&D N 38/2000, ed. Rich Ling and Kristin Trane, 26 June 2000, 2–6, <http://www.telenor.no/fou/prosjekter/Fremtidens_Brukere/seminarer/mobilpresentasjoner/Proceedings%20_FoU%20notat_.pdf> (31 January 2002).

27. Leopoldina Fortunati, "The Mobile Phone: New Social Categories and Relations," in *The Social Consequences of Mobile Telephony: The Proceedings from a Seminar About Society, Mobile Telephony, and Children*, Telenor R&D N 38/2000, ed. Rich Ling and Kristin Trane, 26 June 2000, 9–12, <http://www.telenor.no/fou/prosjekter/Fremtidens_Brukere/seminarer/mobilpresentasjoner/Proceedings%20_FoU%20notat_.pdf> (31 January 2002).

28. Rich Ling and Birgitte Yttri, "Hyper-Coordination via Mobile Phones in Norway," in *Perpetual Contact: Mobile Communication, Private Talk, and Public Performance*, ed. Mark Aakhus and James Katz (Cambridge: Cambridge University Press, 2002).

29. Ibid.

30. Pasi Mäenpää, "Mobile Communication as a Way of Urban Life," in *Ordinary Consumption*, ed. Allen Warde and Jukka Gronow (London: Routledge, 2001), 107.

31. Barry Wellman, "Physical Place and CyberPlace: The Rise of Personalized Networking," *International Journal of Urban and Regional Research* 25, 2 (2001): 227–252, <http://www.chass.utoronto.ca/~wellman/publications/individualism/ijurr3a1.htm> (29 March 2002).

32. Barry Wellman, "Little Boxes, Glocalization, and Networked Individualism," forthcoming in *Digital Cities II: Computational and Sociological Approaches*, ed. Makoto Tanabe, Peter van den Besselaar, and Toru Ishida. Springer Lecture Notes in Computer Science: The State of the Art Series (Berlin: Springer-Verlag, 2002).

33. Leopoldina Fortunati, "The Ambiguous Image of the Mobile Phone," in *Communications on the Move: The Experience of Mobile Telephony in the 1990s*, ed. L. Haddon, COST248 Report, Telia, Farsta.

34. Wellman, "Little Boxes, Glocalization, and Networked Individualism."

35. Haddon, "The Social Consequences of Mobile Telephony."

36. Fortunati, "The Mobile Phone."

37. Ibid., 17.

38. T. W. Adorno and M. Horkheimer, "The Culture Industry: Enlightenment as Mass Deception," in *The Dialectic of Enlightenment*, trans. John Cumming (New York: Herder and Herder, 1972).

39. Jean Baudrillard, "Simulacra and Simulations," in *Jean Baudrillard, Selected Writings*, ed. Mark Poster (Stanford: Stanford University Press, 1988), 166–184.

40. Neil Postman, *Amusing Ourselves to Death: Public Discourse in the Age of Show Business* (New York: Viking, 1985).

41. Robert McChesney, *Rich Media, Poor Democracy: Communication Politics in Dubious Times* (Champaign: University of Illinois Press, 1999).

42. John Leyden, "NTT DoCoMo Pays $217m to Put Spam Back in the Can," *The Register,* 7 April 2001, <http://www.theregister.co.uk/content/5/20182.html> (18 March 2002).

43. Harold Lasswell, in Jacques Ellul, *The Technological Society*, trans. J. Wilkinson (New York: Knopf, 1964), x.

44. Ibid., 82–83.

45. Ibid.

46. Lewis Mumford, *The Myth of the Machine* (New York: Harcourt, Brace, & World, 1966).

47. Joseph Weizenbaum, *Computer Power and Human Reason* (San Francisco: W. H. Freeman, 1976).

48. Martin Heidegger, "The Question Concerning Technology," in *Martin Heidegger: Basic Writings*, ed. David Krell (New York: Harper & Row, 1977).

49. N. Katherine Hayles, *How We Became Posthuman: Virtual Bodies in Cybernetics, Literature, and Informatics* (Chicago: University of Chicago Press, 1999).

50. Mark Dery, *Escape Velocity: Cyberculture at the End of the Century* (New York: Grove Press, 1996).

51. Raymond Kurzweil, *The Age of Spiritual Machines: When Computers Exceed Human Intelligence* (London: Penguin Viking, 1999).

52. Jeremy Lovell, "Briton Wires Nervous System to a Computer," *Reuters,* 22 March 2002, <http://story.news.yahoo.com/news?tmpl=story&cid=581&u=/nm/20020322/tc_nm/britain_cybernetics_dc_2> (27 March 2002).

53. Marshall Berman, *All That Is Solid Melts into Air: The Experience of Modernity* (New York: Penguin Books, 1982).

54. Alvin Toffler, *The Third Wave* (New York: William Morrow, 1980).

55. Lawrence Lessig, *The Future of Ideas: The Fate of the Commons in a Connected World* (New York: Random House, 2001).

56. C. M. Kornbluth, "The Marching Morons," *Galaxy,* April 1951.

57. Sean Griffin, "Walt Disney Programs," <http://www.museum.tv/archives/etv/W/htmlW/waltdisneyp/waltdisneyp.htm>.

58. Jack Valenti, "Home Recording of Copyrighted Works," *Hearings Before Subcommittee on Courts, Civil Liberties, and the Administration of Justice of the*

Committee on the Judiciary, House of Representatives, Ninety-Seventh Congress, 12, 13, 14 April; 24 June; 22 and 23 September 1982, <http://cryptome.org/hrcw-hear.htm>.

59. Electronic Frontier Foundation, "Consensus at Lawyerpoint: Being a True Account of the Undertakings of the Broadcast Protection Discussion Group," <http://bpdg.blogs.eff.org>.

60. Motion Picture Association of America, "Content Protection Status Report," <http://judiciary.senate.gov/special/content_protection.pdf>.

61. Electronic Frontier Foundation, "Hollywood Wants to Plug the Analog Hole," <http://bpdg.blogs.eff.org/archives/000113>.

62. Cory Doctorow, telephone interview by the author.

63. Dan Gillmor, "Bleak Future Looms If You Don't Take a Stand," *Mercury News,* 23 March 2002, <http://www.siliconvalley.com/mld/siliconvalley/2922052.htm> (27 March 2002).

64. Yochai Benkler, "From Consumers to Users: Shifting the Deeper Structures of Regulation Toward Sustainable Commons and User Access," *Federal Communications Law Journal* 52, 3 (2000): 561, <http://www.law.indiana.edu/fclj/pubs/v52/no3/benkler1.pdf> (23 March 2002).

65. James Madison, Letter to W. T. Barry, 4 August 1822, <http://www.jmu.edu/madison/madison.htm#Purpose> (29 March 2002).

66. Steven Johnson, *Emergence: The Connected Lives of Ants, Brains, Cities, and Software* (New York: Scribner, 2001), 100.

67. Anthony Townsend, telephone interview by author, November 2001.

68. Anthony M. Townsend, "Life in the Real-Time City: Mobile Telephones and Urban Metabolism," *Journal of Urban Technology* 7, 2 (August 2000), 87.

69. Jeff Goldman, "The City Transformed," *TheFeature.com,* 22 November 2001, <http://www.thefeature.com/index.jsp?url=article.jsp?pageid=13458> (27 March 2002).

70. Townsend, "Life in the Real-Time City," 104.

71. William J. Mitchell, *City of Bits: Space, Place, and the Infobahn* (Cambridge: MIT Press, 1995). See also: The *City of Bits* Web Site, <http://mitpress2.mit.edu/e-books/City_of_Bits/index.html> (27 March 2002).

72. William J. Mitchell, "The Revenge of Place," in *Proceedings, Third International Space Syntax Symposium,* Atlanta, 2001, <http://undertow.arch.gatech.edu/homepages/3sss/papers_pdf/01_mitchell.pdf> (29 March 2002).

73. Andy Clark, "Natural-Born Cyborgs?" in *Cognitive Technology: Instruments of Mind, Proceedings of the 4th International Conference on Cognitive Technology,* ed. M. Benyon, C. Nehaniv, and K. Dautenhahn (Berlin: Springer-Verlag, 2001), 17.

74. Ibid., 17.

75. Ibid., 20.

76. Ibid., 24.

77. Howard Rheingold, *Tools for Thought* (New York: Simon & Schuster, 1985).

78. Vannevar Bush, "As We May Think," *Atlantic Monthly*, July 1945.

79. Rheingold, *Tools for Thought*.

80. Ibid., 138.

81. J.C.R. Licklider, "Man-Computer Symbiosis," *IRE Transactions on Human Factors in Electronics* HFE–1, March 1960, 4. Reprinted in *In Memoriam: J.C.R. Licklider, 1915–1990* (Palo Alto: Digital Systems Research Center, 1990), 1.

82. M. Mitchell Waldrop, *The Dream Machine: J.C.R. Licklider and the Revolution That Made Computing Personal* (New York: Viking, 2001).

83. D. C. Engelbart, "A Conceptual Framework for the Augmentation of Man's Intellect," in *Vistas in Information Handling*, vol. 1, ed. D. W. Howerton and D. C. Weeks (Washington, D.C.: Spartan Books, 1963), 1–29.

84. Wright, *Nonzero*.

85. Ibid., 16.

86. Ibid., 22.

87. Ibid., 22–23, 24.

88. Ibid., 152.

89. Ibid., 154.

INDEX